HEAD SHOT

HEAD SHOT

VICTORIA NIXON

unbound

First published in 2019

Unbound
6th Floor Mutual House, 70 Conduit Street, London W1S 2GF
www.unbound.com
All rights reserved

Photographs reproduced in this book are from the author's
personal collection except where otherwise credited.

While every effort has been made to trace the owners of
copyright material reproduced herein, the publisher would like
to apologise for any omissions and will be pleased to incorporate
missing acknowledgements in any further editions.

Typeset by PDQ Digital Media Solutions Ltd.

A CIP record for this book is available from the British Library

ISBN 978-1-78352-749-6 (hbk)
ISBN 978-1-78352-779-3 (ebook)

Printed in Great Britain by CPI Group (UK)

1 3 5 7 9 8 6 4 2

In loving memory of my mother, father and brother.
Always in my heart.

CONTENTS

CLOSE-UP

'How vain it is to sit down and write if
you have not stood up to live'

Henry David Thoreau

London 2012. Opening night at a friend's art exhibition draws a good-looking, fast-moving crowd, the flashbulbs so frantic I don't see who's furiously tapping my shoulder. Ah, it's another pal and former model with a towering young admirer in tow. Parking her suitor with me, she skips off into the crowd. I soon discover why.

The lofty one's dark city suit neatly belies his state of mind. Grabbing two large vodkas from a passing waiter, he snorts them both in seconds and they clearly aren't his first. Thirtyish, clean-shaven with hooded slate-grey eyes and a drained face, he fixes me with a deep unnerving gaze:

'Tell me, is it true that you Sixties models all shagged like stoats and married for money?'

He may have been joking, and he wasn't the first to ask.

But he will be the last.

I gave him my best 'bright lights' smile and left him to it.

I'd never given the Sixties or Seventies much thought since living them, life being too full-on to dredge lost memories. Yet that unabashed question from a wasted city slicker delivered the nudge I needed to clear the junk from the trunk which languished in my loft. To put an end to being forever labelled by a vacant stare in a vintage glossy.

That's not how it was, not how I was.

This is how it was.

Before 1963 the British fashion model had a graceful hauteur and fitting name – Fiona Campbell-Walter, later Baroness Thyssen, was its premier beauty. As life changed fast her elegant mode gave way to the startled waif with enormous eyes who looked into the camera as if she'd only just noticed it. By the height of the Sixties this look was so perfected it ceased to be interesting, paving the way for us lot – a motley gaggle of post-Shrimpton, post-Twiggy models whose names were rarely known, but whose faces made us fortunes. Neither pouty hair-flickers nor rich men's trophies, we didn't fit in the box or stay between the lines. Our allure was coltish and unruly, and we wanted to be strong and empowered.

My generation of models never morphed into media personalities, rarely managed pure chic and never fretted about our weight; we just got on with the job. Astounded as I was to be named 'The Face of 68' by the *Daily Mail* it was no big deal. I was happiest working my way around Europe, not focusing on, or deserving of, that Twiggy kind of fame, not wanting my youthful face to be the one defining element of my life.

The unkempt look now reigned because quirkiness and innovation were prized in a time when 'meaning' replaced narcissism. It wasn't what you wore but what you were that counted; our style was never to flaunt wealth, flap labels and drip jewels. That was too frocking far. And why marry for money when we made plenty for ourselves?

We were a fearless, defiant brigade who quickly learned that high-fashion hedonism did not preclude danger and destruction in this radical new era. But we recognised good luck when it waved at us, ever grateful for a ticket to see the world with a paid-for smile, always aware that the minute area of placement and position of eyes, nose, ears and mouth could confirm or cancel a fortune. And so it was – we teenage girls took destiny into our own hands and headed off to work in foreign climes with zero fuss, armed solely with a determination to see new worlds and the certainty that life's best teacher is experience.

We didn't do it to be liberated or considered equal to men – we already thought we were. This was no deep feminist philosophy, simply a desire to find freedom in a different way: to make our own money, determine our own fate, to have adventures in unknown locations before walking away to do something useful, productive and rewarding. We knew photographic fashion modelling would be a career of diminishing returns, ten years max, with the door closing slowly before it slammed shut for ever.

Yet that staccato free-wheeling restlessness, that desire

to escape the humdrum was way more extreme in me than the others. Adventure followed me everywhere, but so did constant tragedy, and as long as I kept on running there was no space or time for memories. I could lock away my tangled thoughts, avoid being ambushed by grief and never be touched by sadness.

But how far did I have to run to leave my past behind?

Now, half a century later, I'm about to open that trunk to dump the modelling junk and be free of the decade I've never ever confronted. It feels strange, bone-close, as I lift the Louis Vuitton lid cobwebbed thick and sticky with age. One glance, just one, is all it takes for my past to howl from every corner. Those ten years of faded tear-sheets ram back into my life as each reveals its real story. Not of pouting lips and vacuous smiles, but of high swings felled by the devastating self-destruction of my family and friends. For also in that trunk is the hard evidence of their too-brief lives: the hand-scrawled letters, the soul-touching poems, the nicotine-stained postcards, the fun-time photos and the dog-eared press cuttings of their premature, puzzling, untimely deaths.

No longer is this just about binning the junk. This is about confronting the psychological agonies of those I loved, and of acknowledging that the shock of unexpected suicide, of purposeful self-death never leaves you. It can happen to anyone, any time and anywhere.

A never-ending absence. That never known reason. The guilt that haunts.

And the confusion in that 'anything goes' era – when it was cool to smell a touch, hear a taste and touch a sound – of separating out those friends who were little more than a pain in the neck from those who had real pain in their heads. Recognising that my independent maverick life was too often splintered by the partners I chose as I tried to rescue them from themselves.

1

MADE IN BARNSLEY

June 1964. Huddersfield Road.

The red MG, hood down, cuts cleanly across the kerb and stops with a jolt beside the school gates. I recognise the local driver's face. Everyone does. He's dating a sixth-form prefect – the car a seventeenth-birthday gift from his father. We all envy the lucky girl whisked away from school each day. And then he looks my way and smiles.

'Would you like a lift home?'

'No thanks, I only live twenty yards away, and besides . . .'

'Can I take you out for a drink then?'

'No, I'm only just sixteen, and what about your . . .'

'Well, what if I take you to the Spencer Arms in Cawthorne and we order a Babycham for you, and if the barman serves you I'll take you to a club to hear some cool music?'

'Okay!'

But what about his prefect girlfriend? She isn't his girlfriend any more.

He said.

My first ever date is the following evening.

The construction of the big date hair-do takes two hours. It's more a hair-don't, part beehive, part bagel and uses enough Silvikrin hairspray to massacre an ant colony. I shimmy into a dove-grey sleeveless frock from Sheffield's Marshall & Snelgrove and perform the perfect three-point turn for my mother. Boy, oh boy . . . Dusty Springfield has nothing on me!

First date hair-don't, 1964

'Well, have a lovely time, darling, and be a good girl.'

Make your mind up, Mum!

The date's a success despite the dodgy barnet; probably

7

because of it. He can't stop laughing and even takes a photo. The jilted prefect pretends she's given him the elbow, and I've acquired my first ever boyfriend. He's bright, handsome, kind – and keen. His parents are charming, his sister an elegant dental surgeon married to a naval surgeon, and all is pinch-myself perfection. My life has changed in a heartbeat. Dreamboat and I waste no time experimenting with exciting grown-up things throughout the next year – most of them at week-ends, down quiet country lanes in his red MG.

'Don't kiss me like that!'

'Sorry, it was just a slip of the tongue.'

'Actually, I quite like it. Do it again!'

The more he teaches me how to kiss with an open mouth, the more I almost vanish down his throat. We're on a teenage high in its purest form, recreational drugs unheard-of and drinking habits tame. The real buzz is an all-encompassing belief in the power of rhythm and blues.

Just off the Barnsley Road to Sheffield, a local self-assured young man named Peter Stringfellow has opened a new club, the Mojo. Formerly a school of dancing, its bouncy sprung floor is excellent for leaping around once you've paid your two and six at the door. The inside space, one huge room, has matt black walls streaked with pop-art murals but has no licence to offer alcoholic drinks, just coffee. Peter's unique knack of booking outstanding groups before their first big hit means the Mojo has live gigs that other UK clubs can only dream of.

Soon he's booking the world's major blues stars – but persuading the talent to perform in an alcohol-free zone is not an easy task. We're waiting for Sonny Boy Williamson to blow us away but when he arrives he's tetchy and confronts Peter.

'Where's the booze, man?'

'We don't have any, SB.'

'Man, I don't go on stage without no booze!'

Peter looks a tad uneasy. Gossip has it that Sonny Boy recently set his hotel room on fire while trying to cook a rabbit in a percolator. The off-licence across the road produces an acceptable bottle of whisky which Sonny Boy knocks back before his performance guaranteeing no-hands harmonica playing that tears our teenage souls apart.

Hours later normality is tardily restored with the upstairs-tiptoe past my mother's bedroom door and her inevitable . . .

'Is that you, darling? Make sure you double-lock the front door.'

Five years earlier, to everyone's surprise including my own, I'd sailed through the 11-plus exam, insisting on attending the local all-girls grammar school rather than being pushed off to board – the only member of my family for generations to turn down a fee-paying education. I wanted to stay close to my pals. We were rebels, not play-safers and to risk losing them was a step too far.

My fate as a non-privately educated Fifties child was sealed by that 11-plus exam, which had one purpose only for the grammar schools' 'pick of the bunch' – to channel us, via intense study, to careers with realistic prospects of academic success. Barnsley Girls' High School's excellent teaching assured us we could be whatever we wanted to be – except perhaps housewives – and we were just as likely to achieve our goals as the boys at the grammar school across town.

After Dreamboat heads off to university in London, it's time for me to face the music at school. I know I've lost the academic plot – my teenage voyage of carnal and musical discovery producing an educational malfunction of humongous proportions – but frankly, it's a relief to retreat from the pressure. Somehow I've acquired an extreme drive and self-assurance to do something more diverse with my life than what is expected. I simply don't see an academic degree as my ultimate goal.

I don't want to do a predictable job in an institutional set-up.

I don't want to go to the same workplace every day.

I don't want to marry Andrew Accountant who will bore me within a month.

I don't want to put money in a pension fund worth little by the time I retire, and descend into old age wondering what life could have been.

A letter arrives from my boyfriend in London. It's clear the exciting temptations of the Big Smoke are not delivering all they promised, because he wants marriage! *'I'll give you everything money can buy . . . Imagine us arriving at the Mojo Club in an E-type Jag . . .'*

I think I do love him, but I feel too young to know how to love him. I simply can't contemplate marriage to the first boy I've loved. I have to love more, to see more, to do more, to discover more. If not, how will I ever know if he is the one or just the one now and not for ever?

We want different things. I hanker, he wants hunker.

I want the freedom to make my own financial way in life. To be 'settled down' and 'looked after' by a man holds no appeal right now, and the humdrum horror of being possessed by anyone ever, holds none at all. I don't want to live like a doll rather than a full human being, in cosy bondage while gratefully accepting protection and approval as reward for my submissiveness. I want the road less travelled – however thrilling, however harrowing.

I hate hurting him, but somewhere deep inside feel a strange delight that I matter so much, and feel a bit ashamed.

It's true that my life in Yorkshire is cosy, settled and safe, but not for a future lived backwards – carpet-slipper stability at twenty and a world cruise with hubby at seventy. If there's a chance for adventure, I'll take it. I want to run down Swiss mountains in early summer, climb Sydney Harbour Bridge in the rain, trek through jungles in Ceylon, cartwheel past the Empire State Building; to see what is far far away. Out there.

'Can't wait to scream at them!'

'Oh, me too! Just hope I don't faint!'

The entire class at my grammar school are off to see the Beatles perform at Sheffield's City Hall. Last week they'd screamed their way through a Cliff Richard concert. Andrea gives me a knowing look. 'Er . . . no thanks, we'll pass. It's not really our kind of thing.'

My best friend and I prefer to see bands in smaller, sweaty venues where it's all raw and less staged. We're going instead to the Mojo to see Manfred Mann, a blues band who haven't yet 'sold out' – their blues integrity still intact despite a hit record or two.

Standing at the back of the dark club to watch the set, Andrea and I adopt our usual detached routine of 'judge and nudge' to appraise the sound and assess the talent. This reticence to display emotion always produces bemused interest. Road managers often approach us to 'meet the band', unable to fathom our coolness next to the ever-present wide-eyed groupies who zip around like bats on Benzedrine. But we don't want to sleep with the band or plead for autographs. We know the score – that most musicians are not sensitive rock poets with beautiful souls, but a bit thick and dull and often drug-addled and drunk.

And a long way from home.

But Manfred Mann and their music strike a chord despite the singer's sexy smirk, tight checked trousers and provocative posturing. When a crew member approaches to say Paul Jones, the aforementioned vocalist and harmonica player, wants to meet, I think, why not? He's mega-attractive and, hopefully, bright. Indeed, as we chat in the club's only quiet recess, he reveals that he read English at Jesus College, Oxford, before dropping out – and comes across as a fundamentally decent guy. Andrea looks at her watch. The last train to Barnsley . . . we must go. 'Don't worry, I'll drive you home,' says Paul. Thirty minutes later, the group's scruffy touring van pulls up outside my house, after dropping

Andrea at her gate. Paul turns from the driver's seat: 'By the way, are you a model?'

'A model! Don't be daft. I'm sixteen and still at school. But I don't think I want to stay on.'

'Yeah, I understand. I got kicked out of Oxford because I preferred singing in a band to studying. I still feel the same way. I couldn't do anything else. You could be a top model.'

'What kind of model?'

'A fashion model. You could really make it. Seriously. Why don't you come to London and give it a go?'

'Nah, I'd be no good at the flicky hair toss and pout, it's all so mindless.'

'Well, only if you allow it to be.'

'Is this one of your chat-up lines?'

'No – I'll ring and speak to your mother if you like.'

And he did.

This fame thing was perplexing. The only time I'd confronted it was at junior school when each girl in my class was asked to stand up and declare what career she would like to have. Quite advanced stuff for ten-year-olds in the late Fifties.

All went swimmingly with the standard answers of 'I want to go to teacher training college, Miss' until it got to Patricia, who leapt to her feet.

'I want to be famous!' she stated emphatically, and promptly sat down again.

'And what, pray, do you want to be famous for?' asked our teacher.

'Anything I can do that will convince people that I am!'

She was never taken seriously again until she scored the

best results in Yorkshire for her 11-plus exams and was presented with a huge silver cup. Perhaps she had a point. Maybe there was more to being a successful model than having a face unclouded by thought.

Paul Jones and I exchanged letters in the following few months and met up whenever he toured nearby. But I began to ignore my first 'rule of cool' – detachment around attractive musicians – and began to fall heavily for Mr Jones. Only to discover, from my mother's *Daily Mail*, that it wasn't just me and Mr Jones. He was married with two children. And that was that. He sent a long, sensitive letter. But that was most definitely that. Paul's endorsement to my mother that being a clothes horse wasn't an entirely ridiculous career choice was his lasting legacy in my life.

Barnsley, age 17

You'll have guessed by now that *my* Barnsley isn't the genteel Cotswold haven so beloved by Prince Charles. It's the other one – that proud, gritty northern town that begat Michael Parkinson, Arthur Scargill and a handful of decent cricketers.

To be a true member of the Barnsley elite, you grew up overlooking the colliery where your father worked. This town was all about coal for over 500 years. To be sure, it enhances the industrial wasteland scene-setting to say you saw the pit from your bedroom window, but I don't qualify for genuine hardship-membership because my father ran our family firm

No such thing as 'being posh' in the Barnsley I grew up in during the Fifties – you were a grateful employer or thankfully employed. Local coal mining produced strong mixed emotions – pride because it was a thriving industry that promised a new, post-war future and anger that it was inhumane and unsafe to use human life to that degree.

Exhausted miners making their way home after an all-night shift in perilous underground corridors was an all-too-familiar sight in my childhood – still wearing their metal-capped boots and heavy protective helmets, their faces smeared with grime and only the whites of their eyes free from the dense sulphurous soot. I didn't have to be from a mining family to know the danger, to see the courage of this hard life in South Yorkshire.

My arrival – just months after the worst Big Freeze of the century into a bankrupt post-war Britain – was a welcome distraction for my parents and a source of bored amusement for Nicholas, my brother, born seven years earlier during the Second World War. Our vivacious mother had fallen for the charms of a dashing army major when she voluntarily drove war-time ambulances, but both sets of parents disapproved of this pairing and neither party turned up for the wedding. It wasn't that the backgrounds of my parents were profoundly different, simply that their parents thought they were. Both had built successful trading businesses but Dad's lot were considered far less worldly. At a perceived hierarchical level, snobbery did indeed exist – even in Barnsley.

My parents in 1940

An unremarkable detached house on a hill, a mile from the town centre, is where I grew up. Informal, with a lived-in feel, it was the kind of place a dog could jump on the sofa and be relaxed and cheerful. My adored, very adorable mother was a

16

drudgery-shy housewife with an offbeat approach to interior design based on what didn't need much cleaning. A jet-black porcelain bath, loo and hand basin emerged from the back of a delivery lorry. To her eternal irritation, every single tide-mark, stray hair, toothpaste smear and shaving-cream blob proudly presented itself on the shiny, uncompromising ebony surfaces from the day they were installed.

She had much the same antipathy towards cooking. No nostalgic stock-simmering kitchen waftings for me, just the crunch of quickly grabbed raw carrots and peas. Mum was never emotionally reliant on repeated assertions of the deliciousness of the meal she placed in front of us. She felt she had better things to do than chop and whip and peel and snip. It was simply food – a vegetable, a protein and a starch – which we all wolfed down and shot off again.

'Do try to masticate your food, darling.'

Schoolboy sniggers from Nick.

'She's only six. Perhaps you should call it chewing,' muttered my father.

Yet her artistic presentation of meals was quite masterly. She could dress a Barnsley chop or lonely chicken breast to look like a dish modern chefs would envy, plates hastily drizzled and sprinkled with all manner of spontaneous, offbeat pickings from the garden.

No foams but lots of forages. Extra sweets and cakes were never used as rewards or treats or bribes and we had little desire to ever seek solace in custard creams and garibaldis.

There were no serious books in the house, only half-read paperbacks. *Lady Chatterley's Lover*, very poorly disguised in a brown folder, briefly appeared after its dramatic trial gripped the nation and Penguin won the right to publish the book in its sexually explicit entirety. Probably purchased for the naughty bits rather than D. H. Lawrence's literary brilliance, it was *not* about the act of sex, Doris Lessing's foreword reminded its readers, but about 'all the power-play between the genders'. Be that as it may, it was outside activities that were unanimously preferred chez our gaff.

Our long, sloping garden had a compact orchard which produced tasteless cooking apples (we encouraged scrumping) and a huge pear tree with a swing. I'd fly up into the blossom and leap off into my father's tiny, treasured rose garden, hoping to miss the rockery en route. A lively lawn scattered with bikes of all sizes and cricket stumps led to the gravel drive by way of unplanned rhubarb plants with leaves the size of umbrellas, and several unruly trees.

We knew summer had arrived when Wimbledon bounced around on the tiny black and white screen in the background, and lemon squash ice lollies and Tizer quenched our thirsts. Racing down the hill to Tinkers Pond which throbbed with tadpoles and sticklebacks and was reputed to have no bottom, I'd wait for the sound of the daily steam train to get closer and closer. As it proudly puffed into view I'd wave furiously at the driver and, when he waved back and blasted the whistle, dance around in my Startrite shoes engulfed in smoke which smelt like a glorious open fire. Being measured for your new shoes was a risky business then. Sliding junior feet into an X-ray machine at the local shoe shop meant the rays shot through your tiny body and out of the top of your head, ensuring the perfect fit, but not always of the type you wanted.

Everything outdoors was exciting, the more dangerous the better – scrambling over treacherous rocks, exploring derelict houses, building secret camps and finding good trees to climb. Oaks were the best with their solid limbs. 'Not that one, Vic, it's a horse chestnut with snappy branches,' yelled Nick, up to five times a day. Most trees were easier to clamber up than down, but knowing how to fall was all part of the fun.

We longed for white Christmases with hard icy snow so we could career head-first down the hill on kitchen trays. Our door-to-door carol singing (Nick on trumpet, me bleating along to it) was once kyboshed when Mrs Bailey at number 26 poured a bucket of water over us from her bedroom window, and Yuletide TV viewing always included that Christmas classic *It's a Wonderful Life*, the tale of a small-town, good-hearted businessman rescued by his guardian angel when looming bankruptcy drives him towards suicide. We felt cosy and safe that this was just a film and could never happen in real life.

It was a time of endless space and wild unsupervised freedom. Our laid-back parents encouraged us to do things by ourselves. They did their thing, we did ours. Scissors, knives, matches – they trusted our judgement. We knew that petrol tended to combust when lit, that bleach wasn't a refreshing drink and that cod liver oil, Milk of Magnesia and TCP cured everything. Collapsing into bed feeling safe, looked after and loved – all the time knowing that the grown-ups were down there taking care of the serious stuff. Knowing that tomorrow would be as much fun as today.

Vic and Nick with cat and mouse

When the holidays ended Nick would pack his trunk and tuck box to face a new term at boarding school while grumbling about its horrid meals and freezing dorms. But it was just a rant. He was a popular student, good at all sports and art (considered the two coolest to be good at) and never away from 'a spellbinding book'. Nick's school overlooked Nottingham's Sherwood Forest, the massive woodland said to be stalked by Robin Hood and his merry men. We'd visit him on open days, take a huge picnic, and sit in the heart of the 4,500-acre forest next to the thousand-year-old Major Oak with its enormous hollow trunk which, according to folklore, served as a hideout and sleeping place for Robin and his bandits. It was here that Nick first addressed my father as 'Sir', the school rule for addressing elders. I naturally emulated everything my adored older brother did (our parents were 'Mum' and 'Dad' because Nick declared that '"Mummy" and "Daddy" was for cissies') but drew the line at calling my father 'Sir'.

With Nick back at school it was Granny who became my family playmate. Small and cuddly, with enormous bosoms, my father's mother Agatha promptly moved in with us after her husband died, and I adored her. She taught me to sing and dance and do the splits. Constantly swathed in 4711 cologne, Aggie didn't believe in washing – 'so bad for the skin'. The largest bedroom in the house became Aggie's bedsit. She rarely left it and all her meals were delivered there on trays, my mother considered an extremely poor cook, not remotely worthy of her son. This stand-off ensued for the full eight years of her stay, my father adopting a 'hands-off' neutrality.

But Aggie and I had a special bond and her face lit up whenever I skipped into her room. I'd find her sitting bolt upright in bed wearing long, white cotton gloves and slowly brushing her silver, waist-length hair a hundred times before twisting it into a neat tight bun. She had a bizarre collection of strange little brooches and rings which I was allowed to wear, but only in her room. Never bored by my repetitive questions, never cross when I broke things or collected very creepy crawlies in jam jars, she was happy to show me time and time again how to knit scarves and crochet handkerchief edges – and was always on my side when 'Mummy is being a bit horrid because she's too busy to play with me.'

Aggie had three famous friends. The international opera singer Mario Lanza was 'a very dear friend' who regularly sent her postcards from exciting distant climes – the heart-lifting flash of colour bearing an exotic stamp making her ecstatic for days on end. Goodness knows where she'd met him. Mario Lanza had a reputation as quite a boozer but it's hard to imagine him popping into one of Aggie's pubs for a quick snifter – even though her family-owned Shakespeare Hotel was, somewhat conveniently, next to Barnsley's Theatre Royal.

Then there was Harry Corbett who made his name on children's television with glove puppet Sooty. Aggie also knew Harry H. Corbett, the actor in BBC series *Steptoe and Son*, who constantly referred to his screen father as a 'dirty ol' man'. As Aggie got older and dottier, we were always in fear of her asking Harry Corbett if his father was still a dirty old man, and Harry H. Corbett whether he still enjoyed putting his hand up Sooty.

On rare occasions Aggie would don her lacquered wicker hat and navy blue suit and step out to take coffee at Barnsley's ever premier venue, The Queens Hotel. In a regal manner that she couldn't pull off, she'd inform anyone within earshot of the pride she felt at 'all that the Nixon-Bookers have achieved in Barnsley'. She was so proud, in fact, that she never once collected her state pension from the post office in case anyone thought she needed it.

The summer of my tenth birthday, Aggie took my cousin Mary and me to stay with her only non-famous friend, Edna Rowbottom (Paddlebum to us) who had a guest house in

Blackpool. God, how we loved Blackpool! Elvis souvenirs everywhere and totally geared to FUN. Its gaudy seaside glitz was made for us as we cartwheeled down the Golden Mile with its three piers and five-mile promenade, guzzled sticks of lurid pink rock and scared ourselves screamless on the Pleasure Beach Big Wheel. Paying sixpence to see the puppet Archie Andrews laugh hysterically in a glass dome made us bonkers with delight, but by far the most exciting place of all was the Tower with its vast aquarium and a proper circus every day with wildly exotic animals in daredevil acts, which we only found fun after Aggie convinced us that the animals 'are really enjoying it'.

The Tower ballroom, still one of the world's most wow ish rooms with its epic dance floor surrounded by red velvet chairs and wide-bottomed balconies caressed by angels and fairytale frescoes, only ever came alive for the afternoon tea dancers. After spookily rising through the ballroom floor, the Wurlitzer organ tackled a melancholic version of 'Oh I Do Like To Be Beside The Seaside' before playing on solo for the waltzing couples, and Mary and I took it in turns to dance with Aggie, who needed no persuading.

It's fair to say that my parents led an ultra active social life with cocktail parties galore. Everyone drank strong alcohol in the Fifties, lots of it, and smoked with unabashed exuberance, waving their fags around like conductor's batons. I was often roped in to help mix and hand out drinks to guests but had to promise not to leap out and surprise them from behind the bar.

'Hello, daarhling . . . my, haven't you grown . . . a G&T

for me and "uncle" John will have the Bell's. Not too much water, sweetie.'

My mother, wearing perfectly positioned pearls and a pretty frock over killer foundation garments, never drank to excess. She had natural high spirits and a total love of life. Tall and unselfconsciously beautiful with an attraction a hundred packs of Benson & Hedges could never corrode, she was also very funny and had a capacity for friendship with a multiplicity of people, so never had need of alcoholic props. Stopped for post-party 'erratic driving' when at the wheel of one of my father's firm's cars – a drop-head, two-seater Jaguar XK140 – she was cautioned by a besotted policeman and whizzed off to the local police station where it was established that it was the quinine in her tonic water that had made her 'feel a little queer'.

My parents at the Rotary Club's Annual Ball, 1952

If my father's side of the family were 'proud and proper Yorkshire folk' who'd worked hard to achieve success with their local transport business, those left on my mother's side bore more allegiance to the Bloomsbury Set. Mum's mother Violet, daughter of an oil and soap manufacturer who invented the scouring pad, grew up in Oakwood Hall in Rotherham, and ran off with a surgeon when my mother was three. Grandpa tracked them down to London's Savoy Hotel and attacked the surgeon in the foyer, shrieking 'You Unmitigated Cad' – the precise headline used by *The Times* the following day when it duly reported these rum goings-on to its readers.

Mum's lot. Oakwood Hall, Rotherham

My mother had been packed off to boarding school at five before her father promptly married a woman she loathed. The feeling was mutual. Never allowed home during school holidays, Mum was just eight when she was taught to drive by her school caretaker – and a Swiss finishing school in Neuchâtel conveniently ensured her continuing absence from home.

After Grandpa died, the loathed stepmother inherited his house, residing there with her daughter Anne, Rufus the long-haired dachshund, and their paying guest – a confirmed bachelor who was a surgeon at the local hospital. Step-aunt Anne, in the Wrens during the war, sported a crew-cut, jodhpurs when relaxing, and a man's suit to go to work. Sometimes she smoked a small clay pipe. We all knew she wasn't remotely interested in finding a husband but weren't quite sure why. She ran New Design, Barnsley's only arts and crafts shop, with stringent professionalism, stocking Heal's fabrics, Scandinavian Dansk glassware, Rosenthal and Wedgwood china and Winsor & Newton easels, brushes and paints.

A slight rapprochement ensued over time, and occasionally we were invited to Tarrawarra, an elegant house just streets away (no clue as to why the name of a house in Barnsley should be that of a small town near Melbourne), with its two-storyed circular entrance hall and towering, loud-ticking grandfather clock – so named, I always assumed, because dead Grandpa was propped up inside. The vast kitchen had meandering dusty larders and a box on the wall that jiggled to inform staff (in bygone years) which room had rung a bell for attention. The 'Tarrawarra Set' hung out in my step-grandmother's exquisite drawing room, overlooking her neighbour's tennis courts, where they chain-smoked, discussed life's aesthetics and nodded furiously whenever an abstract observation hit its mark. I'd watch from a corner as they lit each other's cigarettes with cupped hands, inhaling deeply before flopping back into over-stuffed armchairs. Step-Granny wasn't remotely interested in me but if I behaved well I was offered a humbug from an oval tin and Rufus would stare down his pointed snout and sniff dismissively. My father did not go to Tarrawarra. Ever. Existential conversation was never his forte.

Dad was lean and lofty and always in suits, an ever-present Player's Navy Cut dangling from his lips. His preferred form of entertainment was to team up with his pal, also an Arthur, for impromptu alcohol-fuelled jaunts which could entail driving to Murray's Cabaret Club in London (think British Fifties *Folies Bergère*) if their mood so desired.

When I wistfully pleaded for a 'little sister or brother' (instant raised brows and much intense whispering) the two Arthurs were despatched to Manchester to purchase a cuddly pet and returned with a glass tank containing the most adorable little chap I'd ever seen. We bonded immediately and I named him Ali. Dad had made me the most popular girl in junior school by buying me a twelve-inch alligator at the peak time of Bill Hayley & His Comets' smash rock'n'roll hit which had the catchphrase and playground fave: 'See you later, Alligator!' 'In a while, Crocodile!'

Ali lived in an aquarium several times his length, three-quarters water and the rest tiny logs, gravel and rocks. A docile little chap, he had alert eyes, a permanently smiling jaw, and I adored him. Ali's tiny legs and feet supported his strong, mottled tail which always made him look a tad off-balance.

We fed him small pieces of raw fish on the end of a long fork, always hoping he didn't develop a taste for fresh finger food.

My father celebrated this successful pet purchase with a few strong drinks. Dad only ever became nicer and chucklier with alcohol and found endless fun in pronouncing sturdy Yorkshire surnames. 'Did you play with Johnny Whittlestone and Katie Kettleborough at school today?' he'd chortle. Local place names of Viking origin were favourites: 'Heckkkkmondwike . . . Oswaldttttwistle . . . Clecccckheaton . . .' and throughout the entire year of 1954 we could hear him murmuring 'Facel Vega . . . oh . . . *F-A-C-E-L V-E-G-A*' in wonderment and awe when the French first unveiled their very fast and luxurious car.

Morris Minor didn't quite hold the same appeal.

Dad's lot – the first 'Mail service' using a horse and cart

Dad's family had introduced transport to Barnsley, obtaining the first tender to carry the Royal Mail using a liveried horse and cart. Soon they were operating horse-drawn people carriages and Barnsley's first motorised public bus services.

. . . and Barnsley's first motorised bus service, the charabanc, arrives in 1907

The business continued to expand and to encompass most things with wheels and an engine but by the time my father took over the helm, the company was pared down to a single Morris car dealership, with Jaguars thrown in for good measure because he loved their grace, pace and space.

Far from being buoyant when he took it over in the mid-Fifties, the business was struggling to survive the prevailing harsh climate of strikes. The other directors, Granny Aggie and her younger son John, a dental surgeon, wouldn't hear of the company being wound up. What would people say? The Nixon-Bookers of Barnsley must never throw in the towel!

It was a given that, with his engineering background, Dad would be assigned to run the family business when his father died. But my father's heart, knowledge and expertise were in engineering, not car trading. He wanted to invent, not sell cars. His recent invention was a cup-link that cleverly interlocked and extended professional fire hoses and he was devastated to later discover his design had been copied and patented after he'd shown it to a friend who'd taken it back to his office to 'admire'. Several people became very rich, but not my father.

Dad was never one to sit and mope. Adored by all my school friends, he loved boogie-woogie and jazz (especially blues cornettist Bix Beiderbecke - '*Bixxx Beiiiiiiderbeck*'), taking up the clarinet when Nick began to play a trumpet. When the saxophone replaced the clarinet's place in jazz because of its more powerful sound and less complicated key system, Dad had a welcome excuse to abandon it. The complexity of the clarinet's intricate key layout, its four parts, and a reed attached to the mouthpiece were somewhat difficult to master, especially after several large G&Ts.

Cool, free-fall music by Jerry Roll Morton, Kid Ory and Sidney Bechet is what we played at home – rarely classical or pop stuff. The one exception was American rocker Eddie Cochran singing his ever catchy 'ain't no time for the Summertime Blues . . . ', always guaranteed to produce instant smiles around our house, until Eddie died tragically at twenty-one, on tour in Britain with Gene Vincent, when their taxi crashed into a lamp post in Wiltshire. It marked the first time that I heard death openly discussed at home. The last ever single that Eddie recorded, appropriately titled

'Three Steps To Heaven', became a posthumous No. 1 for him, and a poignant family favourite.

Meanwhile Nick had introduced us to skiffle, forming his own band when Lonnie Donegan's hyper version of Lead Belly's 'Rock Island Line' unwittingly sold millions in 1956. Skiffle was a combo of hopped-up jazz, blues and folk played on homemade improvised instruments including a washboard you scraped with thimbles and a bass formed from broom handles and string attached to a wooden tea-chest base. With Nick on acoustic guitar and best friend Roger on bass, I was sometimes allowed to ping the washboard – far more exciting than my dull old piano lessons. Dad loved Nick's skiffle band and paid for a huge soundproofed garden hut which was put to very good use.

Always bursting with adventurous plans, Dad took Nick and his pals car racing at Silverstone, and me, age eight, on my first ever aeroplane flight to the TT motorcycle races in the Isle of Man. 'Why can't I open this window, Daddy? . . . I want to put my head in the clouds!' He tried to explain but I just didn't get it, and cheered up mightily when a steward came round with a tray of boiled sweets as the plane descended.

When Dad designed and built an imposing American-style fibreglass motor boat, he planned its inaugural launch one April Sunday morning in Filey, the East Yorkshire coastal resort, with Nick and two school friends as crew. Red flags flapped furiously and thundering North Sea rollers crashed onto the deserted beach. A coast guard purposefully marched over.

'No sailing today, sir. The weather is extremely volatile.'

'What better time to test a new boat's endurance!' laughed my father, a dead ringer for Tony Curtis in *Some Like It Hot* in his new sailing outfit, peaked hat, white trousers and navy blazer with gold buttons. But the waves, the size of small mountains, were non-negotiable – the high-performance engine couldn't cope and packed up half a mile out to sea. Standing on the gleaming look-out deck, my father spotted a monster wave heading their way. They survived the first, but the next was massive, unstoppable, it came down on them like a guillotine.

'I think the correct command is "Abandon Ship",' he yelled, saluting his young crew.

The crowd of holiday-makers now gathered on the beach cheered with relief as the four sailors washed up on rocks and the boat sailed into another bay entirely. All were safe and nearly sound after the laundering of a lifetime.

2

FACED INTO LIFE

'Happiness depends on which lens you look through'
Allan Wells

'May I introduce the Pocket Rocket?' hollered my father, steering the first freshly delivered off-white Mini up our crunchy gravelled drive.

Dad's interest in his boat had quickly diminished when he first took delivery of this sensational new Morris vehicle that he hoped would regenerate sales still badly hit by the endless strikes in British car factories.

Nick, Mum and I stare in open-mouthed amazement as this tiny, stylish box pulls up beside us. We leap inside, only half-listening to my father's eulogistic design descriptions.

'Just look at this ground-breaking iconic design and spacious interior seating in a car just ten feet long and four feet wide! It's truly revolutionary and simply conceived as a short-term solution to the Suez oil crisis but I bet it can outgun an Aston Martin away from traffic lights every time!'

It's the summer holidays again and Nick, now nineteen, is just back from Durham (now Newcastle) University, where he was accepted at sixteen for their prestigious Fine Art course irrespective of his A-Level results. Nick's school art master had recognised my brother's creative talent, which delighted our parents as they'd never actively encouraged or discouraged us academically. No anxious, ambitious, competitive schedules at our gaff. And Nick's art master had even persuaded the school governors to commission him to paint a mural in the school's entrance hall where it remained for years. During these term breaks he loves staying physically active by doing full-time labouring jobs.

Brother Nick in 1960

More Minis are waiting at the end of my first solo train journey to Oxford at just thirteen (the ticket collector given ten bob to keep an eye on me) for the annual summer stay with my aunt, uncle and two younger cousins. My granny Aggie is already in situ with her other son, Dad's brother, who is the in-house dental surgeon to 20,000 car workers at British Leyland's Cowley plant near Oxford.

Cars! Cars! Cars! We can't ever get away from cars!

I love these summer visits to see my sparkling little cousins, their mother adorable, competent and giggly; their father strict but fair with a wicked sense of humour.

It's late afternoon, the day after my arrival, when twelve-year-old cousin Mary suddenly squeals, 'Look! There's Nick's Mini!' as we turn into Apsley Road clutching a container of cheap smelly talc we've just bought for Aggie. Sure enough, my brother's racing-green Pocket Rocket is smartly parked outside her house. But why is he here? His labouring job in Barnsley means he only has weekends free.

A familiar, daunting feeling of déjà vu makes my stomach start to churn as we walk the last twenty yards to the house, for it was Nick who was sent to deliver bad news the last time I was on holiday here, after little Ali's tank thermostat broke and he died from over-heating.

The front door is slightly ajar as we approach. A deep, unearthly moan descends from the direction of Aggies's bedroom. In the living room my sweet ten-year-old cousin Barbara appears frozen to the spot, her hands cupped tightly to her mouth, her eyes swimming with terror. My aunt edges towards me and puts her arm around my shoulders. Nick is standing behind her, barely able to look at me.

'What is it?' I say defiantly.

'Your . . . father . . . he's had an accident, darling. It

was at work and . . . he was found . . . and he was taken to hospital . . .'

She can't go on. A sob. A silence.

I remain upright.

'Please tell me he's injured, don't tell me he's dead. Please . . .'

Nick's eyes finally meet mine in a blur of grief.

'He's not in pain any more, Vic. Let's take a little walk.'

Nick and I make our way to the garden at the back of the house which leads to a small wood. I want to cry but I can't. I can feel pin-pricks in my eyeballs but I can't cry. I feel like there's a brick wedged inside me making it hard to breathe. I know my life has changed for ever, that nothing will be the same again but I simply can't take this in.

Dad has killed himself by attaching a hose to the exhaust pipe of a Jaguar in one of his showrooms and inhaling the carbon monoxide fumes. He asked Peter, his favourite mechanic, to leave out tools, saying that he wanted to fix the loose exhaust.

I don't understand. We walk round and round in circles for hours, lost in, consumed by our own thoughts, all reality utterly ceasing to exist. I feel as if I've been knocked over by a massive, cold wave, followed by total, blank disbelief. Numbness encases me. All the certainties of my life just shattered.

'But . . . why? I need you to explain!'

'We will never know why,' Nick says gently, looking way beyond his nineteen years.

My mother last saw Dad alive around 11.15 P.M. when he mentioned going to the showroom office to do some work.

She didn't think it unusual. He often preferred to catch up on paperwork when no one else was around. Nick took the 8 A.M. call from mechanic Peter, who'd arrived at work and found my father lying unconscious on a board at the rear of the Jaguar.

My father's suicide reported in the local press

The piece of hose pipe was under his arms.

When Nick arrived at the showroom he found Dad still breathing. The engine had stalled and his life was holding by a thread. In the hospital lift heading to the emergency operating theatre, Nick and Peter – one each side of the stretcher, both pleading with Dad to hang on – heard the faint, strangled rattle that announced his departure from this world.

At the inquest the following day, the coroner announced that it was quite clear Arthur Nixon-Booker had taken his own life; he had had financial difficulties which he'd tried to keep to himself, and a verdict was recorded that he killed himself while in a fit of depression.

'A fit of depression?'

Dad was the happiest man in the world with no predisposition to suicide.

This good-natured, warm and sunny man with a tremendous enthusiasm for living had no previous history of depression or mental illness. So why was he compelled to kill himself? Was it a moment of madness – one spark of irrationality that caused this catastrophic, cruel outcome?

There was no note. Not a thing.

If only I'd been at home, if only I hadn't been in Oxford.

No time to say goodbye.

Just gone.

The hideous reality began to sink in. Slowly, hazily, I realised, I grasped, that my father's death was a deliberate decision. But why had he done this? Were there any warning signs that could have prevented his devastating death?

The only thing that had seriously annoyed Dad was when our neighbours, also Barnsley car dealers, built a bungalow in their generous grounds. When unveiled it virtually touched our house, but left their own standing in its fully detached glory as they swept up their drive. The value of our house tumbled overnight.

Unrelated to that incident, on the day I'd left for Oxford, I watched another neighbour – a charming retired architect who adored and respected my father – approach Dad as he was tending his beloved roses, and whisper something in his ear. My father stumbled and I heard our neighbour say, 'Don't worry Arthur, it will all be okay' and put his arm around Dad's shoulders. Was he the bearer of news my father couldn't bear to hear?

Little had Dad realised, when he drove that first Mini up our drive, that an idiotic corporate mistake by British Leyland was about to snatch failure from the jaws of engineering success. They'd priced the hugely popular car way too low. Its retail cost was £437, but dealer profit was only £15 on each car. The maverick Mini design, which took just one year from drawing board to assembly line, had not had its engineering costs seriously calculated. The financial margins were a disaster. This groundbreaking little car, my father's one hope for a financial U-turn to save his business, was a damp squib.

Had this fiasco led my father to 'false accounting' – perhaps knowingly receiving hire-purchase payments for vehicles he knew could not be delivered? Had he been caught out by our architect neighbour when falsely using his name? The minimum jail sentence for this type of fraud was seven years.

Although impending financial meetings threatened everything in his world, my father gave no indication of the crisis overwhelming him. He did, however, take out a life-insurance policy which 'paid up' whatever the circumstances, even suicide. Could Dad have sacrificed himself for us, believing that we would gain long-term stability from his life insurance?

My initial shock kicked in again. The very thought that he may have given his life for us to have a better one produced a searing out-of-body agony. This was pain. It's how I imagined war to be – carnage, limbs being torn off and flesh flapping in the wind. I wanted to *know* what in God's name had made him undertake this irrational act? To work out why he hadn't left a note to explain. Perhaps writing a note at that moment would have been as futile as winding his watch. All hope gone. And with it any future. Our future.

I still have vivid memories of him relaxing in his favourite high-backed armchair checking his football pools coupons, the names and teasing tone of the radio announcer making him chuckle:

Tranmere Rovers	*2*	*Accrington Stanley*	*3*
Kilmarnock	*1*	*Motherwell*	*0*
Stenhousemuir	*4*	*Alloa Athletic*	*4*

The radio football results were always followed by the shipping forecast, informing us of 'Wind speed and weather conditions in our coastal waters' and assuring us that 'All is well' even when sailors were enduring a force nine gale in Cromarty. Always read as a kind of poetry, it allowed the non-marine listener to ignore the actual weather conditions and imagine some rustic-looking boats bobbing around on a gentle swell.

A metaphor for my father's life perhaps.

But was it the calm before the storm, or the storm before the calm?

It was thought best that I stay longer in Oxford, but Nick shot back to Barnsley to help organise things at home.

A funeral? A burial? A cremation?

'Surprise me,' I can hear my father murmuring, with his ironic smile.

I still don't know. I have never found any trace of my father's remains; his death was *never* ever discussed and I have no recall of what happened to him from that moment on. I've blanked everything. Not having physical closure kind of keeps him alive. A solicitor pal tried to trace him recently, but couldn't. I have never felt angry or abandoned. Just so sorry.

If only he'd stayed alive he might have realised that his pain was temporary, that human beings *are* able to reinvent themselves and find happiness. Even after the greatest of losses.

Time is stronger than all of us. And pain is meant to be a debt paid off by time. But it's too late for him.

*

The Suicide Act became law on 3 August 1961, ten days before Dad took his own life. This new Act of Parliament decriminalised the act of suicide, so that those who failed in their attempt would no longer be prosecuted or imprisoned. Until 1823 the body of a suicide was directed to be buried at night at a secret crossroads location and a stake driven through it. Now it's usually buried in consecrated ground without a religious ceremony.

Dad's clothes and bits and bobs around the house have all disappeared by the time I return to Barnsley. The glass jar of Brylcreem that lit up the bathroom with its scarlet label and shiny black lid, his lovely old clarinet and its endless spare reeds, the Super-8 home movie camera with reels and reels of family films proudly recorded by him in happier times have all simply vanished. His death is never discussed at home because Mum believes that I can't bear to share our mutual pain. We're both too close to it. She's right.

I still can't believe he thought his death was preferable to his life. His tragedy left a totally devastating imprint on our lives. I try to console myself by thinking he would have found old age difficult – unable to escape to his work-office or the horse races he loved so much. It's hard to imagine this lively, beaming man shuffling around, tripping over furniture, unable to drive.

Today you can have a dead relative's ashes made into jewellery or an egg timer, or added to a firework so that they can whoosh off with a blaze of glory. I'd probably sit Dad's pot of ashes on the drinks shelf in our living room next to some bottles of single malt, the kind of spirits he'd be happy to have as company. I'd raise my glass to him every evening and thank him for being such a wonderful, fun-loving, life-enhancing father.

The kind-hearted folk of Barnsley are completely thrown by Dad's suicide. People they knew had died in wars or from heart conditions. Choosing to die isn't in their repertoire of understanding. No one knows how to react, let alone discuss it. Nice Mr Turner, in his fluffy car-coat and round spectacles, who always waved at me from his Morris Minor, now quickly looks away trying to hide an expression of – what? Pity? Disgust? Embarrassment? Our eyes never meet again. He's not the only one – a number of people briskly cross roads to avoid me.

Essentially I'm now reduced to my own company by all except my mother. Counsellors don't yet exist to assure me that 'One day you're the butterfly, the next you're the windscreen.' This era and culture expects me to hide my pain and not embarrass others with tears and dislocation. And my uncle – devastated to have lost his only brother and a thousand pounds he invested in propping up the business in its latter months – never speaks to my mother again, and all contact with the cousins I love, my only cousins, is promptly severed.

I struggle to sleep in the years after Dad's death. When I do it's with angry dreams of waves crashing against the shore, weeping zombies gathering shells, rivers winding through forests of strange masked creatures. I can't bear to hear the words 'committed suicide'. It makes me scream inside. You commit a crime, you commit a murder . . . not suicide. 'Suicide' or 'Misadventure' – the recorded verdict makes all the difference to those left behind.

I'm dreading returning to school after the summer holidays . . . how to deal with the pain and being 'different'? Knowing where the questions will lead and the shocked and embarrassed silence that will follow. Please don't ask if I'm all right. Please don't say, 'I do understand – I lost my grandmother last year.' It's not the same.

Aware for the first time ever that all living beings must die, it makes me determined to not allow grief to overwhelm and blight my life. Instead it will spur me on to achieve for my darling dad. He's not a suicide in my eyes – the word that defines my dad is *Jaguar*.

From somewhere deep inside, I find a strand of strength, a kind of inbuilt ticking clock which strangely motivates me in an unconscious way. Our kitchen garden backs onto the school's playing fields which are whopping enough to accommodate simultaneous games of hockey, rounders, tennis, netball and athletics, with games periods each day to keep us all leaping around. And as I gaze at their abundant glory I know that sport will be my answer!

My heroine is Dorothy Hyman – the Barnsley girl who won a silver medal for the hundred-metre sprint at last year's Rome Olympics. No guessing who was first in line for her autograph when she and her medal returned to Barnsley. Totally inspired by her (future wins confirmed her status as one of the world's best and still Britain's top woman sprinter of all time, and whose father famously said, 'Now, don't let it go to your head, lass'), I win a weighty cup for 'Fastest Schoolgirl Sprinter' in the region, presented by the Lady Mayor of Barnsley.

Sprint Cup winner, summer 1961

It's only fair to confess that my feat had far more to do with leg length than athletic talent. Already a five-foot-nine giraffe at age thirteen, I pretty well walked it.

But it isn't enough to have sporting prowess at girls' grammar schools in the early Sixties. Academic achievement is the name of the game and our English teachers (both men) focus fidgety classes by informing us that 'Listen!' is an anagram of 'Silent' and that we are each 'unique' not 'quite unique' or 'very unique'. It must have worked despite our giggling attempts to lift their trouser turn-ups with rulers (to view their hairy legs) as they spout Shakespeare up and down the classroom aisles. Anyone who can persuade a class of forty-four teenage girls that H. G. Wells' *The History of Mr Polly* is a riveting read and impart an inkling of joy into *The Merchant of Venice* has enviable authority.

Pouty, wide-eyed, dreamy hair flickers are non-existent at Barnsley High. So is sex education and our imaginations run wild. Between lessons, we take it in turns to draw an imagined penis on the blackboard. Mine has hairs all over it, like a demented hedgehog.

'My brother's willy doesn't look a bit like that,' says Jenny Burton.

'Well, he's just a boy, the hairs will grow onto it later,' I reply.

That remains our template until Wendy Lewis tells us she's 'gone all the way' and sketches the real thing. Her acclaim is short-lived. She gets pregnant and is expelled before she can 'contaminate' the rest of us.

I'm often hauled in front of our Head Mistress for breaching uniform rules. 'You think you're being creative, Victoria, but that black polo-necked sweater you're wearing is not part of the school dress code,' says the urbane and elegant Miss Baldwin. 'It's charcoal grey, not black and the classrooms are so cold,' I offer. But the cane is never forthcoming. A little talk is considered enough.

If we like the teachers we usually excel at the subject they teach. Not so with Maths teacher Mrs Aveyard, her shrill voice commanding us to 'Push on . . . push on, girls' as we try to make sense of some equation that resembles an Arabic poem. Our Religious Instruction teacher, Miss Barber, always refers to God as Yahweh, which sounds to us more like the title of a singalong than the name of the Almighty. There's a no-talking rule on the stairs, in the corridors, in assembly, in classes – anywhere and everywhere except the playing fields.

Nick is still on his Fine Art course in Newcastle. He doesn't ring home often but Mum and I don't worry; his life appears to be full-on work and fun. When he does phone, his lively calls *always* pulsate with thrilling stories of his 'hip' course. His tutors, Richard Hamilton, the 'Father of Pop Art', and acclaimed artist Victor Pasmore, have introduced an innovative teaching method, the 'Basic Design' course, which changes British art education for ever. But much more important (according to Nick) is the news that Hamilton regularly takes his students dancing at the Majestic Ballroom in their lunch hour – a cool pack which soon includes an enigmatic first-year cohort named Brian Ferry.

Lucky Nick. How I envy him. My life is more trimming hedge than cutting edge. But my resilient mum remains as loving, selfless and caring as ever for me and her friends in need, ensuring she's rarely lonely or alone, the house ever-flowing with those seeking wise, non-judgemental advice.

Popular with both men and women, my mother has a sort of sexy confidence that attracts men because it's not flighty and frivolous, and which women admire because it's inclusive and non-threatening. My pals all love her – she digs our music and is surely the only over-forty in the UK who never utters 'what sex is that?' when *Top of the Pops* belts out on screen.

As the months pass after Dad's death, Mum and I become closer than we've ever been, as Granny Aggie never returns from Oxford. After a glance at *Coronation Street*, post-supper and -homework, I meander up to bed with Spider, my adored Yorkshire terrier at my heels. He'd replaced my beloved pet alligator after Ali died. Spider and I snuggle down to listen to Radio Luxembourg on my tiny transistor radio. The faded, crackly '2-0-8 Your Station of the Stars' mostly plays pop music by British singers with forceful names – Fury, Faith, Wilde and Steele – between the ramblings of silly old Horace Batchelor, the pools tipster. Millions of us teenagers listen raptly every night, never realising for a second that Luxembourg is a country, simply assuming the music comes from two rooms out there somewhere.

Sunday night is best because it schedules the *Top 20 Chart Show*. Drifting off to sleep, transistor clamped to my left ear, gently singing along to Helen Shapiro's 'Walking Back To Happiness' . . . 'whoop I oh yeah yeah' . . . I hear the sharp, shrill ring of our house phone.

My mother finally reaches the receiver downstairs in the hall. A short conversation follows a suppressed scream and heavy thud. Then silence. I leap out of bed, crash across the landing and see her leaning awkwardly against the stairs reaching for a cigarette. All colour has drained from her face, the phone receiver is dangling in mid-air.

'Nick's been stabbed. Very near his heart, it's touch-and-go. We need to get to Newcastle.'

We dress in silence in the freezing cold. I snuggle into my camel duffle coat, gather up Spider and we set off for Newcastle in a pitch-black starless night. We both concentrate on Mum's driving. At 3.30 A.M. by the dashboard clock, she drives the wrong way round a large roundabout and tells me not to panic. At 4.15 we pass Newcastle train station and see a giant newspaper placard declaring 'Art Student Stabbed'. I keep thinking that if Nick dies I can have his record player and then detesting myself for thinking that.

The door to Nick's ground-floor flat in Jesmond is opened by one of two policemen who inform us that a knife has been discovered in the garden. They drive us to a nearby hospital where Nick is lying in a cot-like bed, barely conscious, his chest covered in bulky bandages. An exhausted middle-aged doctor ushers us into a tiny side room and gestures towards two white chairs. Mum and I sit awkwardly forward, our hands on our knees.

'He's going to be okay . . . physically, that is,' the doctor murmurs.

'I don't understand. What do you mean *exactly*?' asks my mother.

'I'm extremely sorry to have to tell you this, but the knife wound was self-administered. We need to transfer him to

Collingwood Clinic, a psychiatric hospital, and give him a course of ECT treatment.'

'But what is ECT?' Mum asks. How does it work?'

'We don't exactly know. It's best to think of it as reshuffling the inside of the brain, like a pack of cards.'

Electro Convulsive Therapy is one of the most controversial medical treatments ever invented. An electric pulse will be placed to Nick's head causing him to have a controlled fit or seizure. This will not be done under a full general anaesthetic (it is today, but not then) so he will be fully aware of the seizure. Muscle relaxants will be given to him to reduce shaking movements and prevent injury. A course of six or twelve treatments is normal.

We stay in Newcastle to be close with Nick during treatment, carefully avoiding the few patients with their wild, distracted eyes. For this ward has nothing of the conviviality and camaraderie of a usual hospital visit. It is a silent, intense flurry of white – coats, screens and doctors' faces. Grave looks and whispers prowling the recesses of damaged, lonely, tormented minds. Male nurses checking the whole ward every fifteen minutes to make sure nobody's done a runner, or worse. Fragments of conversation drift from the nurses' office, then more sedation, turning patients forever inwards, eternally trapped by the pain in their own minds.

'This ECT treatment is making me confused,' Nick announces on the third day. 'I want it to stop. I've got to get out of here.' He springs out of bed and makes for a ground-floor open window. There's a scuffle. Two male nurses floor him, hold him down, pressing so tightly their knuckles turn white as they roughly wrap and tie him into a white coat with fake sleeves. Frog-marching my brother to a tiny room with bloated walls like giant pillows, one of the men locks the door leaving Nick inside.

'What are they doing to him, Mum?'

'They've put him in a straitjacket and thrown him into a padded cell until he changes his mind,' whispers my mother in utter disbelief.

Witnessing this face-down restraint and imagining my brother being given ECT treatment is beyond horrifying. Nick doesn't appear mad. He makes perfect sense. How can this be happening to my wonderful brother? Who is making these disturbing decisions about his sanity?

It transpires that since Dad's death, Nick has been attending Bible meetings with an old school friend who is preparing for priesthood, and he was given a book about Martin Luther, the German theologian who initiated the Protestant Reformation in the sixteenth century.

And apparently Luther instructed Nick to self-destruct.

My thirteen-year-old head is pounding. Did the shock of finding Dad on the showroom floor do this to Nick? Has the manner of our father's death planted a contagious seed – or is my brother's mental condition the direct result of a self-destructive gene? Does this mean I have it?

During our journey back to Barnsley, Mum and I try to stay jolly for each other and when our little car finally turns into the gravel drive, crunching and crackling through the clinging branches of the weeping willow my father planted shortly before his death, we both sigh with relief. Mum opens her mountain of mail while I make us cups of tea.

Approaching the living room with two mugs of piping PG Tips, I can see Mum's head is rolling in her hands. She takes a deep, heavy breath and reaches for yet another cigarette. 'The insurance company won't pay out for Dad's policy. We're broke – we'll have to sell the house immediately, and I'll have to find a job.'

An estate agent is summoned who tells us, 'It's a lovely property, but the market is severely depressed right now.' The following day he rings and informs us he's found a buyer. 'Done deal,' says my mother quietly. But hours before the contract is signed, the buyer threatens to pull out unless the price is drastically reduced. Our agent says 'take the offer' and she reluctantly does, only to find out later that the buyer was the agent's brother.

A letter from Nick in the Collingwood Clinic cheers me up: 'I'm feeling much better now and feel so sorry for the distress that I've caused you and Mum,' he writes. 'Yesterday I had to go in front of a committee of doctors and professors and they seem to think I am making rapid progress. Eight friends came to visit me and everyone is being so kind. Thanks for asking which record I'd like for my birthday – Mozart's Symphony No. 40 in G Minor would be great.'

I ask my music teacher at school to tell me about Nick's chosen record. 'It's a symphony of grief depicting feelings of insecurity, anxiety and urgency written when Mozart was at a very low point of his life. It's intensely emotional and tragic in tone.'

Not exactly Louis Armstrong's 'What a Wonderful World' then. C'mon my wonderful, special, funny, handsome brother, my friend, my hero, my life, my . . . everything. Please, please, get better. Let's laugh again soon.

Mum is offered a job in a jewellery shop owned by a friend and we look at a small featureless house twenty yards from the gates of my school. 'I'm sure we can make it look lovely with some window boxes, and it's useful to have a bus stop so close now that we don't have a car,' I say in an upbeat voice as we complete our viewing. My mother stares blankly ahead. 'Yes darling.' We move in, acquire a lodger – or PG (Paying Guest) as Mum insists on calling him – and both pray that Nick's past does not become his future. Making the house as cosy as possible over the next eighteen months, we mostly spend our evenings watching telly and styling our hair with gigantic rollers and frenetic back-combing. Barnsley's answer to Vidal Sassoon is way too pricey for us.

Cuddled up with Spider, and half watching some late-night BBC programme after Mum has gone to bed, I'm gob-smacked when I hear a theatre critic called Ken Tynan say *fuck* live on air. I can barely believe it and run upstairs to tell Mum, giggling loudly. 'You must have misheard, darling.' But I haven't. Hell breaks loose in the press. It's a first. Politicians go bonkers and Mary Whitehouse writes a complaining letter to the Queen. Yet Tynan's career soars: this, I later realise, is a seminal moment in this radical 'new thinking' Britain that is finally shaking off its former taboos.

And Nick has turned his life around and is now super-active, positive and happy. He has a lecturing job at his former university in Newcastle and an enchanting girlfriend he met on the same Fine Art degree course. She's warm, right and bright and Mum and I adore her.

Friday evening is always *Ready Steady Go!* time in this house, and ITV's hipper answer to the BBC's *Top of the Pops* has as its opening theme tune Manfred Mann's '5-4-3-2-1' co-written and sung by my one-time-crush pal Paul Jones, which makes it my must-watch of every week. Spider always jumps on my knee whenever he hears the intro. He loves good sounds and I rest my chin on top of his head, smell his soft, warm fur and we sway in time to the music. He hardly leaves my side these days. But tonight I can't find him anywhere.

'Hey Mum,' I shout through to the kitchen, 'where's Spider? *Ready Steady Go!*'s starting.'

She opens the door to check the garden. Then I hear it. The screeching of brakes, loud voices, a hollow scream. Rushing back through the front door, my mother returns with trembling hands, her face deathly white. She can hardly get the words out:

'I'm so, so sorry, darling . . . Spider's been run over. He managed to get through the gate.'

Please tell me this isn't really happening. I try and react calmly to not upset my mother. I've been here before. At sixteen I know more about death than I do about life. The reality of losing my beloved little pal shatters and splinters my heart. I can't imagine life without him. No more waggy tail approval when he sees my walking shoes go on. No more deep sighs of disapproval when I dress up to go to a dog-free zone. My little friend is gone.

Mum knows it will utterly devastate me to see Spider's lifeless body, and asks the car's driver to take him away and dispose of him. But where did he go? Handed to a vet, thrown in a ditch, slammed in a dustbin, fed to the foxes on the Yorkshire Moors?

Gently stroking my hair, desperate to give me strength and a new focus, my mother whispers, 'Darling, I think it's time to make some enquiries about your possible modelling career in London, if that's what you still want to do, and Paul Jones thought you could.'

It's what I want to do more than ever now. To suppress this mordant pain. To get on with my life. To run free from all emotion. Nothing to complicate my running. No obstacles, just opportunities.

According to Mum's research, only one institution in the UK has the fully respected credentials for training a fledgling model. The Lucie Clayton School and Model Agency in London's Bond Street offers a month-long 'Charm Course', and, if thought suitable for modelling at the passing-out parade, girls automatically go on the agency's books. Lucie Clayton, the person, doesn't exist. The founder, a former Blackpool model who started it as a kind of non-boarding finishing school, invented the name because she thought it sounded 'posh'. She sold the school for a pittance to former barrister and magazine editor Leslie Kark and when I was growing up it was Britain's leading model agency, turning out such illustrious pupils as Fiona Campbell-Walter and Jean Shrimpton.

Mum makes an appointment for my assessment interview. The 39-shilling bus fare from Barnsley to London is loads cheaper than the train fare, but takes two hours longer. She works overtime so we can do the journey by train. 'Less time to get nervous, darling.'

Arriving in Bond Street, we tiptoe up the narrow flight of stairs a few doors down from Fenwick's. My mother and I are then ushered into a light, ordered office to await Mr Kark's assessment of my modelling potential. The tall, dapper proprietor enters with a pretty assistant who begins to measure me. Yet to be schooled in 'preparing a face to meet the faces that I meet', as T. S. Eliot would have it, I giggle nervously. 'Do you ride horses?' enquires Mr Kark.

'Not any more, but I *can* take it up again,' I respond a tad too exuberantly.

'No, no, no – quite the opposite! Your thirty-six-inch hip measurement is a little big for us, but your five-foot-nine-and a half height is good and you have a face which could photograph well.'

'Are there any other requirements?' asks my mother.

'Yes, something behind the eyes, a sense of humour, a spark, a personality that will last through hours of being kept waiting by photographers, of boredom, repetition and long hours.' Damn. Nobody warned me about that part. Not quite as exciting as I thought.

The course – 28 guineas for a month of mornings consisting of Deportment Instruction, Dress-sense,

Make-up, Diet and General Health – is enough to make my Maths mistress squirm. But first I have to keep my side of a bargain with my mother and complete a six-month secretarial course in Leeds . . . 'Something to fall back on if it doesn't work out, darling.'

The shorthand reminds me of algebra and the ten-fingered typing of my former piano lessons, but the months fly by in a constant whirlwind of London anticipation and a sense of the wild, unfettered freedom that beckons my future. My amazing, much-loved mother has given me a solid platform from which to launch myself. She understands my need to go, to control my own destiny. By watching her I know about self-sufficiency, self-preservation and self-respect. And the art of being self-contained and happy on my own.

She's taught me how to be strong and brave and true to myself. Never to make decisions in the hours of darkness, always to be curious – and that life is a matter of freedom that needs your full control. She's shown me how true pleasures come from things that no one can take away: a wondrous sky, the rhythm of the seasons, a love of art and beauty. And that humour bonds everyone regardless of age, class, geography and race.

She understands, from her own childhood, how the early patterns of opportunity and deprivation can make or mar our lives, and that there is a point where you – and only *you* – can decide to play victim or not, that you can't avoid pain but you *can* choose to overcome it. And most important of all: if you want to find happiness, you must first find gratitude.

On the morning that I head for the train to London my mother hugs me tightly and we say our goodbyes. As the taxi driver crams my worldly goods into the boot of his car, Len the miner yells from the bus stop across the road:

'You show 'em lass! Where there's pluck, there's brass.'

Leaving Barnsley for London in 1966

3

FRAMED IN LONDON

'A goal without a plan is just a wish'

Antoine de Saint-Exupéry

I feel like a dog being groomed for Crufts. Day one at Lucie Clayton and we've been taught to roll around the floor to reduce our hips but not to get hot and sweaty because 'low perspiration can be exciting, sexually, but only in the right place,' explains Mr Kark. Learning to emerge elegantly from a low-slung sports car (a mock-up E-type Jag) without showing my knickers is nearly as taxing as balancing four books on my head. Tomorrow we'll discover how to sit with our ankles crossed – never legs – and Mr Kark will lecture us on etiquette, or 'Thoughtful Manners', as he sweetly puts it.

I can hardly wait to phone home:

'Hello Mum, can't talk for long, it costs a fortune before six and I might run out of coins . . . I'm ringing you from the payphone on the landing of my bedsit in Holland Park. The house itself is very grand, and my tiny room in the gods is cosy, but sheet-bitingly cold. There's a shilling-in-the-slot gas ring thingy but it doesn't last long. Could you possibly send me an electric blanket? Quite enjoyed my first day but most of the girls are here to learn how to model for the Berkeley Dress Show which will launch them as debs – which of course could be a huge advantage in Barnsley! There's no fridge in my room so I've stocked up on Dairylee cheese triangles, Ritz crackers, Campbell's tomato soup and Butterscotch Angel Delight. Last night I tried Heinz oxtail soup but spat it out when I realised what it was and stuffed myself with Twiglets instead.'

Mum is thrilled that 'you're doing what you really want to do', she'll send an electric blanket, she misses me like crazy and 'Home is always here whenever you need us.'

Day three and Miss Edison's barking voice stops us in our tracks, 'Girls! Girls! Girls! We are very privileged today. This is Michelangelo Antonioni, an important Italian film director and he's looking for the right face for a film he's making about the London fashion scene.' The tiny man, fiftyish, in navy suit with narrow lapels peruses us all, then asks me to put my hair up and smile without showing my teeth – it's half a muscle from a leery sneer. '*Va bene*. You will be 'earing from me,' smiles Antonioni. Yeah, sure.

The following afternoon, Vidal Sassoon drops by the school to invite us all for haircuts at his salon in New Bond Street and appears irritated when I decline his free offer. But I can't imagine my unruly mane cut into his neat, geometric bob. 'Why not?' he asks, and when I reply, 'Because it makes everyone look the same,' Miss Edison nearly chokes in horror. Make-up classes have us all looking like Danny La Rue –

mud-thick pan cake, terrifying false eyelashes and a thunderous line of brown blusher intended to make our cheekbones stand out. But mine want to leap out and run away.

Varsity Newspaper, www.varsity.co.uk. Photo: Vladimir Vinski
Third day at Lucie Clayton Model School

This time it's Mr Kark who interrupts our make-up lesson. 'Girls, this is Albert Locke, the ITV director, who is looking for girls to model in the fashion show section of *The Glad Rag Ball*, a variety show to be broadcast in December. Locke picks twelve girls. I'm his hesitant twelfth choice. The Who, Donovan, Lionel Blair, Jimmy Tarbuck, Frankie Vaughan, Georgie Fame and Wilson Pickett are also appearing. 'What a line-up!' laughs Mum when I ring to tell her. 'You don't let the grass grow under your feet, do you, pet? It's like reading the gossip column of the *Daily Mail*.'

The four weeks are soon up and tomorrow is the Passing-out Parade. 'Sounds like a cross between Sandhurst and a night on the tiles,' chortles Mum. We'll be graded A to E according to our potential as we float along the catwalk. No girl's ever achieved an A and an E is 'Forget it!' The other girls rush off to buy pastel-hued suits and frocks from Selfridges but I gallop over to Biba where owner Barbara Hulanicki *gives* me an achingly beautiful black dress in an art deco/art nouveau combo embossed fabric. We've been instructed to wear delicate shoes on the catwalk but I can never totter anywhere in high-heels without stumbling into passing strangers, so it's the Russell & Bromley purple suede boots for me.

I phone home from a call box on the corner of New Bond Street:

'Oh Mum . . . I don't quite know how to tell you this but . . . I FAILED! I was the only one who didn't pass in the entire school! Not even an E . . . an eFFing . . . TOTAL FAIL! I'm so sorry. I wanted to look so cool, clever and sort-of-ironic but it backfired. Mr Kark said that black is NEVER worn in daytime except for funerals, my hair is too wild, I don't wear enough make-up, and I walk like a carthorse!

He's offered me another two-week Improvement Course . . .
to fucking tiptoe, saunter, bounce, shimmy, sway, stride,
stagger, lurch and plod.'

Not even a runner-up at Crufts.

My mother gives this devastating event a positive twist, as
always. 'Darling, never worry about any disappointments. When
one door closes, another always opens. Take advantage of this
extra fortnight at Lucie Clayton – they'll admire you for it.'

Late for the extended course, I take a short cut to Holland
Park tube station through Princes Place where an enormous
white Rolls-Royce is attempting to reverse, totally blocking
the narrow street. I'm rendered swear-less when a familiar-
looking short man hops out of the back seat and says 'Ciao!'
It's Signor Antonioni who informs me he's planning to shoot
the interior scenes of his new film 'right here' in photographer
John Cowan's studio. He wonders if I can return later today
for Cowan's assistant to take headshot stills, followed by a
film test.

YES!

Antonioni's film, *Blow-Up*, is an awesome and delicious
satire on the flamboyant working practices of a misogynistic
fashion photographer. But this doesn't impress a soul
at Lucie Clayton, and two weeks later no one has time to
offer me a revised grade – or a much-yearned-for PhD in
Thoughtful Manners and Drag-Queen Make-up.

However *Blow Up* turned out to be the cult film of the
decade. It took an observant Italian film director to put a
finger on the pulse of Swinging London. And I didn't get a
part – but Jane Birkin did. No contest. And his choice of six-

footer Veruschka to play herself and leggy-writhe around the studio floor with David Hemmings for three throbbing minutes, was inspired. The only line she uttered was 'Here I am' – surely the ultimate cinematic example of 'Action!' speaking louder than words.

Photo: John Hooton, 1966

And what became of the girl from Barnsley whose dreams were crumbling fast?

Um, well, she became a typist. You were right, Mum – a useful fall-back.

My salary is £8 a week and consists of typing invoices in the accounts department of an advertising agency in Mayfair. At the top of the building, Accounts is isolated from the Suits and Creatives buzzing around beneath. But here's the thing . . . I kind of enjoy it. The clatter of my manual Olivetti with its noisy carriage return and bell ping, the predictable routine, the un-madness and normality is strangely comforting and clannish, particularly the office humour directed at the hyper staff below.

And Accounts couldn't care less when the 'oh-so-pleased-with-himself' Radio Caroline disc jockey Simon Dee regularly swooshes up to the pirate station's offices next door in his white E-type Jag, and have no opinion whatsoever when *Vogue* snapper David Bailey appears stonkingly drunk during his interview on the BBC's *Eamonn Andrews Show*.

'Superficial types, eh! Have you finished typing those invoices, love?'

Six months into the job, while dashing for the lift, I crash full-whack into fashion photographer Mike Berkofsky. His finished prints, destined for the Creatives, scatter like cheap confetti around our feet. 'Ever thought of wearing glasses . . .' he mumbles, looking up and hearing my bumbling apology, '. . . or of modelling . . . ?'

'No!'

No way am I falling for that bloody line again.

'Seriously,' he continues, 'I could use you next week for a magazine shoot: you look a bit like Faye Dunaway. You'll need an agent. The best one right now is next door to my studio in Bruton Street. Here's my card – I'll tell them you'll drop by later.'

Damn. Damn. Damn. It would be so easy to give a cool 'no, thanks' but not when the shoot's for Quorum, the most innovative boutique in the market place.

Askew Model Agency is buzzing when I spiral down to the basement premises, the slightly chaotic club-like atmosphere poles apart from well-mannered Lucie Clayton just round the corner. Not a deb in sight, and the visual diversity of the models unexpectedly refreshing. Two wacky, over-caffeinated Americans, an exquisite slow-blinking black girl with endless limbs and a vivacious brunette who's a dead ringer for Claudia Cardinale are all sprawled on well-worn banquettes, their portfolios and accessory bags randomly dropped where they flop between bookings and go-sees.

The Askew sisters, Gloria and Valerie – mid-forties, neat suits – preside over the room from two colossal typewriters at far-side desks. A hip young booker, Dinah, shares a joke with Valerie's excitable Italian boyfriend Fulvio who deals with accounts and swears in Milanese at any opportunity. Everyone appears to be nicely bonkers. I feel instantly at home.

A few questions from Gloria and then 'Right, first you'll need some composite shots. And a name change. Victoria isn't remotely catchy. How about Vikki with two *k*'s – like Twiggy has two *g*'s?' followed by a huge smile. Blimey, I think I'm on the books! But will Accounts think I've sold out? My top-floor associates appear to be thrilled and wish me 'all the luck in the world. You'll fucking-well need it!' Thanks, guys.

Promising young photographers take composite shots free of charge, the model choosing prints in exchange for posing – giving both parties 'what the camera sees' experience. This essential marketing tool for models consists of an A4 format printed card with her statistics, agency info and face-on/profile/full-length shots in a variety of moods, ranging from the 'cute and flirty', the 'flicky hair toss while gazing meaninglessly into the middle distance', the 'leapy through the air for no apparent reason', the 'disdainful (who's just farted?) raised eyebrow' and the 'full Macleans toothpaste laugh'. But by far the most popular is the 'wide-eyed vacuous stare with lips slightly parted as though in the preliminary stages of flu or unable to acknowledge or understand that one breathes through the nose'.

Try as I might, I can't master any of the desired poses, least of all the 'pert and pouty in a decolletagey, clingy thingy' but manage a *'Don't Mess With Me!'* glare in every shot which appears to satisfy the snappers but not Agent Gloria.

'Look, love, it's important to understand that versatility is what it's all about.'

'Surely a unique look makes people remember you.'

'Well don't blame us if work is slow,' snaps Gloria, clearly regretting that her new product isn't a bottle on a shelf. It talks back.

But the composite works with immediate effect. Fortuitous timing sees Yves Saint Laurent introduce the most ground-breaking, revolutionary fashion innovation ever – a cool, alluring trouser suit for women. *Le Smoking* tuxedo and later *Le Safari* prefer square, marching shoulders and a 'don't-mess-with-me' leer to make them work on camera. Lucky indeed for this gauche new model, Vikki Nixon, with two *k*'s.

The studio shoots can last for twelve hours and I learn on the job. Lights blaze endlessly and Vaselined feet are forced into heels two sizes too small. More light readings. More hair fiddling. The corset's so tight I can hardly breathe. This sure ain't a piece of cake. (What I'd bloody give for a piece of cake!)

It's not long before I can count the clicks of the camera without knowing I'm doing it. Twelve exposures, then relax muscles until the snapper's ready to shoot again. It's all automatic reflex: turn on – stop – sit back – wait – turn on again – until it's a wrap. The professional patter goes like this:

'Right, babe, now first I'm gonna take some head and shoulders. Turn your head to the left, babe. No, no, camera left! Watch my hand! That's it, darling. Now bring your eyes round to me. Yes! Lovely! Fab! Hold it!' Flash! An explosion of lights. 'C'mon, less glare, more happy . . . yeah, good, come on, concentrate, that's nice, more like that.' Flash 'Give us another of those, love. Yes! Yes! Yes!' Flash again. 'Put your chin down. Too much! Eyes back to me. Yeah!' Flash. 'Face round to me more. No! No! Too much, too much! Relax your face, soften your eyes, loosen your neck. You look stiff, babe. Gimme a grin, yeah that works! Now keeping your head in exactly that position, look right into the middle of my lens. Oh, yeah! Don't move an inch. Give me a hint of a smile, no, too much, too much. Yeah. Yeah, Yeah! Fab!' Flash. 'No, your eyes are staring and cold. Look away

67

for a second and come back to me, straight into the lens. Oooohhh, yes, bloody fabulous.' Flash. 'Now a teeny, weeny smile, more teeth, yeah.' Flash. 'Your neck's too tense. Don't hunch your shoulders, it makes 'em look even bigger! Turn away, look back. Stay. Like. That! THAT'S THE SHOT!'

Flash. Flash. Flash.

Job done.

No 'How was it for you?' from our snapper. Simply . . . job done. Now bugger off.

Needing an excuse to celebrate my busy first month after joining the Askew agency, I'm drooling over yet another pair of purple suede boots in Kurt Geiger's Bond Street window when a black cab pulls up and a tiny, delicate creature jumps out. She has jaws of steel and a thousand clinking bangles.

'My name is Marit Allen and I work for *Vogue*, and this is photographer Helmut Newton who would like to see you at Vogue House. It's just round the corner, we can take you there.' The taxi's rear window winds down and a pair of penetrating chestnut eyes emerge, then a tanned proboscis, followed by a wicked smile. Mr Newton, I presume.

Vaguely thinking my mother would disapprove, I leap in and we whizz round the bend to Hanover Square and up to *Vogue*'s top-floor studios where Mr Newton's eyes strain slightly from their sockets under ultra-bushy eyebrows as he concentrates on assessing his latest prop. He finally yells, 'Book her!' and I feel like a racehorse arrested for drink driving.

Newton's peculiarly stylised fashion photography is already ultra controversial and immediately recognisable. He specialises in, and has a reputation for, going that bit too far. His work sometimes conveys a kind of cruelty that cuts through the elegance of his glamorous, wealthy settings. But proudly liberated, as I most certainly am, I choose not to focus there because Helmut Newton's models always look spirited, decadent, restless, independent and sexually confident – and a booking for this magazine is the very best.

It's the morning of the *Vogue* shoot and I'm nervously making my way to Leonard's salon, a tall grand house just off Park Lane, for a hair and nail gloss. Leonard is now the *coiffeur du jour* having usurped Vidal by inventing a superb cutting technique based on the geometry of Buckminster Fuller's geodesic dome that mirrors the shape of the head. The hair is sectioned into triangles before being cut and it is a flawless technique where everyone ends up with a cut that suits their head shape as well as their face.

I'm ushered up an elegant staircase to the first-floor salon where Leonard is commanding the central position in front of enormous shimmering silver mirrors. His team of stylists – handsome, manly guys well-honed in flirtatious client-exchange – are all sporting ubiquitous embroidered shirts and ties from Mr Fish with their wide-lapelled green velvet suits, the ever-flapping bell-bottoms hiding two-inches-taller Cuban-heeled boots.

Waving warmly and waiting to be nailed and curled are three other models booked for the shoot – the divine Willy Van Rooy who is currently Helmut's favourite model, the

Biba model Vicki Wise and Kari-Ann Muller, soon to be Chris Jagger's wife, and Roxy Music album cover star. We giggle and ponder what naughty theme Helmut has in mind for us today. No doubt we'll be all-powerful and sensual and our careers will continue to sizzle and explode when we appear in *Vogue*'s February issue. Oh, the glory of it all!

Hang on, what's this? Two adorable tiny blonde girls of around three and five skip up the stairs and into the salon. They're also booked for the shoot. We're calmly informed that the *Vogue* fashion story is 'Grey Flannel Family – A Sweet, Endearing Tableau of Garments'. This is about as far removed from Newton's sexy, sizzling *beau-monde* as my old school uniform. On set, back in *Vogue*'s studio, my tightly curled hair has a charcoal beret plonked on top, the sombre slate-grey coat is buttoned to the neck and sensible flat shoes slip easily onto my huge feet.

Bugger! This *is* my old school uniform!

Helmut has a unique way of getting the best from his models in a group shot. Instead of the usual 'Yeah, girls, gimme more of that' approach, he coldly informs us that 'One of you is not giving me what I want and is letting us ALL down.' Of course we each think we are the one to blame. This shoot isn't much fun; we're simply anonymous bodies moved around like toy soldiers, but the kudos of having Helmut Newton tear-sheets in our portfolios can launch an international career. Not much money in editorials per se, but an appearance in a prestigious glossy is what keeps a girl a visible feature in this high-stakes, high-budget business of high fashion.

70

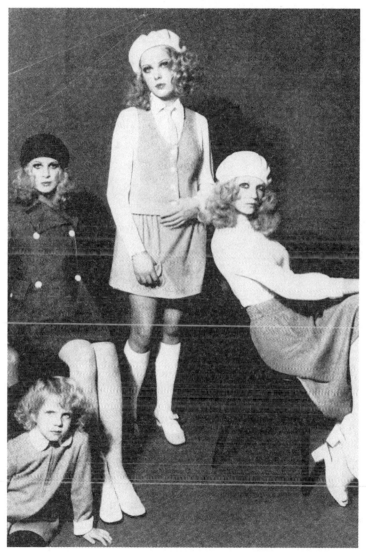

British Vogue, 1968 (© *The Helmut Newton Estate / Maconochie Photography /* Vogue © *The Condé Nast Publications Ltd.)*

Vikki Nixon, Vicky Wise and Willy Van Rooy

71

The next day's booking is more fun. An ad shoot for the widest bell-bottoms I've ever seen, let alone worn. And it's a rare shoot indeed when the snapper commands his model to 'Pose like you're stuffing your face with nosh.'

Try a little
French Dressing
by Lady
at Lord John.
T Shirt £3.95
Trousers £16.95
Selection of
French trousers
from £12.95

Back at the model agency, accountant Fulvio is beside himself with excitement.

'*Ciao, bella.* I have fabulous news. *Un amico* Riccardo, he has opened the *prima* model agency in Milano. We sent him all our girls' composites and he has a *molto prestigioso* campaign for *you* – and the pay is *fantastico*!'

Thanks to feisty Fulvio, I'm all set to be the first British model to work directly with an Italian model agency.

No city in Europe offers more prestigious work to a photographic fashion model than Milan in the mid-Sixties, for Italy publishes more fashion magazines than any other country. There are, however, two tiny problems I'm unaware of. All model agencies in Italy are illegal. The prevailing Napoleonic law declares that it is not legal for model agents to work for a percentage of someone's earnings – hence no indigenous models – and anyone attempting to work must have an approved permit.

But there are ways round this which have been discovered. Riccardo Gay operates quite openly, as he is canny enough to realise he can offer clients an ever changing supply of new models if he books girls through agencies in Paris, New York and London, pays top rates, and splits commission with the 'mother' agency.

My first working trip abroad – and I'm totally up for it. Boy, am I up for it!

4

EXPOSED IN MILAN

It's not what you look at that matters. It's what you see

Henry David Thoreau

It's six in the evening when I arrive at the sparkling offices in Via Revere. Printed head sheets of the world's top model agencies line the walls with endless exquisite faces beaming out, pleading to be booked, but oddly appearing more like convict mug shots.

'Vikki . . . *cara* . . . *ciao* . . . *bella!*' shriek the delightful Riccardo and sister Lucetta in unison, rushing forward to surround me with hugs and kisses in the all-collective embrace.

'Toscani, he is waiting to see you now to confirm for the job.' And with that I'm thrust into a waiting cab and a scribbled address flutters through the window.

Milan itself looks a tad disappointing – this northern industrial city producing cars, books, fabrics and magazines looks more like a compact town than a major metropolis.

It doesn't appear to possess the imagined visual charms of Florence or Venice or Rome – but does appear to be a shopper's paradise. And the women have a certain style. Indeed my Alitalia flight was packed with polished Milanesi sporting perfectly coiffured hair, precisely tied silk scarves, all manner of fur coats and sunglasses they never took off.

As I approach the door of Oliviero Toscani's studio, a monster Harley motorbike screeches to a halt beside me and I find myself staring into the seductive eyes of the most astonishingly beautiful man I've ever seen. Tall and sensual, he smells of fresh, tingling sweat in his exquisite, steaming leather jacket, and tight, tight jeans.

Ushering me into a tiny anteroom, he flicks through my portfolio of photographs. His eyes dance. Mine are fixed. 'I will ring the agency,' he utters. I nod and make my exit. This is going to be a breeze, a piece of cake. Sorted!

Flopping onto my bed in the Hotel Carlton Centro, watching the leaves dancing wildly in the deserted street below and pondering the curious impetuousness of fashion decisions, I leap in the air when the bedside phone rings sharply. It's agent Riccardo.

'*Bella* . . . Oliviero . . . he like you very, very much in the person, but not in the face. He has cancelled the job.'

My enticing, magnetic aura thrown to the wind – the bloody features don't fit!

Oliviero Toscani goes on to create the most audacious and controversial fashion advertising campaign ever produced in the Eighties and Nineties, as far removed from selling clothes as is possible to get.

For Benetton, one ad features a duck coated in black oil, another a newly born baby covered in blood. Spurred on by outcry, his next ad features condemned murderers. But he is forced to resign over international protest. When art flirts with life too heavily, it's a step too far. I never see him again.

A telegram arrives for Riccardo from my French agent. It's for a *Vogue* booking with Helmut Newton. Well, at least someone still wants to book me!

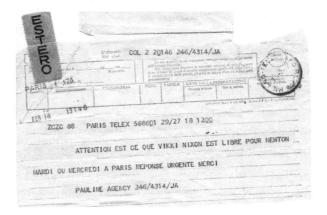

'Not possible, *cara*, I have four more bookings for you here in Italy,' says Riccardo.

I leave Milan by train and arrive at the Grand Hotel in Venice prepared to experience all manner of unearthly visual treats. But the ultimate slide-show backdrop gets lost in a surreal bubble of hair, frocks and what goes with the red suit – no time to see and explore, only to stand in front of yet another background masterpiece and pose sweetly. No one ever came to Venice and saw so little. 'How ungrateful of you, darling!' I can hear my mother muttering.

On the road again – Kerouac *deluxe* – for an ad campaign in Camogli, for sure the quaintest fishing village along the coast that leads to Portofino. The hotel is surprisingly smart, but damn! Why hasn't anyone told me that a hotel room in Italian is a *'camera'*? When the five-star manager asks me if I enjoy the camera I reply, 'Yeah, it's my job to smile in all of them,' which causes winks and sniggers from the reception desk crew for the rest of my stay.

Now it's a magazine shoot in Porto Ercole with jolly Falstaffian photographer Alfa Castaldi and his fashion editor wife, Anna Piaggi. The second I set eyes on Anna I know this one will be different. She arrives for dinner wearing luminous paisley silk pyjamas under a peach satin cape with scarlet elbow-length lace gloves. She's tied a purple bandana around her head with a marabou feather perched on top and her tiny feet are encased in flamingo-pink sandals with huge sewn-on buttons.

Upon discovering 'You are English!' she's in heaven, prattling on about the Chelsea Antique Market and all her King's Road pals. But I'm too visually enthralled to listen, transfixed by her shimmering red lips painted into two sharp peaks with thick blobs of the same vermillion on her eyelids. And that blue-streaked hair is styled into Marcel waves ending in a kiss curl that sits on her cheek like a tame tarantula.

Lying awake, imagining what sartorial splendour Anna will bestow on me tomorrow, I see from my bedroom window that our mega-expensive Pellicano Hotel has no beach – just two long, whitewashed levels carved from rocks onto which guests and their sunbeds precariously squeeze and stay until sunset. I can't quite believe I'm here – it's a heck of a long way from Barnsley but how Mum would love it. My gaze drifts to the sleeping speedboats and gin palaces anchored in the bay beyond which will, no doubt, blast into life first thing.

Sure enough, I dress to the din of a thousand outboard motors crashing onto the tide, their occupants' laughter thrown to the wind as flesh and salt water meet in squeals of summer ecstasy – duly trumped by my loud squeaks of armpit/razor agony. But I get off lightly on the shoot, apart from my hair which Anna insists is styled into tight blonde curls that resemble an explosion in a fusilli factory. But for all her mass of personal sartorial contradictions, Anna's chutzpah and originality and her surprising lack of Milanese fashion xenophobia turn out to be a true breath of fresh air.

This sure has been a *prima* journey of discovery, but resurfacing in Milan for the final *Vogue* booking, I'm knackered and covered in spots. Not quite the pristine canvas that Gian Paolo Barbieri, Italian *Vogue*'s highly respected photographer (twenty-four covers!) has in mind for a close-up headshot. His last resort is to snap a knackered-less profile. The flawed model is disguised with fuchsia lips and a frizzy coral wig.

There's just time to scrawl a postcard to my mother before departing Milan. 'Hey Mum, I've made a fortune here . . . will take you on a slap-up holiday the minute I get back.'

It was not to be.

I had earned a stash of lire – around £9,000 in today's money – and was paid in cash. That was a first. Having heard on the grapevine that I should conceal it from airport customs officials, I stuff the endless notes down my pants, in my bra, round my belt and padded around my purple ankle boots. With immaculate timing, as I sashay through the departure lounge, a whacking huge wad crashes out of my left boot, scattering around my feet.

I'm done for.

The entire amount is confiscated by officials.

Strangely enough, few questions are asked and even less paperwork processed.

I don't retrieve my money and I'm powerfully ushered onto the plane.

Back in London word spreads fast in the industry and Riccardo is embarrassed. He flies over to sort out the mess, and a few months later I'm back. No city in Europe has more work than Milan.

It's best not to hang around for long. Those of us staying in Hotel Arena become used to raids by the 'authorities', always around 8 A.M. and always looking for girls without work permits. Fierce competition between rival model agents is rumoured to be behind these raids, and soon international agencies begin to form worldwide chains to give models more payment security.

And then there are the playboys. Oh God, those ubiquitous, ridiculous Milanese playboys. Each new arrival guarantees a horde of handsome admirers hanging around the hotel bar or lining up outside in their Lamborghinis, and that odd experience of finding phone messages from total strangers at hotel reception the first morning of arrival. One aspiring playboy is known to us for greeting models on incoming flights with an empty suitcase, to look the part as he mingles with passengers before offering the girls lifts into town.

La vita can be very *dolce* in Milan if you like that kind of thing, but it's only the naïve girls who play ball. Not remotely fascinated by rich and stupid men, we British models stick together socially, occasionally joined by Anjelica Huston and photographer boyfriend Bob Richardson, also banged up in Hotel Arena and both here to work for Italian *Vogue*.

Anjelica has an intelligent, striking face with deep twinkly eyes the shade of coffee beans and a proud nose with neat nostrils I envy madly. A small dog could live happily in mine. I've grown quite used to 'Hair & Make-up' handing me a Kleenex on shoots before whispering, 'We've been joined by the Colonel', their euphemism for nasal visitors. To which I always reply, 'Well, if I go on strike I can always picket.'

Apart from being a great-looker, Bob Richardson is an extremely radical American fashion snapper – the first to strip away artifice, under-expose film purposely, and not prioritise the clothes. Women with real lives and real emotions are his heroines, bringing a melodrama to fashion photography not currently found in magazines and challenging every photographer who comes after him to take different pictures. He's the only fashion photographer who ever made Richard Avedon (considered by many to be the best) question his own work.

Handsome yet troubled, Bob looks like a wounded eagle. I'm drawn to him but his only love interest is Anjelica; they'd met when he was forty-one and she seventeen. Her mother had just been killed in a car crash, while listening to Vivaldi – and Anjelica was sent the mangled, bloody cassette tape from the car wreckage. She then found herself wanting adrenalin over security and it started a pattern of being attracted to difficult men. Their intense relationship would last four years, but she didn't know he'd been diagnosed with paranoid schizophrenia at twenty-two after one of four suicide attempts.

In her memoir she wrote: 'I loved him tremendously but knew if I stayed with him I would die.' Bob's version of their break-up was simpler, and equally sad. 'Anjelica and I part . . . I never told her I was schizophrenic . . . shame and fear . . . silence . . . she would have understood.'

Models continued to pour into Milan, most of them nonchalantly ever-derisive about the annoying playboys. Riccardo's agency reigned supreme until the early Eighties, when an event occurred that stopped the never-ending party in its tracks.

A beautiful twenty-six-year-old girl from South Carolina stepped off a plane intending to give modelling 'one last shot' but was fragile and got snared into the scene. It proved lethal. Surrounded by drugs and alcohol, she shot and killed playboy Francesco D'Alessio with a .38-calibre five-shot Smith & Wesson held at arm's length with both hands.

Strung out on Valium, cocaine and vodka, she maintained it was her fear of him stalking her that made her aim the gun. The first shot hit the bedroom wall, the second ripped through D'Alessio's chest and left lung, followed by a shot into his left temple. The fourth bullet emerged just above his right eye and blood and brains spattered the carpet.

Francesco's friend Carlo Cabassi – his house-guest, business partner and companion in cocaine-fuelled romps – found the body and removed all drugs from the scene before calling an ambulance.

The Riccardo Gay Model Agency was partly owned by Cabassi.

When Carlo made his early-morning phone calls to find out who had shot his pal, one of the first people he rang at 7.30 A.M. was Riccardo Gay, who informed him with whom the model had been out that night, and where.

Found guilty, she got fourteen years reduced to twelve years six months – a record low for murder in Italian judicial history, probably to pacify a shocked nation and avoid international outcry, and because of her fragility in such extreme circumstances. Carlo Cabassi was acquitted of obstruction of justice and theft and given a suspended sentence of twenty-one months for possession of cocaine.

For a year or two after the shooting, the models in Milan were mostly left alone. But soon the relentless playboys were on the warpath again. The party never really stopped. Weekends in at the country villa continued, cocaine still flowed freely, and naïve young models continued to arrive – some unable to ever call the shots.

Milan photographers were always respectful in those exquisite locations, the fashion editors excellent, those locations exquisite, and the other models were good fun. It was self-awareness that made those great and memorable times possible. We can't blame others for our own behaviour. But perhaps it was easier to call the shots in the Sixties than in the Eighties.

5

RE-VIEWED IN LONDON

'If you lose the plot you never build the house'

Despite 'walking like a carthorse' at the Lucie Clayton model school I was booked to appear in ITV's iconic Glad Rag Ball fashion show six months later. Here at Wembley sports arena this chaotic event mightily over-runs, producing well-known hyper-sweating 'talent' bursting for their opportunity to 'get out and knock 'em dead!' and bring the house down; which doesn't stop Frankie Vaughan, Lionel Blair, Georgie Fame, The Who and Jimmy Tarbuck – all household names in British popular culture – from waltzing in and out of our dressing rooms, trying on our hats and telling us weak jokes. After I'm chosen to close the fashion show in a shimmering metallic gown (carthorse my arse, I'll show 'em!) Roger Daltrey marches over, kisses me on the cheek and christens me the Silver Surfer. Flattering then. Not so much now.

GLAD RAG DOLL

THE glad rag doll with the willowy blonde charm is Vicky Nixon, a young girl from Shepherds Bush Green with her sights set firmly on a top photographic modelling career.

Just three weeks after graduating from Lucy Clayton's Bond-street school, 17-year-old Vicky is one of 12 models chosen to appear on I.T.V.'s December 8 production, "Glad Rag Ball."

Also appearing in this annual student carnival at Wembley will be Lionel Blair, Jimmy Tarbuck and many other big name attractions.

"Lots of super things have happened in just three short weeks," says Vicky breathlessly. "Since I threw in my secretarial course I've modelled at four guineas an hour and now there is talk of a film test."

In "Glad Rag Ball" Vicky will model clothes from all the top boutiques in London.

From carthorse to rag doll, London Evening Standard, 1966

One guy stands out for me in all this mayhem. Thirteen years older than me and a rock publicist who began his music-biz career as the Merseybeats' road manager, he's about to become my first London boyfriend. His ex-wife had walked out years ago because 'the music business is not a proper job for a man'. But it suits us just fine. Bill Fowler and I get each other. He makes me feel safe and loved without reining me in. When he suggests that I move in with him, I agree immediately without telling my mother or even viewing the flat. I'd already viewed him quite considerably – good-looking, easy to love, funny, reliable, practical – the kind of guy who always opens difficult jar lids without making a fuss.

His flatmate Barrie Marshall and girlfriend Jenny are quite simply the kindest, most grounded people I've met since arriving in London. Barrie seems way too nice ever to be a success in the cut-throat music business. How wrong I was. The founding chairman of Marshall Arts, he's been a legendary rock concert promoter for over thirty years. To his long-time pal Paul McCartney he's 'dear old badger – the coolest promoter in the world'. And still one of the finest men I've ever met.

But the flat. Oh, the flat!

In Enfield, where outer London finally surrenders to Middlesex, it's situated down a muddy back alley behind the local tube station, which is the very last stop on the line – and it sits above a bathroom fittings shop exotically named Awash. Over-shiny shower units and avocado suites are their speciality. But once it even sold a bidet – specially ordered for a local *femme française*. Ironically, the flat itself has no bathroom – the huge bath is in the kitchen and the loo's in an old outbuilding on the roof.

No wonder Bill's wife left home! But none of us care. We make sure we're hardly ever there.

Within months Bill and Barrie both become act bookers for Arthur Howes, the UK's leading rock tour promoter, and their jobs include launching the hottest acts – currently the Kinks, The Walker Brothers and the Beach Boys – onto the international concert circuit. When they start to tour early in 1967, I find myself living alone above Awash for weeks on end. It's not much fun and Dinah, my super-cool agency booker, has the answer. A crash pad in Earl's Court. 'We've a spare room in our flat,' she says. 'Come and take a look.'

Dinah's current flatmate and best friend Rosie has just arrived from Newcastle and leaps up and down like an excitable new puppy when we meet. Wide-eyed and open-hearted, there's a compelling child-like innocence about her, an endearing vulnerability that also gives me slight cause for concern. Parking my belongings the following day between draped Moroccan hangings and lamps adorned with scarves, I see that Rosie has the latest Pink Floyd album, *Piper At The Gates of Dawn*, tucked under her arm, the first record to announce a new musical diversity that (when accompanied by an appropriate drug) makes you instantly hip in this 1967 Summer of Love. Yet popular music across the country is still split between cosy car-coat wearers driving Morris Oxfords who prefer tunes sung by Des O'Connor and the Seekers, and the others in paisley flares, antique waistcoats and purple capes, tripping out with mega-imaginative existentialism to 'Strawberry Fields Forever'.

Yes indeed, the preferred drug around town is LSD derived from lysergic acid and sold on the street mostly in liquid form – usually absorbed onto a piece of blotting paper divided into several squares: one drop, or 'dot', per square. This opens the doors of perception beyond the rim of the knowable, introducing its users to a world of cosmic harmony or schizoid paranoia, depending on your trip. But it doesn't take long to realise that my Gates, here at Redcliffe Street, are beyond being Piped at Dawn. Flopping into bed in the early hours after a long and late shoot riding a stuffed tiger for *Queen* magazine, I find a bedraggled guy under the blankets clutching a tambourine, and another on the floor gurgling 'far out man . . . far fucking out'.

The new crash pad appears way more suitable for opening my inner metaphysical self for inspection than removing make-up and trying to grab eight hours' sleep before a close-up Revlon shoot tomorrow. I'm wary of acid. Part of me wants to get as high as a kite, but I know I'll keep reaching for the string. I'm not entirely convinced that a twelve-hour trip will grip me with all the awe of a traveller returned from a mystic land, or that heading to the local shop while tripping will take me to a staggering new realm of mental consciousness. I get the vibe and look the part for this Summer of Love but, to be honest, I'm a bit scared that I'll be the one who won't come back, the one who experiences extreme paranoia and lengthy stays in psychiatric wards. That the edge will be closer than I think, especially when I don't mean to jump.

My shoot for Revlon is with the same off-the-wall, wildly brilliant young snapper Clive Arrowsmith who snapped me riding the tiger yesterday. And what a shoot that turned out to be! You never know what awaits you on Clive's shoots – he always gives the impression he's permanently stoned, but his work is so fabulously precise that's hardly feasible.

The Summer of Love. London Evening Standard, *1967*

Yesterday's shoot was ultra bizarre. 'Okay, Clive, so what's the look? Wistful waif, elegant bitch, lonely resident of Cannes who's just poisoned her lover, vivacious vamp, naughty child or tigress?' It *is* tigress, but not as I know it. In a 'forest' location, late at night, astride the stuffed tiger, with a fake moon and any other prop that presents itself. 'Oh, look, there's an orange,' which model Greta nonchalantly flings in the air, while I touch the moon. 'Can you believe that this is for *Queen*?' I whisper to her, only too aware that this glossy magazine is far more familiar with deb balls than fashion with balls.

For today's Revlon shoot with Clive, the master *maquillager* Guy Nicolet has flown in from Paris to transform my face to launch a new range called Nuance. Ah, Nuance, one of those weird words that takes ad agencies months to think up, that means bugger all but promises so much. And yields . . . just what, exactly? I try to spot the key differences from last season, or any season in the entire history of make-up.

Dewy skin, pounding luscious lips, come-hither eyes – it is forever thus. Except that every new season enticing new promises are added. How long before we can buy every conceivable dream in a labelled jar, I wonder.

'Keep your head down, love. You've got a chin that could slice salami,' laughs Clive.

Ah, the delights of Nuance – such a delicate shade of difference.

Pink Floyd are still doing their cool thing on the turntable when I return to Redcliffe Street that evening, hoping events have calmed. But several strung-out bodies are sprawled across the floor encased in the overpowering stench of burnt brown rice and joss sticks. Two of the best known faces in the British heavy rock scene are on all fours gnawing the cabriole legs of the tapestry-covered sofa. Ah, this must be the elegantly wasted rock star lifestyle I've heard so much about. Sadly, the stark reality is a dehumanising blur of bodies in an achingly empty oblivion. I pack my bags and head back to Enfield.

Dinah leaves the model agency to work at Granny Takes A Trip, the first psychedelic King's Road boutique to sell crushed and hammered velvet clothes to soporific slinkers – their strokable trousers incapable of holding any tactile promise other than signalling 'We're heavy dudes who hang out at the Roundhouse.'

And Rosie, dear, gentle, sweet Rosie, dies from a heroin overdose four months later.

The worst kind of accident . . . just waiting to happen. She didn't see it coming.

But others should have. If I'd stayed, I could have helped. I wish to God I had.

The back-breaking accessory hold all that I cart daily from Bill's outer-London pad now seems more appropriate for a month's holiday in Sydney. Models are expected to arrive for work in full make-up and every outfit demands a new hair-do, which means packing Carmen rollers, hairspray, two different-length hairpieces, three full wigs in different styles and shades (always looking like spooky old wigs no matter what clever, twirly, bandana, scarfy things you do with them), a stash of our own accessories – shoes, boots, scarves, gloves, underwear, costume jewellery, mostly having sticky encounters with half-eaten sandwiches and false-eyelash glue – plus a huge diary to write our assignments *and* a sack-sized portfolio containing tear-sheets of our most flattering work. Only the up-market glossies have hair and make-up done on set with stylists to personalise each photo with their on-trend accessories.

So when my Agent Gloria suggests I take a short-lease flat at the inner-London block where she lives, I jump at it. Portsea Hall, a smallish art deco building in a one-way street within easy reach of Marble Arch, has glistening chandeliers in the entrance hall and a uniformed chap to open the door, but seldom has a space looked so gloriously full of its own emptiness. My first-floor flat has zero character and no redeeming features. But there are no groaning groovers under the bed in a profound state of relaxation, and no drugs on the draining board. It's compact and practical and with a couple of bean bags and a potted palm, it's perfect.

In this oasis of calm, I'm a bit surprised to discover that my next-door neighbour is that lively old hell-raiser George Brown, Deputy Prime Minister and Foreign Secretary in the current Wilson government. George is known to like a drink or two – his agent originating the phrase 'tired and emotional' as a euphemism for Brown's frequent unruly behaviour under the influence. (Oh, God, no all-night raves George, please!)

Curiosity finally gets the better of me and I find myself often pausing – faking a struggle to find my keys – outside our virtually touching front doors, hoping to hear a juicy titbit or two. I long to knock and ask to borrow some sugar, hoping he'll say, 'Oh do come in for a drink or four.' I briefly see Mrs Brown open her front door to receive a parcel. She's wearing a pink rayon quilted dressing gown with a fetching Ena Sharples hairnet, and has a Silk Cut dangling stylishly from her lower lip.

I never get the invitation, though direct access to A-listers is easy. PR over-protection and VIP separation areas simply don't exist. The famous are less precious and more approachable in Sixties London. It's what you're celebrated for that counts, not the fame itself. And sometimes these people even approach us!

19 *magazine, 1968.*   Photo: Mike Berkofsky

Shortly after *Bonnie & Clyde* is released I take to wearing a beret and maxi-skirt, à la Faye Dunaway, and, paying a fleeting visit to Browns boutique in South Molton Street, find myself face to face with Warren Beatty, in London to promote the film. He proposes a date. Blushingly, stutteringly accepting Mr Beatty's compliments while gazing over his shoulder and thus avoiding the bluest eyes I've ever encountered, I manage to utter, 'Sorry, I already have a boyfriend. But thanks a lot.'

He's deeply unfazed. Plenty more lanky larky blondes around.

It's an icy day in October 1967 when I drag my bulging model kit up the wide stone steps leading to Chelsea Manor Street studio. I know this will be a quirky shoot. *Nova* is unique in Britain for breaking the mould of women's magazine publishing. Alongside the artfully designed fashion pages are serious and often controversial features on raw new subjects – feminism, homosexuality and racism. It's politically radical and intelligent, and has an intrepid fashion editor, Caroline Baker, who's always looking for the alternative 'wow factor' fashion story.

Today she's on another shoot. The clothes have been left on a rail for us two models and photographer Michael Cooper to bring to life. He's not an obvious choice for fashion; he's best known for his brilliant 3D photo on the Rolling Stones' *Their Satanic Majesties Request* and the cover of the Beatles' *Sgt. Pepper's Lonely Hearts Club Band*, shot in this studio just five months ago.

Michael introduces himself. Unshaven and stunningly attractive in that sensual, long-haired and slightly bruised and fragile psyche kind of way, he appears pretty stoned. When his two models walk onto the stark white studio set, wearing Ossie Clark's latest, he has little idea how to place us. Highly respected as the long-time chronicler of the Rolling Stones, his tenacious eye recording the triumphs, tragedies and fears of the nascent rock'n'roll legend, he's not comfortable as a fashion snapper freezing the perfect pose. Although his photos have a cool honesty, they're reportage not fashion.

I waggle my foot to ease the pressure of an unbearably tight shoe.

'Yeah, that's great! Now look over your shoulder doing that.'

What?

Much as I respect Michael's work this doesn't work – the click of the shutter too late, or way too soon. And his hands are trembling, constantly trembling. He keeps disappearing into the dark room at the far end of the studio to engage with a delicate, fine-boned man with a winding silk scarf, whose face I recognise. The smell of dope gets stronger and stronger.

'Isn't that Keith Richards?' I whisper to my fellow model, a sleek and stunning brunette with enviably dewy skin and an alert twinkle in her eye.

Indeed it is.

Keith and Michael appear preoccupied, talking in hushed tones, and we try to guess their subject matter.

'Is it the integration of the esoteric and exoteric approaches to alchemy?' I say to impress.

'Nah, much more likely to be the police drugs raid at Redlands, Keith's Sussex home. Michael was there,' she whispers with knowing confidence.

'Hang on, that was eight months ago,' I remind her.

Finally Keith draws up a chair and watches the rest of the session. He makes faintly louche exchanges with us, yet is always gentlemanly, introspective and polite. I think he's pretty impressed with the dewy brunette. He quietly encourages Michael and they occasionally share a joke. It's endearingly obvious that they're close pals.

'*Nova* will never use the pics,' I murmur to the twinkly-eyed one as we pose for the last shot. But they did.

Photo: *Michael Cooper*

Giving it some back bone. Nova *magazine, 1967.*

The resulting fashion spread was *so* unflattering and *so* lacking in image sharpness and all-round focus, that it wasn't very funny.

Except that it was . . . we had a Stoned story to tell.

It was only rock'n'roll and we loved it.

Frankly we models couldn't care less what's on-trend this season – 'Spots Are In But Stripes Are Not!' etc. We're simply the blank canvas for other people's musings and hardly ever covet the clothes, jewellery or shoes. Off-duty we prefer to walk into rooms before our outfits. Most of us prefer poems to extravagant possessions. I still do.

Real style has little to do with grooming and seasonal fashion. It's an attitude – you can't manufacture it. Apart from Browns in South Molton Street – which we support because Mrs B always sources and champions the newest, most talented home-grown designers, the only shop in London to do so – we also love and salute Biba with its cool, all-black interior, potted palms and hat-stand clothes rails, until it evolves into a soulless five-storey high-street department store adding wallpaper and soap flakes to its product range. And we never even set foot in Carnaby Street – it's a tourist con trick to lure in foreigners desperate to emulate the 'London Look'.

But the London Look is not simply about fashion. It's about a free-wheeling restlessness heralding a new world of freedom, romance and escape. That aloof, lady-like sleekness and glacial hauteur is long gone; the wide-eyed early Sixties waif has also had her day, paving the way for a new type of girl. Now it's all about a lack of self-consciousness, a languid ease of movement and the ability to light up a room in a slow burn kind of way.

She's never been to a salon to be pampered, painted, preened, pummelled, and plucked; you don't notice the label on her dress – it could be a size 8 or a size 16. The key to the look is an illusion of artlessness. And she's not necessarily a model, actress, party showstopper or singer. She's a girl's girl, quick to laugh and safe in her skin. She's the woman strong men fall in love with, not the one they just want to shag.

Forty-eight boutiques now line the half-mile stretch of the King's Road between Chelsea Town Hall and Sloane Square. Even Thomas Crapper at number 120, loo maker to King George V, has morphed into Skin but R.Soles pops up to shoehorn back some soul, producing the best cowboy boots this side of the Atlantic. I still have a pair.

Soon everyone wants a slice of the profitable cake – and rents and property prices rocket sky high. The King's Road has simply become a vast theatre, an open-air stage along which artful exhibitionists parade and pose, jostling for space on crowded pavements, spilling out on the road and being narrowly missed by Mini Mokes, white convertibles and pop star Rolls-Royces.

One car that never fails to stop us in our tracks is the 1966 Ford Mustang owned by Mr Freedom entrepreneur Trevor Myles. It's the world's first furry car, the entire coachwork boldly streaked in tactile, weatherproofed yellow-and-black flock tiger stripes.

As I pose in front of this faux-fur-covered car on a shoot for the *Sunday Times* magazine wearing a pair of tiger-printed 'soft panne velvet Oxford bags' designed by James Wedge, the owner of Countdown (at number 137), I can't stop thinking how tickled my father would have been to see his daughter posing with a tiger-flocked Mustang.

And then tears begin to flow. I can't stop them. Such a rare, beautiful car jolts me back to being ten years old, travelling with Dad in his Jag and playing our game of 'who's the quickest to add up the registration plate numbers of the car coming towards us?' He always let me win. James Wedge, who is also the magazine's photographer, is a sensitive man and fully understands. It's what made Helen Mirren fall in love with him during this era.

This formidable King's Road fashion fest began when I was still a Barnsley schoolgirl. Mary Quant bought the freehold of Markham House for £8,000, turning the basement into a restaurant and the rest into the King's Road's first ever boutique Bazaar. At first it stocked clothes by art students, had whisky on the counter and naked people everywhere (customers simply changed on the shop floor) and its lively window displays caused delighted traffic jams – and so scandalised old colonels passing by that they threw bricks through the windows.

But now, approaching 1968, they beckon us into a composed space with a corporate air that doesn't tolerate much 'Just looking'. Organised professionalism is taking over and rent-stretched independent boutiques begin to sell out to the familiar multiples which stridently move in and threaten the whole 'Chelsea Idea'.

Our sanctuary is Quorum, just off the King's Road, the only shop that boldly anticipates the mood of the hippie years and defines the ethereal look of the decade. Ossie Clark, the one designer to cut on the cloth and never use a paper pattern, creates the ultimate, delicate, easy-to-wear dresses which, combined with his wife Celia Birtwell's nature-inspired prints on wispy chiffons in washed-out tones, are desired by us all. The very idea of a long, soft dress, herbaceous all over, feels *now*, radical and bold, despite its material delicacy.

When I take my mother to meet Ossie (so nicknamed because he grew up in Oswaldtwistle in Lancashire) in this tiny Radnor Walk boutique, she's so overwhelmed by the beauty of the clothes that she steps backwards into a mega-expensive box of chocolates Ossie has placed near the door for his customers. Mum is beyond mortified. Ossie laughs until he cries.

Later, sipping real coffee in the wood-panelled Guys 'n Dolls on the corner of Lincoln Street, my mother nudges me. 'Isn't that . . .?' I look up to see Mick Jagger leaning over a pretty blonde at the next table. She's wearing a black and yellow PVC miniskirt and reading French *Vogue*. 'You've got it upside down, love,' he says and flounces off.

Back in Mum's cosy Barnsley house for Christmas, I'm woken by a gentle knock on my bedroom door.

'Darling, there's a phone call from London. It's your model agent.'

'Tell her I'm still asleep, Mum.'

'I've tried that, but she says it's urgent.'

Creeping downstairs to pick up the handset in the hall, I attempt to focus. I'm sure I told Gloria I wanted to 'book out' for two weeks to spend precious time with Mum.

'Hello, Gloria.'

'The *Daily Mail* needs a head shot. Can you return to London as soon as possible? You're about to be named "The Face of 1968".'

'But I've just over-plucked my eyebrows and I've got an enormous spot on my chin.'

The damned spot throbs away for the entire journey to London. By the time the train pulls into St Pancras I can feel zit's the size of my nose. Maybe Clearasil can sponsor me. (Photoshop wouldn't have known where to start.) Covering the erupting volcano with my hands and hair, I'm pronounced 'The Face of 1968'.

I don't 'worship Monroe' as stated, but the 'All woman, not dolly' is spot on! I'm ultra grateful – such lucky breaks are the stuff of dreams – and I want to feel flattered, thrilled and triumphant, but feel somewhat trapped by expectation.

At my happiest stomping around Europe, using modelling to explore foreign climes, I never fear time spent alone, but to be permanently on show, losing all privacy, scares me. I'm no big deal and don't want, or deserve, that Twiggy kind of fame (The Face of '66) with prospective managers beating down my door, and press paps snapping me shopping as I'm blowing my nose, or product endorsement deals when I'm no big deal whatsoever. I don't want my youthful face to be the one defining element of my life – forever the Face of '68 until I reach sixty-eight. I simply see these modelling years as a fortunate way to view the world before doing something useful.

THE NEW FACE
OF '68 Who is she?

VIKKI NIXON ... "All woman, not dolly."

WOMEN   by JEAN ROOK

VIKKI NIXON, I predict, has the Grown-Up Girl face of '68. And I predict further that Vikki, a new model girl, will set fire to the pages of the glossy magazines in the New Year.

Aged 18, and born in Barnsley, 5ft. 9½in.

tall, and 34-24-35, she worships the late Marilyn Monroe, and believes in "a new type of model girl, who is all-woman, not dolly."

A former £8-a-week typist, she was photographed three months ago by fashion photographer Mike Berkofsky, who told her: "One day you'll earn

that much in an hour."

Now Vikki is on the books of a leading London model agency.

Why this face out of the millions? Because it's sexy. Because it's as womanly as the now Gertie Lawrence fashions which, we forecast, will take the kink out of Carnaby Street.

And because she has

a mane of blonde hair, massive grey-blue eyes, and a tall, square-shouldered body, like Garbo.

Being Yorkshire helps. As the one-time Barnsley High School girl puts it: "If I make good, I'll tell people about Barnsley. T h e n maybe they won't ask me if it's in Scotland."

My grimace of '68. Daily Mail, *1968*

This accolade has been kindly bestowed on me by a feisty journalist from Yorkshire who wants to raise the professional profile of 'the lass from Barnsley'. That woman is Jean Rook,

'First Lady of Fleet Street' and Britain's highest paid female journalist, so well known she's the original model for *Private Eye*'s Glenda Slagg. Jean embraces this privileged position, revelling in her success in what is a totally male-dominated industry and labelling herself the 'bitchiest, best known, loved and loathed woman in newspapers'. No subject is too taboo for Jean – she interviews scores of public figures in her down-to-earth forthright style.

Jean's two other favourite models are Vicki Hodge, the sparkling and spirited blonde daughter of baronet Sir John Hodge, and Hazel, the exquisite, long-limbed black girl I first saw at my agency. Fleet Street's First Lady books us at every opportunity when she becomes the *Daily Mail*'s fashion editor as well as its trenchant columnist, and we adore her. Vicki and Hazel are also blisteringly forthright and we always have riotous times on Jean's shoots.

Vicki has fallen for the charms of one of the most dangerous men in London, a small-time gangster called John Bindon. Worlds apart from her privileged background, she met him after director Ken Loach spotted him in a Fulham pub and cast him in *Poor Cow* in 1967. Tall and broad, though boyishly charismatic, John is fearless, a great storyteller, and very bright. But it's probably his sense of menace that makes him irresistible to our rebellious adventuress. He's also prodigiously well-endowed and regularly shows his primary asset, slapping it on a bar after whirling it around like a helicopter, and then displaying five half-pint mugs along it.

It's a spectacular sight.

John and Vicki move in together in Fulham, but that doesn't stop others from falling for his obvious charms. When she takes John to Mustique it is Princess Margaret, also a guest of Lord Glenconner, who takes a shine to John. Much to Vicki's irritation, PM and JB continue their liaisons in London where phone calls to Fulham summon him to Kensington Palace and a car picks him up, but they never arrive '*à deux*'.

Vicki once spotted them at the Gasworks, an eccentric restaurant off New King's Road, where the mad proprietor tells you to 'Fuck off' at the door if he doesn't like the look of you, an erotic chess set can amuse pre-dinner, and table guests often include a giant red setter with a napkin tucked into his collar.

This unlikely friendship was, for years, the subject of intense speculation. Compromising pictures taken on Mustique were said to be at the centre of a bank robbery at Lloyds bank in Baker Street in the early Seventies. Mysteriously a D-notice, a government gagging order, prevented media coverage of the raid in 1971.

After yet another bracing booking with Jean in Fleet Street, Vicki offers to drop me at my next photo shoot in Chelsea. As we approach her souped-up ice-blue Mini, dragging our overflowing model kits, I notice the bonnet is badly dented, the front windscreen splintered, and the back seats have been torn out. 'Have you been in a crash?' I ask, somewhat bewildered that she hasn't mentioned it before now. 'Oh no, that . . . that's just John. He got a bit cross with me last night.'

When John won the Queen's Award for bravery in 1968 after rescuing a drowning man from the Thames, it was rumoured that he'd pushed the guy in, and only pulled him out after a policeman appeared. He also, allegedly, once cut off a man's arm with a machete. We are all mightily relieved when Vicki finally turns her back on him and takes up with a nice guy called Ian, who works in advertising.

That doesn't stop the Gangster Look from blasting into style.

On set again for the newspaper's fashion page, Jean scrunches my hair and hands me a shoulder holster. 'It's for carrying your cigarettes in,' she explains, 'an exact replica of Legs Diamond's and it's the latest thing, lovey. Now, hang it on your right shoulder and get into gangster mode.'

Right on cue, Vicki walks into the studio for our next shoot.

'Great news, everyone! Ian and I are getting married next week.'

I'm really pleased for her. I've met Ian several times; he's a good guy. The studio phone rings.

'It's for you, Hodgie,' yells the photographer.

'Oh, hello darling,' giggles, whispers, sweet nothings and a final 'Yes and I love you too. See you at six.'

'How sweet of Ian to ring and calm your nerves before the wedding,' I sigh to Vicki.

'Oh that wasn't Ian. It was John.'

John is arrested for stabbing to death a fellow gangster, Johnny Darke, in a Fulham pub. Put on trial for murder at the Old Bailey, he's acquitted after actor Bob Hoskins stands in for him as a character witness. But his career never recovers from the adverse publicity of the trial, his criminal activities garner more publicity than his acting, and he dies from cancer in 1993. Vicki has wisely married Ian, though continues to see John as a loyal friend.

MEANWHILE, BACK ON THE GANGSTER SCENE

THE gangster look is getting sharper every minute. Slouch hats, tight belted rain-coats, dark chalk-striped suits for boys; berets, maxis and broody Bonnie looks for girls are, of course, essential.

But now the Under-world Look has gone one further, with basic gangster accessories.

Like this drop-dead shoulder holster.

As a matter of fact it's for keeping your cigarettes in. (Gangster Girls don't carry bags, lovie, except to shove the bank notes into).

AND this is not just any old shoulder holster, you know. It's an exact copy of one belonging to rum-racketeering Legs Diamond, whose last whispered words have

Daily Mail, 1968

Why is it that the highly successful models – who won't allow themselves to be over-objectified, abused and humiliated in their chosen work – often pick abusive duffers for their personal lives before getting it right? Countless girls at the top of this game choose to be with unsuitable, extreme men whose sole aim is to splinter them on a gradual, cruel journey from independence to subjugation.

Even Jean Shrimpton reveals in her memoir that she 'just kept picking the wrong men' – staying with and financially supporting poet Heathcote Williams for two years and paying for everything as he was 'becoming alarmingly crazy'. He set fire to himself on her doorstep while practising fire-eating before being rushed to a mental hospital. Twiggy's first husband was, in her words, 'a chronic alcoholic' and who can forget, years later, Kate Moss and Pete Doherty.

But a stable, well-balanced partner who adores you can appear too safe when your life is surreally wired to this kind of work. And the ones who want us as arm candy, to match their latest fast car, leave us cold. It's the dangerously exciting, creative guy waiting round the corner who gets inside your head. He often has all kinds of 'issues' but this allows the model to transfer or deflect the focus from her own purely physical issues to his complex mental ones.

We models rarely think we're beautiful. There is always someone, professionally, who doesn't like a physical feature, and lets us know. Our qualifications for work are based on how we look for a job, and it takes a sky-high level of confidence, self-esteem and strong coping mechanisms to offset the fear of not living up to expectations, and to accept valid criticism when necessary.

It's a matter of getting the shot right that counts, of not letting down the photographer and his team. But bad photographs can make us feel that the main prop wasn't up to the task. It's nothing personal. And yet it is. It can be hard to keep in context, to separate the snapper who says he doesn't like your legs, from your partner who does.

When Jean Shrimpton, for years the world's top model, tells of 'having terrible bags under my eyes', and of fashion editors constantly telling her to go to bed earlier, she sums it up superbly: 'God has given me bags under my eyes in the same way he has forgotten to give me a bosom and shoulders.'

Of course, choosing partners with complex problems can also mean that some of us are ultra-compassionate, too trusting and have a particular empathy for the lonely and lost – and are easily taken advantage of. Whatever, it won't ever happen to me, will it?

6

CONFUSED IN SPACE

'And remember, no matter where you go, there you are'

Confucius

It's the summer of July 1969, a scorching one, and I'm eating breakfast with Bill when the phone rings. It's his old pal Tom Keylock.

'Can you both make it to Sharon Tate's wedding to Roman Polanski tomorrow? It's at Chelsea Register Office with a reception at the Playboy Club, and Sharon's worried there are too few guests and asked me to bump up the numbers. They don't know that many people in London and you'll be very welcome.'

I'm off to Milan the following day and Bill isn't that fussed, so we decline. How could we ever have imagined that within a year Sharon would be dead, murdered by Charles Manson and his evil group when she was just twenty-six and eight and a half months pregnant?

I like and respect Tom, and feel guilty about letting down

109

this former paratrooper who survived the carnage at Arnhem in the Second World War. But this is nothing. Soon Tom has far greater problems to negotiate. Initially employed by the Rolling Stones as their driver, he quickly assumes a key role in their entourage as fixer and protector par excellence. He's capable, a generation older, looks more like a schoolmaster than a driver, and is a safe and trustworthy pair of hands. When the news of Brian Jones's drowning in his Sussex pool reaches the Stones at their recording studio in west London, Tom is instructed to 'get down there and sort things out'.

It's assumed that Brian has died an all-too-predictable death because of his excessive drug taking and a police investigation endorses this account, the coroner recording a death by misadventure. But rumours persist of foul play by Frank Thorogood, one of three others there at the time.

Tom parted from the Stones several months later, but in 1993 he was phoned by Thorogood's daughter who knew Tom. Her father, she informed Tom, was now gravely ill in hospital and wanted to see and tell him something about the night Brian died.

According to Tom, he said: 'Well, I'll be honest, I done him up.'

At this dramatic point a nurse told Tom that Thorogood needed to sleep and Tom said, 'Look, Frank, I'll see you tomorrow.' But by the time he reached home, Frank's daughter had phoned to report that her father had died. But Tom never believed that Frank had drowned Brian deliberately. 'It was an accident. They were playing around, Frank ducked him and wallop!'

The details of Brian's death are still talked about obsessively with sometimes preposterous scenarios proposed. One outrageous version is that Tom arranged the murder at the Stones' behest but the substance of Frank's confession – that Brian died through horseplay that got out of hand – is by far the most plausible. Now our dear friend Tom Keylock is dead too, so we'll never really know. The key has well and truly locked.

It's still July 1969 when I meet Jean Rook in the BBC Lime Grove studio canteen at 5.30 A.M. She's going live on air to talk about the influence of Apollo 11 on earthly women's fashions. They need some froth between the live coverage of man's first landing on the Moon.

'Now, lovey, you'll be wearing this green Afro wig with matching emerald lipstick, a silver lamé catsuit under brass breastplates, and a skirt made of rattling brass chains with gold moon-hopping boots. Don't look so horrified, you won't have to say anything, just moon around a bit.'

But this is a big deal. It's one of the great highpoints of television broadcasting. Three days after the giant Saturn V rocket blasts off from the Kennedy Space Center, and thirty lunar orbits later, two astronauts, Armstrong and Aldrin, have made history by becoming the first humans to land on the Moon and complete the Moon walk as part of the Apollo 11 mission.

It's a logistical nightmare for the BBC production team who need to keep the levels of viewers' excitement constant for several hours. After repeatedly showing footage with edited highlights, there's tangible relief in the studio when Jean starts to do her thing. She begins to describe my outfit and I can feel the camera slowly panning up and down my body, zooming in and out of the ludicrous ensemble.

Suddenly Cliff Michelmore, the UK television's foremost presenter/anchorman, turns to me and says, 'Now tell us, Vikki, what does it feel like to be a glorious moonstruck creature?'

The crew smile, Michelmore nods encouragingly and twenty million viewers wait to hear the profound reply of the first green-haired moon child. My mouth opens but nothing comes out. I look as though I'm knitting with my teeth.

Suppressing an almost irresistible desire to 'moon' at the nearest camera, I murmur, 'Oh God, I wasn't expecting this. Er . . . frankly I feel a bit spaced.'

Cue bemused glare from Michelmore and loud sniggers from all the crew.

A week later and undeterred, Jean Rook invites me to dinner at the Kensington Roof Gardens, the lush 1.5-acre rooftop oasis above Biba, to celebrate David English's new editorship of the *Daily Mail*. But I hardly recognise any of the assembled celebrities bestowing blessings, barbs and *bons mots* and am initially relieved to be seated next to comedian Benny Hill. At previous events like this I'd observed that the public personalities of television stars, especially funny men, often become the template for their off-screen behaviour, their character reduced to a series of predictable expressions and catchphrases. Hopefully Benny Hill will maintain more than a semblance of humanity.

Sadly not. Having viewers splitting their sides in Norway doesn't stop him from being possibly the most miserable man I've ever encountered. As the evening drags on, polite exchanges exhausted, his eyes bore through me until they're boring me to death. After several glasses of wine I try to liven him up with a David Attenborough approach.

'Have you ever watched a bee entering a foxglove?'

This doesn't achieve a nature lover's intake of breath, but a filthy look as if I've just asked to hold his penis.

Okay, so let's try an abstract, pseudy one.

'Did you know that if the Earth had no clouds, the sea would evaporate?'

'Can you pass the salt, love?'

Oh well. Last one. My oft-used cliché:

'And where do you intend to spend eternity?' Previous answers have ranged from 'I'm in panto at Skegness next week', 'Dunno, love' and, very rarely, 'In your arms, for ever.'

'Not sure,' he mumbles. 'I live with my mother.'

I feel a bit sorry for Benny Hill and just manage to avoid saying 'I'm not surprised' by giving him my best 'fake sincerity – pose number three' smile.

Surely it's a strain to feign slapstick when you're so bloody sad in real life.

My mother is not often sad. Her letters pulsate with life and fun . . . 'I took Margaret to lunch yesterday, frightfully nice little restaurant, but we went a bit mad and had gin and tonics and half a bottle of wine, and tried this thing called couscous. It tasted like old cobwebs and when Margaret said she thought it was made from semolina I nearly spat it out; reminded me of school! And, don't laugh, but the little chap who lives opposite is being a bit of a nuisance. He bought me wallflowers for the garden, then a box of chocolates on Friday, and now he's asked me for dinner tomorrow night. I wouldn't mind if he was forty-five and dashing, but he looks about ninety and is deadly dull!'

Mum is soon offered a highly prestigious job as the live-in bursar of Bretton Hall College, and is responsible for the finances and welfare of the attending Performance Art students who, needless to say, all adore her. And Nick has resigned from his lecturing job at Newcastle University to design amazing state-of-the-art furniture – desks, chaises longues, screens, and tables in Perspex and stainless steel. The prototypes are exquisite, though expensive to make, and Mum and I send spare cash whenever we can. It's an exciting, busy time for him.

London life with boyfriend Bill is pretty full-on too. His agency has launched the Kinks' career by making them the support band to headliners Dave Clark Five and arranging their first TV appearance on *Ready Steady Go!* I get to know the guys in the band but it's Pete Quaife, the bass guitarist, who becomes a real pal. He's funny and bright, a clever cartoonist, and when Bill's away touring or busy at work, I often see new movies with Pete. Bill has little inclination to view the latest London West End releases, so Pete and I arrange to meet up at Bill's workplace in Lower Regent

Street, walk to a big-screen cinema nearby and grab our popcorn from the foyer.

When Pete breaks his leg in a road accident – four days before their European tour – we're all in shock. It's a relief to hear his leg will mend, but touring's out and Bill must find a quick replacement. His old Enfield pal, John 'Nobby' Dalton, fills in and fits in – mainly because he's also, most importantly, an Arsenal supporter.

Pete's leg repairs okay, he rejoins the band, but I know things are getting tough for him. He and Ray Davies are the band's founding members, yet he says he feels constantly sidelined by the continuous aggressive interaction between Ray and younger brother Dave. Initially this boosted the band's drive, but gradually the psychological conflict becomes too much and Pete becomes utterly exhausted with the internal feuds, and with being the permanent peacemaker.

Ray does indeed have a reputation for being volatile, gloomy and difficult, but it's obvious to me on the occasions we meet that he's an unhappy and deeply complex man and I fear for him. He seems to hate all the attention that fame brings, and some years later, while performing on stage, he produces an empty bottle of pills and thanks everyone for all they've done. Rushed to hospital to have his stomach pumped, he later admits it was a suicide attempt.

Leaving the cinema with Pete, after we've seen *Easy Rider* together in April 1969, he appears somewhat distracted and suggests a drink at Hatchetts Club in nearby Piccadilly. Bill joins us later, and Pete eventually drops a bombshell. He's really had enough, and wants to leave the Kinks. Hatchetts owner, Hughie, sensing our shock, offers us dinner with champagne, and several low-key musicians pop up and play an impromptu gig behind us.

Suddenly Pete stops talking mid-sentence; he likes what he's hearing. At the end of the number, Bill is asked to approach the singer, an unknown Canadian who has walked into the club by accident, and bring him over to our table.

'Hi, my name is Bill Fowler from the Arthur Howes agency. I'm with Pete Quaife, of the Kinks, who'd like to have a word with you.'

As they both stroll over, Pete whispers to me:

'This is the guy; THIS is the singer for my new band.'

And that IS the end of the original Kinks.

I feel sad about the break yet strangely privileged to be the first to know.

A centre-page spread in *New Musical Express* is how the other band members find out:

'"KINKS SPLIT" says Pete Quaife – sitting contentedly on Hampstead Heath with three unidentified musicians, his new band Mapleoak.'

It's Bill's task, once again, to re-approach John Dalton to replace Pete, whose new band sadly never makes it big. He leaves London to live in Denmark where he becomes a graphic artist and continues to be an accomplished cartoonist. I really miss my cinema pal.

When meeting Bill's contacts in the music business I often find the managers as interesting, or more so, than the band members. Robert Wace, the Kinks' manager, has that clipped, well-bred reserve that usually hides chronic shyness

or a majestic self-assurance. In Robert's case it's the former –
a particular sensitivity that always draws me to him.

The Who are managed by two guys who couldn't be
more different. Chris, brother of Terence Stamp, is the
tough Cockney son of a tugboat captain; Kit Lambert, the
Oxford-educated son of an esteemed classical composer.
Chris is the great-looker, even more so than brother Terence,
but it's always Kit that I beeline for at social events. Tiny,
giggly, bespoke-suited and with huge cushion lips, he's
totally, endearingly, mega-intelligently . . . bonkers. He
knows just how to pitch his patter and we often titter away
together, completely oblivious to events taking place around
us. Always encouraging the band to be visually extreme in
their stage shows, Kit loves egging them on to smash their
instruments to the hilt. In one year alone Pete Townshend
shattered seven Rickenbackers and several Gibsons as Kit
fondly tossed endless fire bombs on stage.

One evening at our fave low-lit club, hanging out at a
small table laden with drinks and forgotten food, Kit nudges
my arm and says, 'Just listen to this guy.' An unknown
guitarist pops up from an adjoining table and plays his first
ever impromptu gig in the UK. He's wearing an antique
military jacket, green velvet loons and is playing the guitar
with his teeth.

I'm speechless, but my face says it all. The guy is American,
yet unknown in the States.

Kit wastes no time in signing him to Track, his own record
label.

The guitarist's name is Jimi Hendrix.

And yet. And yet . . . I watch helplessly as Kit's gilded life slowly descends into drug-ridden chaos and finally self-implodes. His Knightsbridge house burns down, his Venice palazzo is badly damaged by fire, and he only escapes a prison sentence for drug offences thanks to a canny lawyer. Bankrupted, owing millions, he always insists he's owed stacks of royalties from albums he's produced for The Who and Jimi. This is later found to be true.

But it's all too late now.

He dies at forty-five (the same age as his father when he died) after drinking heavily and falling down stairs at his mother's house. Father and son are buried in the same grave. Oh, Kit.

It's increasingly obvious to me that fame and what it entails is not all-desirable; it's hollow, not real, and this girl from Barnsley has to stay real. I'm disappointed with myself when a platonic man-pal rings and says, 'How do you feel about Tramping tonight?'

Bill is away and I jump at it, but Tramp is the last place I should be rocking up to if I want to stay real. It's a glitzy new 'members only' nightclub with a sparkling international clientele, quite different from the dimly lit Speakeasy, our usual late-night hang-out frequented by smashed music industry execs and assorted musicians who jam together hoping to be discovered.

But I'm lonely. Bill is overseeing the Beach Boys tour after the international success of *Good Vibrations*. A sprinkle of glitter should cheer me up, however far removed from my comfort zone. And at least it's not Annabel's in Berkeley Square, that elite but soulless club for the posh Brit brigade, with its revolting Turtle Soup costing eight and six, and Vintage Sardines at a whopping twelve and nine! And where Eric Clapton was turned away for not wearing a tie and – I ask you – the Beatles refused entry because they weren't wearing shoes.

Platonic pal and I join a table in Tramp's sumptuous dining room lit by a line of shimmering chandeliers and urbane faces with eyes that never focus, constantly darting from side to side in case they miss some glister. I'm introduced to a man who offers a spare chair next to him. He's probably an international banker or a young Hollywood movie hotshot.

'Hello, my name's Kevin.'

'Oh hello, are you in the movie business?'

'Nah . . . footballer.'

'Which team? Real Madrid?'

'Scunthorpe.'

'Well, I'll be jiggered! That's more like it, lad. Did you know, Kev, that football was invented by Sheffield FC, just ten miles from where I grew up? A game took two hours and there were twenty players a side. And I helped organise a school strike when we weren't allowed the day off to attend an important Barnsley FC cup game.'

'Get away! I'm from Doncaster!'

We get on famously. A lovely guy, that Kevin Keegan, and attractive – pre bubble perm, when it's more of a modified mullet – and he's funny too. Right up until the moment he asks, 'Do you fancy a dance?'

Underneath the lavish chandeliers we slowly unwind from our gilt and velvet chairs.

'C'mon, Kevin, stand up properly!'

As I gaze down at the top of his head, I realise he is.

'I think I'll pass,' he sighs, flopping back in his seat.

It's late-Sixties London and the modelling scene is changing fast. Top agencies have raised their commissions and are demanding a percentage from clients as well as models. This effectively doubles their earnings. Models wait three months to be paid for each job, the maximum time it takes for clients to pay the agency, but we can beg advances if our invoice books look healthy.

Yet I'm mightily frustrated that Fulvio, my agency accountant, won't advance his models any funds whatsoever until clients have paid in full – much like a bank only offering an umbrella when the sun's shining. This doesn't make sense when I'm saving to buy a house for my mother. Although she loves her bursary job she often talks of moving closer to me in the future. A sale of the Barnsley house would barely buy a courtyard in London. And Nick is having problems selling his self-designed avant-garde furniture, which is affecting his relationship at home. I need to help.

A canny snapper suggests an approach to a Knightsbridge-based agency which pays quicker than most in London and has prime international connections, especially with the Ford agency in New York – the first, best, and most prestigious model agency in the world. Blimey, if I'm ever lucky enough to work with them in Manhattan I could make

The don't-mess-with-me glare in 1966.

Quorum Boutique, Chelsea, 1966   Photo: Mike Berkofsky

Thanks to photographer Mike Berkofsky for rescuing and restoring these badly damaged images from the 1994 L.A. earthquake.

Quorum Boutique, Chelsea, 1966

Photo: Mike Berkofsky

Queen magazine, 1969   Photo: Clive Arrowsmith

The Summer of Love is gone. Time to discover the dark side of the moon.

Sunday Times Magazine, 1970   Photo: James Wedge

Matching your pants to your Mustang is a must in 1970.

The new age of **British Steel**

It's an old adage that the customer is always right, but now they call it marketing and teach it at universities.

Providing the customer with what he wants, when and where he wants it, is an admirable, not to say essential, science in which the British Steel Corporation sales forces are all set to major.

Like any organisation that attaches the utmost importance to customer goodwill, BSC is taking pains to evolve a marketing set-up which will promote efficiency without sacrificing individual needs and preferences. This is not just a question of going on exactly as in the old days—buyers are as eager as anyone else (including sellers) to recognise the advantages of new ways of doing things, provided the advantages are real. This simple truth will not be lost on BSC.

Steel is a most versatile material with plenty of potential for exciting, new applications. By imaginative product development and by intensive market research, BSC aims to widen the appeal of a material shaped to its customers' requirements.

British Steel shaped to the customers' requirements.

British Steel Campaign, full-page ad in the *Sunday Times Magazine*, 1969

This Yorkshire lass knows how to wear a steel dress with pride.

L'Officiel magazine, 1970, The Collections – Spring issue

Photo: Roland Bianchini

Paris precision. Improvised movement not advised when holding this mega-heavy mirror at 3 A.M.

Ricilsoie Cosmetics campaign, 1970

Lashings of product with a touch of the blues.

Italian Vogue, 1970 Photo: Gian Paolo Barbieri

When my hair needs a rest this wig works best.

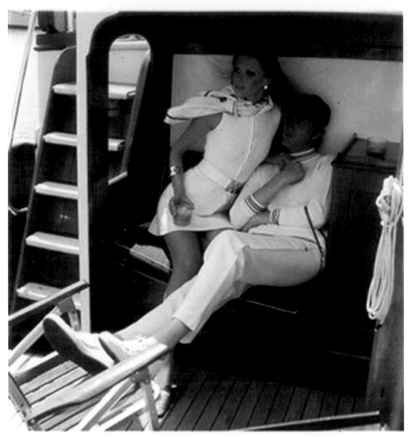

British ad campaign, 1970   Photo: Norman Parkinson

A welcome break during a tense day's shoot on a boat off the Kent coast –
not knowing if my brother is alive or dead.

enough dosh to buy my mother an impressive dwelling – and one for me too.

Right on cue Mum phones and laughingly tells me, 'Guess what, darling. I saw your old maths teacher Mrs Aveyard at the bus stop yesterday and she said, "We hear Vikki's doing very well for herself in London. You must be very proud of her." I just had to phone and tell you, as she's the very last person you'd have expected a compliment from!'

How true. On my final school report she'd written: 'I doubt if Victoria will make a success of anything in her life.' And Mum's advice re my 'new' agency approach: 'Entirely without prejudice, you look terrific, darling. But don't be too ambitious for your lovely conscience. Do approach this new agency if you feel it will make life easier financially, but don't worry if they say no. Everyone in Barnsley thinks you're doing marvellously.'

Running the show at the Peter Lumley model agency, a stone's throw from Harrods, is Jill Rushton who managed the Lucie Clayton agency for five years during its early, most successful 'Shrimpton' era. She turns away fifty applicants a week. I'm nervous.

Novelist's daughter, barrister's wife and charismatic career woman, Jill sits surrounded by nineteen phones, which are also manned by trilingual Penny and Joan who have an advanced system of cross-referencing cards to pinpoint in seconds a request for 'an Amazonian blonde to wear a bespoke metal dress manufactured by Sheffield foundry workers for a British Steel advertising campaign'.

Yeah, that sounds like a job for me.

Who else but a South Yorkshire girl could wear that dress with so much pride?

I'm signed up.

Jill's heart matches her well-screwed-on head. She's tender, direct, brusque and splendidly kind – always ready to offer a spare bed to any of her models with boyfriend troubles in the five-storey Chelsea house she shares with genial QC husband Robin Grey. A safe pair of hands, she welcomes me into the fold.

Bursting to tell her an amusing post-booking titbit the following day, I leap up the stairs to the first-floor agency and barge into the bookings room. But Jill's not at her desk – she has a caring arm round a stunning brunette in tears because photographer Terence Donovan has told her she's too shapely to work in fashion and cancelled her booking. He said exactly the same words to another of Jill's models, a certain Jacqueline Bisset, who went instead to Hollywood, was hailed by *Newsweek* as 'the most beautiful actress of all time' and is still an in-demand actress. A lifetime's blessing in disguise.

Terence was right. You're the correct height and shape for modelling, or you're not. And models in this era don't stay slim because we snort endless lines of coke, munch Kleenex, have disorders – or whatever current story is doing the rounds. Nor are we automatically gifted with some genetic template for weight control that eludes other women. We simply eat wisely because we have to sustain a consistent weight for the long term in order to make a living. It's a learned ability to stay the course, not simply to get in shape for a family wedding or a forthcoming holiday.

Jill turns away 'under eaters' instantly. The giveaway signs can't be hidden – dry hair, sallow skin, brittle-looking bones and a deadness in the eyes. It's all there to see if you know how, and why, to look. No reputable agency will keep a girl, however beautiful, on its books if she exhibits emotional baggage with drugs or food. It simply doesn't need the hassle.

Nor does it need the model who gets 'sick' more than normal, usually before an important job, with headaches, stomach upsets, colds, food intolerances, and whose bathroom cupboards overflow with potions and pills – but thinks nothing of getting wrecked at the bar.

Modelling isn't brain surgery, but it can be a damn sight harder than it looks. You need more than a photogenic face to get to the top. And staying there is the true test of a girl's character. It takes serious drive, determination and resilience to travel the world alone, to be a team player on set and to immediately understand what is expected of you in the big picture.

We'll be booked time and time again if we're punctual, organised, get on well with the client and crew, and have a great sense of humour. Especially on location, where we need to be one of the boys who can lug a suitcase into the jungle, change behind a bush, knock up a sandwich, make the photographer laugh, the client swoon, suggest the answer to a lighting problem and photograph like a dream. All this counts as much as an ability to understand camera angles and lighting. To be focused; to have good strategies to cope with stress: to make it all look easy and fun.

Jill has her favourites. Her 'most beautiful model of all' is Sarah 'Sally' Crichton Stuart with whom she shares a last cigarette in the Ladies, to help calm Sally's nerves moments before she marries the Aga Khan, Prince Karim, in Paris. How we love hearing about the bride's white sari, and the pearls thrown at her feet, and the reception at the thirteenth-century Île Saint-Louis pile, and how bitchy Sarah's mother was to Jill by declaring, 'I nearly bought that suit but it made me look so old.' And of how Princess Margaret was Guest-of-Honour. 'I do hope she didn't bring John Bindon,' I stop myself from saying just in time.

It's not long before Jill books a job which brings *my* first regal experience. 'You have a Munich booking, darling – your ticket's waiting at Heathrow as usual. The Hotel Splendid overnight, and then a 10.30 A.M. start from Willy Bogner's studio. He'll be driving you and two other models to St Moritz for a week, for ski-wear fashion. You don't need accessories, just boots and your warmest underwear!'

Willy Bogner Jr. Hmmm . . . that name rings a bell. Of course! Bogner ski-wear – it's the haute designer label of the snow. But, hang on, isn't he also the Olympic skier who went off-piste with his fiancée and an avalanche killed her? I must remember never to mention this after a few drinks, which can often loosen my tongue. Willy turns out to be handsome, very *simpatico*, in his late twenties and the cameraman on several James Bond films that require complex ski footage. This is to be the launch of his first ski collection Formula W, a statement to Bogner Senior that he can cut the mustard in the family business.

A robust, utterly breathtaking blonde from Munich called Karin, and Ulla, a delicate Swedish beauty based in Paris, complete the model trio. The car journey's fun, the scenery gob-smacking and Willy takes a shine to me because I make him laugh.

It's obvious when we arrive in St Moritz that the glamour of this infamous post-war alpine home of Hollywood stars, playboys, European royalty, Greek tycoons and the *dolce-vita* racy British still glistens. Designer boutiques cram into the higgledy-piggledy streets between ski shops, patisseries and fondue restaurants where fur-clad shoppers of uncertain nationality and age wave huge big-carat diamonds and sport blond highlights. And that's just the men. As we unload our cases outside the Hotel Au Reduit, Willy suggests that I stay in his luxurious family chalet instead, which he insists on showing me around. It is, indeed, the last word – but his sister, already in situ, takes an instant dislike to the British model who's never skied in her life.

After completing the fourth day's shoot, Willy invites his three models for an early evening drink at the Palace Hotel, perched on the edge of a frozen lake and the grandest place in town. The foyer hums with elegance and leads to a great hall that could be the Gothic centrepiece of a Scottish castle with its open fires, high-backed armchairs, antlers and the mountains as backdrop. *Fin de siècle* opulence made über-cosy.

Our swanky bar feels like Bond habitat, but there's not a soul around until we get up to leave, then a tap on my shoulder. Fully expecting Sean Connery with a Martini and cigar, and wearing a polo neck under his blazer, I'm surprised to see it's a haughty man in a soft grey suit who enquires where we're staying. I tell him, he nods and leaves. After work the following day, the phone rings in my hotel room. The 'grey suit' invites us three girls for drinks with the Shah of Iran who is staying in the penthouse suite of the Palace Hotel.

When I tell Karin and Ulla they go nuts.

'Wow, the Shah . . . my Mom won't believe this.'

'Oh my God, what shall I wear . . . the Dior blue or the Chanel sample?'

I haven't the remotest idea who he is – don't even realise that Iran is the new Persia – so tiptoe back to my room to ring my pal John, who'd been propositioned to join MI6 while still at Cambridge, but became a doctor instead. I know he'll be up to date on these matters.

'Christ! You mustn't go. He's the blood sucker of the century!'

The Shah's request to meet us is not remotely within my realms of understanding. What on earth are we supposed to do – pout and flick our hair? Discuss world politics? The two other models appear to know the form and are already planning their outfits. For Karin it's a toss-up between the lapis-blue Dior cocktail dress and the lilac-frost Chanel sample with sequins. Ulla has her 'killer' version of the little black dress.

'Sorry, I can't go. I haven't brought a cocktail frock.'

'You've *got* to come with us!' Karin says, tossing me the Chanel.

My rebellious streak kicks in and I agree to go, but will not dress up. I don't *want* to look over-excited – surely an unassuming sartorial approach is more fitting. Wasn't it

Lauren Bacall who said, 'Always give people, visually, a little bit less than they want of you'?

The girls totter to the Rolls-Royce, sent by the Palace Hotel, with their trinkets tinkling, giggling at my purple suede ankle boots, ebony drainpipes and embroidered belt worn as a headband. We climb into the back seat of the longest car I've ever seen. If we'd been sitting in the front, we'd already be there. We're ushered up to the Presidential Suite which is the entire top floor of the hotel with a wrap-around balcony.

Crikey! There's a line of dignitaries, or henchmen – I can't decide which because they all look daunting and wear similar suits. The two girls curtsy to the Shah, but which one is he? I choose the tallest most imposing suit and make an embarrassing dip. Oh dear, he's not the Shah, he's security. Polite chatter, champagne, an unobtrusive four-piece band playing softly . . . 'Would one of us like to dance with the Shah?' enquires a suit.

Ulla steps forward, pouts at the Shah and they begin a slow waltz. We all watch transfixed. Then it's Karin's turn. The bodyguards follow her every move in her lapis-blue Dior. Now it's me. Oh God, how I hate this kind of dancing! What the hell am I doing here? What's the point of all this? My feet keep treading on his toes in these stupid boots. Luckily no one is now remotely interested.

'Where are you from?' asks the Shah.

'London. Do you know it?' For the first time the Shah appears animated. His troubled eyes light up and his bold black eyebrows bounce up to his receding silver hairline.

'Yes, I was at university in Cambridge. I'm very fond of England and British cars. I have a Bristol at home.'

Now you're talking.

'Oh, really? What year?'

'It's a 1956 Drophead Coupé.'

'Wow . . . what colour?'

We stop dancing and talk cars; his command of English is perfect. Completely forgetting the 'stick to small talk' rule, I find myself telling him about my father. How the sheer incompetence of the British Motor Corporation, selling cars at a loss and not knowing they were doing so, may have contributed to Dad's suicide. The Shah asks whether political intervention would have rescued the BMC situation and I inform him that all the directors walked away with generous severance payments but every worker lost his job.

I'm on a roll now, the family history that I know by heart and expound without pausing for breath: 'What annihilated great chunks of the British car industry from the 1960s was a poisonous mix of politics – from communist-agitated unionism to catastrophic government meddling and cost-obsessed management. It's still in disarray and earlier this year [1969] a nationalised British Leyland lost five million hours to strikes, doubling to ten million. The government invested £1.3 billion, but only the spending of the cash, not the growth, has happened so far . . . '

The Shah is transfixed, stunned that I'm not talking kittens and ball gowns, and seems eager to continue our discussion, but a suit heads over and whispers in his ear. It's time for us girls to return to our hotel.

Back in London, Jill hands me a package delivered to the agency. It contains a colossal sapphire-blue tin of Iranian Royal caviar, the inky, soft, huge eggs from the Caspian Sea which borders Iran, and a note from the Shah: 'I enjoyed our conversation very much.'

Eight years later 'The King of Kings of the Peacock Throne', as the Shah was known by his followers, was alone and isolated by his enormous wealth and sent packing by the Ayatollahs for being an American stooge. The USA, which had failed to foresee the Islamic revolution, promptly ignored him, and in 1980 he died a friendless death in Cairo.

Now, I'd have more in common with Shah Mohammad Reza Pahlavi than our mutual love of British cars and my father's suicide. His daughter Leila was found dead in a London hotel from an overdose of barbiturates in 2001, and his youngest son Alireza later died from a self-inflicted gunshot wound.

A tiny kiosk in London's Bond Street sells foreign magazines. Not many places do in 1969. It's snowing when I slide by and see Jane Birkin's exquisite *visage* on the cover of French *Vogue*. Next to her is another Parisian glossy featuring a maxi-skirted model with a fake plait like roof-lagging wrapped around her head which brings to mind the Queen Mum on an off-day. She's grasping a full-length mirror. All it needs is the kitchen sink. I stop to buy Jane Birkin and 'that weird one next to it'. The Cockney seller, a dead ringer for Terence Stamp, looks stumped. A sale is a sale, but why am I buying the weird one?

'Er . . . it's me,' I gurn, holding up the non-Jane before stuffing it in my bag.

'Never!' says the seller, suppressing a throaty chuckle.

''Fraid so,' I shrug.

'Well, keep it real, love,' he giggles.

'Yeah, I'll try, but that's the hard bit.'

7

POSED IN PARIS

'Know first who you are and then adorn yourself accordingly'

Epictetus, Greek philosopher

It's one of those bleak London mornings when water gushes down shiny streets sweeping litter into mini-fountain drains. You know the kind. My Marigolds squeak as I rip them off and dump the half-washed pile of tights in the kitchen sink before dashing for the phone. Let's hope it's an exciting booking – a trip to sunny Rio would be good.

'Hello darling, just ringing to say the Paris collections are confirmed for you next week. It's for five nights. *Vogue* wanted you but *L'Officiel* magazine got in first.'

'*L'Officiel* . . . never heard of it. And why five nights?'

'It's the French high society bible, sweetie – has been since the 1920s – very glossy, very upmarket. It made Balenciaga and Dior. And you work through the night because the clothes are only released to the magazines after the catwalk shows. A room's been reserved for you at L'Hotel in the sixth, right in Saint-Germain.'

'What's the name of l'hotel?'

'L'Hotel! It's where Oscar Wilde died. You'll love it!'

You stupid, ungrateful girl.

Penny, my fresh-faced agency booker, all sparkling eyes and neat short bob, would never say that aloud, her patience and charm both legendary. But she's nobody's fool – an irresistible combo that would later attract barrister and author John Mortimer who promptly fell in love and married her.

'Is this your first trip to Norway?' asks the chiselled young chap seated next to me as we taxi down the runway.

'Very funny, I'm off to Paris – don't know about you.'

'Ah . . . well this plane is going to Oslo,' he adds, promptly blasting my dreams of chain-smoking Gauloises with the wrong fingers, sipping café noir and wearing existential black from head to toe.

Oslo to the left. Orly to the right. Whoaaa . . . waved through the wrong gate and didn't think to check! A robust leap in the air, a loud expletive, and three stewards rush towards me.

'*Sit down, Madam!*'

The silver machine grinds to a halt. Dodging audible tuttings and a salivary missile, I'm ushered into a small vehicle already alongside the plane, and returned to the terminal.

'We're just locating your luggage, Madam. Can we offer you our first-class facilities while we organise you on the next flight to Paris?'

Good old BEA. Those were the days.

It's a beautiful, creamy dusk when we touch down. Narrow, winding streets bordered with sedate houses and super wide tree-lined boulevards gradually emerge to peer out of the twilight. The air is fresh and clean. Just time to drop my luggage at L'Hotel before legging it to the studio where the team is already assembled – classic French-charmer snapper and two models – towering English redhead Sarah and American beauty Anna. France's Vidal Sassoon, Alexandre, is *maître coiffeur*. He's the one who originated the *chignon* as an art form, but appears to have moved on to plaits – a scary collection now draped around the massive make-up mirrors.

We sit and wait. And wait and wait. And wait . . . for the star garments, the hand-cut one-offs desired by every fashion publication in the world and never ever released by couturiers until after they've performed on the catwalk to rapturous applause. A magazine's status dictates who gets each garment first. Usually it's the *Vogues*, and, more often than not, the snapper and fashion editor hold on to the garment *très très* long before despatching it on.

Frozen to the spot in this vast, dark, empty space with our perfectly coiffed hair, we wait. But Alexandre, around fifty, can't sit still and adds his fake plaits at every opportunity. Oh no! He's wrapped one round my ears that's frayed at the edges and smacks of old roof lagging. I'm now a spiky sludge-brown brunette with a surly smile.

Spending entire nights with complete strangers quickly warms hearts and makes our instant friendships already seem ancient. When Sarah produces two bottles of Bolly fizz from her kit, we're giggling in seconds and inventing impromptu word play to avoid slow brain death.

'Is cardiology the study of knitwear . . . ?' (It gets worse with every glass.)

'Are you a Socialist?' . . . 'Yeah, I love to go out with my friends' (hic, slurp)

'Do you like this sham-poo?' . . . 'Non, I prefer a proper-poo' (aghhhh!)

Thereby endorsing the widely held belief that God evened up the playing field a little when he bestowed the precious gift of stupidity upon us models. When Sarah informs us that her deodorant stick instructs her to 'push up bottom' and bends over to illustrate, poor Alexandre has to completely redo our laughed-out hair. Damn it, I'm even more roof-lagged now.

Way past midnight and Bing! Bang! A door bursts open. Instant music, lights, urgent adrenalin as four magazine girls stagger in with armfuls of impossibly expensive clothes and every hand-stitched designer original is allocated to its most suitable wearer and draped around a hanger on the rail beside her chair. I can smell the heat of the previous models trapped in the linings. Each girl's scent still recognisable . . . the lighter Chanel . . . Hmmm, expensive Joy . . . that one's Lauder's horrid Youth Dew . . . oh no, this one reeks of old patchouli oil and dope. They're all smelly and soggy round the armpits, models being a bit gung-ho in the personal hygiene department. The catwalk girls sweat the hardest, prancing down the runway after impossibly quick changes, convincing buyers and editors before we get a look-in. Runway models. Photographic models. Completely separate beings who rarely cross the floor in this era.

'Which shoes for the Balenciaga?' shrieks one mag girl to another as if her life depends on it. Stylists don't exist, just low-paid assistants deciding these globally important decisions. For heaven's sake, the gold ones go with everything.

And then there's the story. Every editorial shoot has a fashion narrative to make sense of the feature. Ours is *L'imprimé reflet de la mode* – 'Prints Reflect Style' – each outfit chosen for its outrageous pattern, notoriously difficult to photograph at the best of times.

But, what's this? Oh bugger . . . the cover shot: a huge mirror arrives on set which I, the foreground model, must prop up so that the far side of my garment and Sarah, the background model, reflect through the mirror. But the camera must never be spotted. No room for improvised movement – an inch in any direction makes me and my outfit look twice its size and the other model is wiped out. This is precision overload – virtually impossible when fresh as a daisy at nine in the morning and totally effing bonkers when off your head at 3 A.M.

Yet I should be grateful the snapper isn't ultra perfectionist Guy Bourdin. The latest fashion gossip is that he reportedly left a naked Ursula Andress freezing on a glass table for seven hours while he went off in search of the perfect roses to match her skin tone.

Next up is a printed floral trouser suit in satin-back crepe, with another fillip of a built-in scarf to fling Isadora-wise over one shoulder. But is the scarf 'emerald, peppermint, apple, bottle, chartreuse, jade or lime?' (It's hugely important to know.) A shame we're not in Tokyo; only one word in Japanese for blue *and* green. Or Moscow; words for dark blue and light blue in Russian, but *no* word for just blue.

Now it's a 'café au lait and vanilla tree-bark crepe vamp dress' worn with highly traumatised lurex sandals in 'soft caramel' or is it oatmeal, dark sand, honey, putty or pebble? Well, anything but beige. And bulldog clips pulling the garment up, out, down and in. I can almost hear Coco Chanel scream, 'Look, if a dress doesn't fit on the shoulder, it will never fit!'

Yeah, let's not forget that for a period between the two world wars it was women, not men, who dominated Parisian haute couture. Schiaparelli and Chanel were the first females to turn fashion into global brands, liberating women from the tight laces and frills of the nineteenth century and putting them into clothes that allowed them to move freely and be themselves. Paradoxically Chanel despised fashion. 'Fashion,' she said, 'is what goes out of fashion.' Instead she aimed for timelessness.

Exquisite they may be, but once you've modelled all night for the collections you don't ever want to see these clothes again. Slipping into your tenth chiffon/georgette/organza and tulle evening gown, however sensational, means nothing beyond it being the last to be snapped before you can crawl home.

Finally it's time to locate my comfy old coat, or as some might say, the swashbuckling, burnt charcoal maxi-coat in smooth wool jersey, with its rakish collar, bold side buckling, matching buckled cuffs worn with a broad-brimmed slouch hat and ebony leather, gilt-studded knee-high boots.

No tottering killer heels with a wee twinkling leather handbag in the crook of an arm for us models. A robust fisherman's tackle bag draped from our shoulders or a simple straw basket with long leather handle is as good as it ever gets.

Before heading off for our hotel homes, drained but strangely wired, it's time for one last girly bonding word game. 'Okay, so the theme is: which guy's name would most turn you on? Or off? Like you'd divorce Hugh Miliate to marry Percy Vere. Get it?'

'Rich'ard Grafter!' says Sarah without missing a beat. 'Samuel Pepys,' I snigger. 'Buddy Rich!' yells Anna, banging her hands on the studio exit door in the convincing manner of the world's greatest drummer. 'Game over. It's been a blast.' Goodnight, girls.

It's nigh on day-break when I reach the hotel. That isolated time of urban solitude when this profession gets most lonely. Only the self-contained can hack it at international level where birthdays spent in hotel rooms mean your only card is a note from laundry apologising for a lost sock. The needy and neurotic don't last long. Everything and everyone is temporary in this strange life of permanent transit. The chances of being rebooked with Anna and Sarah are remote. We'll send cards, but never know if they hit their target or the intended recipient has moved on. I'll sure miss those half-cut heart-to-hearts and girly confidences.

Hundreds of us constantly travel the world alone; three

countries in a week, sometimes in a day. We're not feted like The Shrimp and Twiggy – that era of the English Model has gone. The Supermodel not yet launched. We are nameless but vaguely familiar faces, perpetual nomads – all possessions are practical, thrown into a case at five minutes' notice. No excess, no hoarding, no stuff and this strict editing stays with us for life. But we never throw away our letters – they don't take up much room. The tactile pleasure of ripping open an envelope from a far-flung shore with its instantly familiar handwriting and teacup stain, several red wine splodges, a stray hair, and the elusive smell of the distant sender, acts as a precious memory tag for a life that is always, always on the move.

L'Hotel is situated slap bang in the middle of the Left Bank. Approaching through a veil of early morning mist, it appears tiny, perfectly formed, the classic exterior promising a milky haven of expensive neutrals. But how wrong could I be? The flamboyant, eye-watering explosion of *chinoiserie* that hits and envelops me has remained unchanged since Oscar Wilde was a permanent guest in room sixteen.

As I crash into bed, a shaft of morning sunlight beams onto two velvet chairs with angels and cherubs dripping from every corner. 'Either that wallpaper goes or I do!' was the last sentence poor Oscar ever uttered. But I love it. The mega-patterned flock almost leaps off the wall to kiss me goodnight.

Collections over, my Paris agency suggests staying on for more work. The commissions a post-collections girl can generate by sticking around when most models have left town has not gone unnoticed, but L'Hotel is priced way too high for this twenty-year-old saving to buy her mother a lovely house. Chewing the fat with my booker Paulene, we're interrupted by Michel, the agency's sole backer and astute businessman. He's overheard our conversation.

'I 'ave a very small apartment above mine, in Rue Jacob. He is free at the moment, if you would like?'

'*Merci*, Michel! I would like him *beaucoup*.'

A stroll away from L'Hotel, Rue Jacob turns out to be the prettiest rue on the entire Left Bank. We smile as we spot '*les touristes, n'est ce pas?*' drinking wine in cafés; the French never drink wine before or after a meal, only with food and never mid-afternoon – their loss if you ask me. Michel leads the way through imposing iron gates to an internal, cobbled courtyard, we turn left, scramble up four storeys of winding, poorly lit stairs and *Voilà!* my attic studio with its almost clichéd loveliness, way up in the rooftops, the tiny bed-sitting room leading to a slender roof terrace where I'll sip wine after work, inhaling the unmistakable essence of Paris: *parfum*, *Pernod*, *pissoirs* and *Gauloises*, drifting up from the streets below.

Meandering along the river between bookings – gazing at the battered-book stalls and the extraordinarily designed bridges that cross the Seine, up through the narrow streets that climb back to Boulevard Saint-Germain, through ancient archways to spy into courtyards now housing modern companies – it never ceases to amaze me how clever the French are at keeping their architecture intact, preserving their ancient beauty while ensuring they still function as purposeful buildings and not simply museum pieces.

There are no superior smiles when this gangly blonde browses in La Hune, the bookshop so beloved by *les philosophes*, hoping her existential potential will be noticed before her battered tote jammed with essential accessories for her next booking. And no hassle when she pauses to buy a wedge of mature, divinely stinky Comté cheese and wafer-thin slices of *jambon de Bayonne* to devour in her favourite corner spot in the Jardin du Luxembourg. Mmmmmmm Paris! From drab Fray Bentos tinned pies to orgasmic pistachio macaroons without inhaling.

A tiny café in Rue Saint-Jacques is my evening haunt, where a basic meal costs five francs for a bowl of soup with bread, plat du jour, a quarter of a carafe of wine, cheese and coffee. Perfect! Then, nightcap glass in hand on my tiny rooftop terrace overlooking a scrawl of zinc-covered roofs, I marvel at this free-spirited, lively, bohemian city and reflect how near France is to Britain in miles but how different in every way; the proud nationalism, the flag draping, the Marseillaise singing – all without a wince of irony. Unlike us, the French take food, manners, bureaucracy, beauty, politics and philosophy entirely seriously.

Philosophers are moody heroes in Paris, not smelly old men in decaying cords. Intellectuals and academics here even get hitched to models! In Britain a model rarely meets a 'brain' and is perceived, it appears, to 'shag like a stoat and marry for money'. It does surprise me that the French don't have an actual word for home; at the house (à *la maison* and *chez*) but no actual word for home. To further console us Brits they're also reassuringly bad at popular culture. Just look at their telly! And surely Johnny Hallyday should call it a day.

The playboys here are a little different to those in Milan. They don't line up in expensive cars outside our agencies and hotels to ogle and engage, but think nothing of stopping us in the street. A guy called Gerard Perrier, considered the most successful 'modeliser' in town, leaps out of his car and starts 'the chat up' whenever he spots a lanky girl carrying her model kit or go see portfolio. He's so bad at it that I find him irritatingly endearing.

This time he has a *petit* Englishman in his car, an unprepossessing chap who shyly invites me to dinner the following evening. Oh, why not? It makes a change from eating alone or joining the predictable, xenophobic fashion throng. His name is Alan Clore and his choice of restaurant, the 400-year-old Tour d'Argent, couldn't be more different to the see-and-be-seen La Coupole where the tightly knit gang of hyper-stylish poseurs hang out. 'Traditional and stuffy' is the fashion pack's flat feedback when I announce my evening's venue.

But the grand sixth-floor eaterie turns out to have the most jaw-dropping view in Paris, a staggeringly illuminated Notre Dame cathedral with the twinkling Seine as ultimate backdrop, close enough to lean out of the picture window and caress it. Oh, and its cellar stocks 450,000 bottles of wine. How reassuring. Alan's well known to the maître d' and as we glide to the table with the ultimate view, I whisper that models always insist on very expensive restaurants because they give you so little to eat. 'Wait and see,' he smiles.

Duck is the speciality – very bloody duck. A numbered tag, certifying its origins, is presented when we place our order. They're way past the million mark now; the Queen, Winston Churchill, JFK and Henry IV having all done their bit. Our bird is ready and the maître d' stands on a pedestal in the centre of the room theatrically removing the breast and legs as waiters in full tails scuttle noiselessly around. Now the carcass is placed inside a solid-silver duck press and, as the bones and internal organs are crushed, the blood and juices ooze into a silver dish gently warmed over a burner. The blood coagulates and a little cognac, Madeira and *foie gras* are added to the still almost-red breast meat before it's brought to the table.

Oh God, I've suddenly lost my appetite, too squeamish by far to tuck into something that still looks like road-kill. Another drink, quick! Now which one of the 450,000 bottles shall we try next? When Alan nips to the loo and our waiter is distracted, I neatly slip the contents of my plate into my napkin to slide down the table leg into my '*très un-chic sac à main.*' Michel's housekeeper's Chihuahua will love it. '*Quel plaisir de boire du vin sans preservative,*' I giggle to our waiter as he refills my glass. 'You've just told him how nice the wine is without a condom,' smiles Alan. In his early twenties, amusing and introspective, he divides his time between London, Switzerland and France, where his mother lives. He's bright and read politics, philosophy and economics at Oxford but 'hasn't done much since'.

Why not? Quietly informing me that his father owns Selfridges, he leans over and, in a voice I can barely hear, reveals that his father also withheld his twenty-first birthday present of a seven-million-pound trust fund until he'd heard the results of Alan's Oxford finals 'because anyone can be twenty-one.' I don't know whether to laugh or weep.

So does Alan work at all? Well, he invests in films, and backed the recently released *Wonderwall* starring Jane Birkin and is about to back Chekhov's play *Three Sisters*, starring Joan Plowright and directed by Laurence Olivier, but seems somewhat resentful that he puts up the dosh but is never part of the creative process.

It's endearing that he doesn't come across as an acquisitive money-man. Quite the opposite, he appears somewhat lost and lacking in purpose. I feel a bit sorry for him and we become long-term pals, nothing more, often meeting up in London where it's always Claridge's for dinner and occasionally to Paris to watch his French-trained horses race at Longchamp.

He has a friend, Michel Taittinger, who is his French double – diminutive in stature, awash with wealth and, similarly, a bit adrift. This young champagne scion also invests in cinematic productions – his latest venture *5 + 1*, the film of the Stones concert in Hyde Park only a few days after Brian Jones's death. As with others in my growing stable of platonic man-pals, it's plain to see that Alan and Michel are comfortable and relaxed with a female who can't be bought. It fascinates them. Apparently it's a rare occurrence.

'Surely you like jewellery?'

'No, I really don't. I only ever wear a watch.'

'I'd love to give you fifty cases of vintage Taittinger?'

'Nah, I'd only drink them all and feel dreadful.'

But this doesn't stop me ringing my mother.

'Guess what, Mum? I've got these two well-off suitors. Now, would you like to free-shop forever in Selfridges *or* drink Taittinger champagne for the rest of your life?' I expect squeals of delight.

'Not impressed, darling. Don't play around with the feelings of these poor chaps. It's not fair. It's an awful burden to inherit lots of money if you haven't got the strength of character to deal with it.'

'But, Mum, don't feel too sorry for them. They're "modelisers", they live to be seen with beanpole leggy cover girls. Their gene pools need us, but in the end we're simply status symbols, as disposable as their last sports car.'

'Look darling, the one thing money can't buy is a sense of purpose. These poor chaps have everything, except a goal to aim for and a real sense of achievement. And besides, you would never be comfortable with too much luxury. You're not the type!'

She's right. Walking down an empty beach at sunset in Cornwall trumps five-star luxury every time. And you need to look a certain way to pull off huge wealth. I've always been a bit too 'chipped-nail-polish' for that.

It's a fact that long-term relationships are tricky in this world. A model often earns as much, if not more, than her man who must totally accept that fashion photography is an intimate game of make-believe; the all-seeing lens, the exposed subject, the powerful snapper, the cunning disparity between fantasy and reality that fashion plays with delusions of desire and dreams. I'm lucky that my boyfriend Bill travels as much as I do and is not threatened or fazed by my job.

Yet away from home, in this surreal bubble of eternal transit, I often feel sexually puzzled. Not by the ploys of the snapper to get the shot; the mild teasing and nudging is never serious and we learn quickly to spot the tricks and ignore the passes. If he tries it on we know exactly how to cope. This is not a victim culture. We can always call the shots. A flirtatious compliment is recognised as simply that, rather than a portentous knee-groping entrée. But the stray hand that adjusts your shirt too many times, followed by a 'this would work so much better without your top' leads to a walk off set and a call to your agent. And we make sure that word travels around the biz about 'that greasy old perv'. It always does the trick.

No, what I'm most confused about is the paradox of love and sex. Not that thing of thinking you're in love when you're really in lust but something more complex than that. It's when you meet someone, genuinely fall in love and as time goes by you blissfully almost merge with them, feeling all cosy and peaceful.

But eroticism needs separateness. Desire, let's face it, is unfulfilled anticipation and is at its most powerful at the start of a relationship because we're not sure if it's reciprocated. Once we discover that it is, the distance disappears and all the uncertainty, edginess, anxiety, and jealousy that kept us in feverish longing is suddenly removed.

Risk boosts desire. Love wants the opposite: intimacy, working as a team, friendship, romance – and one destroys the other.

The moment I walk into photographer Jeanloup Sieff's studio, I know it will lead to something dangerously exciting. He is, without question, the most attractive, mesmeric man in Paris. Today's booking is for *Vogue*, and the shoot goes well. Total synchronicity; we are as one. At the end of the day, alone in the studio, our eyes meet yet again and lock with mutual longing. Perhaps I would like to stay on for some test shots with him?

'Test shots' are occasionally used as a snapper's euphemism for 'I fancy you and if you feel the same, you could stay on, or come back later, and we could end up having a *Blow Up*-type photographic session where you writhe around on the studio floor wearing not a lot and I, the photographer, lean over you snapping away, and if it feels good you allow me to invade your personal space and we both enjoy it.'

I choose to stay. I'm glad I did.

If my *Blow-Up* screen test had been this exciting, I might have got the part.

But as we lie next to each other, the most attractive man in Paris and I, in this fragile post-coital cocoon of sweat, semen and smoke, we know there is no future. Jeanloup and I both have long-term partners with whom we are happy.

We are simply two right people doing the wrong thing.

And as the throbbing urgency of the before gives way

to the inevitable melancholy of the after, our eyes meet yet again . . .

'*À bientôt?*'

'*Non. Au revoir.*'

'*Oui. C'est ça.*'

'*Adieu.*'

If the phone doesn't ring, that'll be me.

8

FLASHED IN TIME

'Music is a safe kind of high'

Jimi Hendrix

Boyfriend Bill has found a spacious mansion-block flat to rent in Maida Vale. It's four flights up, no lift, and sandwiched between a maze of identical mansion blocks. It's easy to forget which one is ours. Now Head of Promotion at Warner Bros Records, Bill needs a roomy place to put up music-biz pals overnight. Sure enough, the week after we move in, half the London music scene skip the light fandango and flop here too. Bill's lifelong friend Stanley Dorfman co-created BBC's *Top of the Pops,* but it is the current producer Mel Cornish, a witty, quick-thinking, warm-hearted man, who stays every Thursday night – too knackered to make it back to Hertfordshire post live-show celebrations.

The perceived industry wisdom about *TOTP* is that if you don't appear on it you don't have a hit. Fifteen million viewers ensure that record sales can, and do, quadruple overnight so the cutting-edge bands and tacky, uncool acts all appear together – the content of the show entirely controlled by the whims of that week's record buyers. When an act is unable to appear in person because of a tour, illness or the cost of flying in from the States, the programme's resident dance troupe Pan's People perform an appropriately choreographed dance to the song. But if a record slips out of the charts they must scrap the routine and invent a new choreography in an absurdly short space of time. Music video promos do not yet exist.

Mel has an idea that will minimise the chaos. Filmmaker Tom Taylor will make a weekly film clip of a likely chart-mover and, if the performer is unable to appear live, I will be the resident *TOTP* model featured in it – paving the way for the first music videos. Hmmm, could be fun: a Bob Dylan muse one week, a Beach Boys surfing babe the next.

Pan's People turn out to be real troupers and one of them, Ruthie, often stays overnight at our flat, but the DJs who present the shows mean nothing to us. They're just shouty irritants that link one act to the next. If we ever thought about the most irritating one of all, a certain Jimmy Savile, which we didn't, it was how appalling and embarrassing he was in his ridiculous loud nylon tracksuits and weirdly wiggy platinum hair. The concept of him – or any of them – being remotely sexual in any way never crossed our minds. Creepy Savile never homed in on confident girls from stable backgrounds – it was always the most vulnerable and voiceless. He is known for licking the hands and arms of those he's introduced to, so I bristle when he approaches me

149

in the BBC bar (he's heard I hail from Barnsley, he's from nearby Leeds) and deliver such a repellent, piercing groan to his repulsive face that he slithers away sharply.

My film-clip fame is short-lived. The first, for a record called 'Something's Burning' by Kenny Rogers and the First Edition, the next Andy Williams' 'Can't Help Falling In Love' are dull manufactured singalongs, though some folk like that kind of thing: the latter spends a whopping seventeen weeks in the charts which summons a call from my agent, Jill.

'Darling, we don't think that *Top of the Pops* is great exposure for you. You're losing your mystique by appearing in these films every week. We think it cheapens your image.'

So that is that!

No more hilarious Green Room fly-on-the-wall experiences of watching a female singer's manager arguing with Mel because 'she won't do stairs!' Or seeing John Peel (who considers himself way too elitist for the show) grudgingly preparing for his debut, and then forgetting the name of the act he's supposed to introduce, or poor old 'Diddy' David Hamilton fluffing his lines following the LSD spiking of his drink by a record plugger. Or most unnerving of all – in an early show where all songs are mimed 'so that we hear discs exactly as recorded' – seeing Jimi Hendrix inadvertently given an Alan Price song rather than 'Purple Haze' to mime to.

Bill has an eclectic set of friends and another regular pad crasher is Dave Dee, the front man in a band named Dave Dee, Dozy, Beaky, Mick & Tich, who are not even ironically cool or ever taken seriously by the rock establishment. But they've managed to notch up eight Top Ten hits and spent more weeks in the singles charts than the Beatles. Their songs and performances are idiotic and a trifle rude, but Dave is ultra straight – a former policeman who was called to the scene of a 1960 car crash only to discover that the car's occupants were American rock'n'rollers Eddie Cochran and Gene Vincent. When Eddie (my first ever rock hero) died Dave took his Gretsch guitar home from the police station for safe-keeping before returning it to Cochran's family two months later. The moment he played the guitar at home he got the calling – and the cop turned to rock.

Dave and Bill are both anti-drugs, but Dave's strong views don't extend to the suggestive content of his music. 'Bend It', a monster hit in the States, has him wiggling his finger while singing the risqué lyrics and is initially banned until Dave tells them 'it's a dance' and they believe him. He enjoys his stardom, lives the flamboyant celeb lifestyle, drives a Bentley and dates buxom beauty queens. I'm not Dave's type at all.

'Vikki's a nice enough bird, Bill but, sorry mate, she's about as sexy as a stick insect. Now you take my Carol – corrr . . . she's a blinder!'

Yeah, Dave, more shape – less edge.

An ancient wardrobe arrives at the flat to hold his reams of shirts, and I can't help noticing that most of them have sleeves tacked at the shoulder so that they come away with one quick tug when he's mobbed by fans. Around ten pairs of replacement sleeves per shirt patiently await their turn to be tacked in and torn off. When Dave branches out with a solo career, it's surprisingly (to him) short-lived, so Bill gives him a job at WEA Records, newly named when Warner buys

Elektra and Atlantic. Much later, Dave becomes a magistrate and returns to touring – the only Justice of the Peace to be found on stage in his mid-sixties cracking a bull-whip and singing of doomed love in the Mexican desert with the band's vintage international hit 'The Legend of Xanadu'.

At long last I'm seeing more of Bill. WEA Records is less frenetic than his previous jobs. Finally realising that permanent touring is 'risky' for our relationship, he'd moved on from his former job at Carlin Music, next door to Apple in Savile Row, which entailed placing songs with singers (representing Michael Jackson, the entire Tamla Motown catalogue, and securing constant hits for the Four Tops, Diana Ross and the Supremes, Marvin Gaye and Smokey Robinson) to becoming Head of Promotion at WEA. Bill knows that achieving great promotion is all about charm and persistence and the minutiae of detail – mixing records with heaps of bass because the BBC's producers' playing equipment is ultra trebly, and that the end of 'Tumbling Dice' has nine choruses before Charlie Watts comes in again.

But our time together continues to consist of constant chart confrontations – Bill earnestly demanding my 'Yeah, this one's a hit!' assessment after playing piles of demo/promo discs because '*you* are the prime-target-consumer, babe, I need your feedback' – the entire flat forever strewn with undecided vinyl 45s. 'Babe, which of these shall we release as the A-side in the UK? First up is The Four Tops. Tell me, should it be "Reach Out I'll Be There" or "Standing In The Shadows Of Love"?'

Boyfriend Bill Fowler – Head of Promotion at WEA Records

Summoned to help in a different way when American singer Lou Christie arrives in town to promote his American hit 'Lightnin' Strikes', I'm to be his 'English girlfriend' to boost media interest. I like Lou instantly so this won't be too hard. Our 'big moment' is to arrive together at the London Palladium (where Lou will sing and later meet Princess Margaret) holding hands and gazing into each other's eyes. Walls of cameras greet us, limo doors fly open, flashbulbs explode. But Lou and I lose each other in the crowd and I'm left stranded. He makes amends by flying over to Paris where I'm working, taking me to dinner, and becoming a loyal, treasured friend.

The most rewarding part of Bill's work (for me) is seeing his bands play live. We decide to take my mother to meet Stevie Wonder backstage before a show. As with everyone she meets, he promptly adores her and she him – but during the performance, to everyone's horror, he accidently heads lemming-like over the edge of the stage with a fifteen-foot drop into the orchestra pit in front. He's okay, resumes the show and the entire audience rise to their feet. 'Thank God he's all right, darling,' whispers Mum, 'but what a shame he can't see the standing ovation.'

The most ground-breaking (a)live concert I ever heard and saw, to this day, was the Stax European Tour of 1967 which Bill helped plan, and which made Stax recognised as a mainstream force in its own country. 'I can't believe this. We're just session musicians back home, but here we're being treated like the Beatles,' Steve Cropper told me backstage. It was this British tour that made *all* the noise and made those back in the States realise its *full* worth.

The Stax sound's most powerful element was the unique co-ordination of black and white musicians working so seamlessly together, a far-sighted approach at the time. Stax delivered a beacon of racial harmony and artistic authenticity that lit the way for a more equitable music business. Presented by ultra-cool DJ Emperor Rosko, I recall every sexy second of it . . . nothing could beat this . . . the super-long 'Green Onions' intro before the curtain slowly opened to reveal Booker T. and the M.G.'s on stage, the dazzling, unique Memphis sound of Steve Cropper's less-is-more guitar breaks, bassist Donald 'Duck' Dunn and Drummer Al Jackson with Booker T. Jones – and the ultimate climax of Otis Redding closing the show with 'Try A Little Tenderness', a twenty-minute mass-orgasmic sensation never experienced again. Otis died in a plane crash a few months later. He was just twenty-six.

*

It's early June 1970 – birthday time. Skipping down the staircase into the crisp basement of Hatchetts nightclub in Piccadilly expecting a cosy dinner with friends, I'm confronted with the most bizarre crowd of odd-bods ever encountered. Bill has secretly invited every single name in my address book to a surprise party.

My step-aunt from Barnsley in a striped man's suit and newly trimmed crew-cut is in deep conversation with Dennis Wilson of the Beach Boys. To the left of him, Keith Moon is being frisked by Hugh, the owner of Hatchetts, for stink bombs. My mother has brought her best friend from Barnsley, Joan Pratt, a solicitor's wife, who's just accepted a spliff from one of my old school friends. 'So this is a roll-up . . . jolly nice it is too.'

The best surprise of all is seeing my adored brother Nick and his lovely wife for the first time in a year. We've barely kept in direct touch – all so busy with our projects – but Mum keeps me informed whenever she gets a rare inkling. I know they've had their problems and that Nick has been mentally erratic, but they arrive looking happy. They have brought along a tramp because Nick thought 'he looked so sad standing on Victoria station'. Hugh's let him in thinking he's a family member down on his luck.

It's a surreal and odd evening. But good odd, fabulous odd, and when the Beach Boys creep out of the darkness to sing 'Happy Birthday' as a favour to Bill, no money involved, it's the coolest few moments of my life.

Models of my era are simply recognisable faces without voices, so when I grab the phone next morning, nursing one helluva hangover, and hear a highly respected journalist suggesting an interview, I'm flattered. Ray Connolly has a 'must read' Saturday newspaper column. I've met him before on the music-biz circuit and am an avid reader of his work, but 'the interview' is not an art of my acquaintance.

Ray is delightful when we meet – over several drinks he takes notes, and a week later . . . uh oh . . . I pay the price for my media naivety. I'd been hopelessly, stupidly unaware of the caution needed to ensure a statement is not plucked out of context and made into a provocative headline by a canny sub-editor. The bold newspaper by-line screams:

'All models are neurotic. They must be because they're selling themselves. Their faces and bodies are their qualifications – a bit like souped-up prostitutes in a way.'

Yes, I said it. But not intended as a stand-alone statement. That's no excuse because I should have known better. It's taken the modelling profession years to overcome the Christine Keeler model/prostitute euphemism and I go and blow it with one thoughtless interview. I stare at the phone, willing it not to ring as the open newspaper ripples in the draughty room, taunting me to read it again. The phone judders . . .

'Hello, Vikki, Jill here. We've seen the interview. Why the hell didn't you tell us it was taking place? It's absolutely crucial to know how to handle media relations before talking to the press. PR is all about your reputation – the result of what you do, what you say and what others say about you.'

❛ All models are neurotic. They must be because they're selling themselves. Their faces and bodies are their qualifications–a bit like souped-up prostitutes in a way. I mean their whole lives are devoted to their physical attributes ❜

—Vikki Nixon

Picture: James Wedge

Connolly on Saturday

London Evening Standard, *1970*.   *Photo: James Wedge*

How right she is. By 1970, Public Relations, that disciplined and sustained effort to influence behaviour and opinion, is becoming prolific in public lives, rigidly managing the flow of information between a brand/organisation and its public. But I'm not a bloody brand! I'm a vaguely known face.

'I think I have the answer.' says Jill. 'A quick exit from London will make you unavailable. Eileen and Jerry Ford are in town from New York so I'll organise dinner at the Star of India tomorrow evening. Drinks at my place first, at seven. And don't worry.'

Thanks, Jill. That's what makes you the best agent in London. But what the hell is happening to me? This life could get way beyond my control if I don't wise up.

Eileen Ford's ambitious vision in 1946 had given birth to a brand-new industry, which she co-developed with devoted husband Jerry. Her steely manner built an empire and at the beginning of this new decade she is still the world's leading model agent, known to demand the highest level of professionalism from models privileged enough to be on her books.

She's holding court, drink in hand, at Jill's house when I arrive. Jerry is a surprisingly handsome six-foot-two-inch former American football player with a slow, relaxed smile and a good sense of humour, the perfect antidote to the tiny, freckled ball of energy who moves and talks with the speed of lightning. Eileen has an open, blunt honesty that I can only admire, but such a forthright manner that her fashionable wig moves independently every time she shakes her head. It's obvious she's a toughie.

'It isn't beauty alone that counts in my New York agency. It's how well you project your personality and your own unique look. Looking like someone else is the kiss of death. I want an agency of individuals. That's what sells. *You must be yourself.*'

After copious drinks we make our way to Jill's beloved local Indian restaurant. Conversation flows, drinks glug down, chicken korma melts into mouths, and Jill and husband Robin make it easy for me. I don't feel that I'm being physically assessed, but I am.

A particularly animated nod of Eileen's head and it's clear that I'm to be a Ford Model.

It's also clear that her wig has moved to a somewhat un-flattering position. And Jerry's seen it too. Nonchalantly excusing himself by 'going to the wash-room' he brushes past Eileen and deftly nudges her wig back into place. Eileen's quite sloshed. We all are. Time to go.

Thrusting one hand out to me, the other to hail a cab, Jerry proclaims, 'Welcome to the agency. *You* are a Ford Model!' Eileen gives me a hurried hug. The wig stays perfectly in position. 'Yes dear, get those New York composites printed and sent to me as soon as possible.'

Bill laughs heartily when I relate the evening's events to him. 'No wonder the Fords have no rivals.' He has a nip of Scotch. 'It's truly amazing babe – over three billion people in the world, each with a different set of facial features, and yours have been chosen by the top model agency in the world.' Good old Bill – trust a Head of Promotion to eye it like that. Then he sighs, and pretends to fiddle with his belt buckle. 'But three months away. God I'm going to miss you babe.'

Dozing in bed, three sheets to the wind, listening to Bill's gentle breathing, I groggily, blearily, woozily ponder what the East Coast fashion fraternity will make of a girl from Barnsley with the same surname as their current president – to date the least popular, most loathed leader in American history.

9

UN-FOCUSED IN NEW YORK

'Life begins at the end of your comfort zone'
Neale Donald Walsch

'Strewth, a pommie hoping to make an impact in *La Grande Pomme*,' chuckles Dennis, a science teacher from Adelaide. Conversation appears inevitable now that I'm almost sitting on his knee. We're scrunched together in economy Pan Am seats about to be served compact trays of 'luncheon'.

'What's he on about?' giggles Sally-Ann. She's on my left.

'It's just larrikin lingo, Sal. But what the heck is Jell-O?' I mutter, staring at the fluorescent contents of the plastic pot in front of me. Our air hostess, all azure tight-skirted two-piece with jaunty matching pillbox, gives a bemused smile and moves on down the aisle. 'That's the dessert, silly,' laughs Sally-Ann, 'it's the American version of jelly.'

'Yeah, gelatine, made from the connective tissues of cows, pig bones and hooves. Add artificial sweetener and food colouring and you have Jell-O! Will you be leaving yours?'

'Be my guest, Dennis. Are all their puddings this weird?'

'Oh, mate, wait 'til you try their puds made with veggies – pumpkin pie and carrot cake, eh Sal? And did you know that the difference between a 747 and a pommie is that the plane stops whining *before* it gets to New York?'

Sally-Ann giggles. She giggles a lot. We share the same agency in London and this is her second working trip to the States. Her infectious laugh, feisty Essex twang and open fresh beauty encompass the Twiggy-esque charm that Americans love and Sal immediately cracked the huge teenage market last time round. She's with a new agency developed by former model Wilhelmina, who bravely stepped in to try and snatch business from the giant Fords.

We arrive at JFK to find a chauffeur waving a Ford Model Agency sign with my name on it. Shrieks and more giggles as we climb into the limo, clink, clink, clink, and drive into Manhattan. There's a note from Eileen Ford on the back seat: '*Dear Vikki, here are the keys to your apartment. There will be a couple of others staying with you as it is emense* [sic] *and would be much too costly for one person. I am looking forward to seeing you, so give me a call here at the agency, or come in as soon as possible tomorrow. The most important thing I want to say is WELCOME!*' Blimey, I wasn't expecting this. Most new models in town stay at Eileen and Jerry's East Side town house in happy chaos with their four teenage children, or in underwhelming small hotels vetted by the agency.

But here we are, floating down the freeway, gazing

through lean limo windows, barely able to contemplate what awaits us on the flip side of the glass. Through the Lincoln Tunnel and *WHAM!* It's all bumper-to-bumper fat cops and yellow cabs using sirens and car horns instead of brakes, steam billowing from pavements, screeching ambulances, purposeful punters. New York looks solid, invulnerable and unarguable. That tangible end-of-an-era melancholy that has recently appeared in London isn't present here. No one is stoned and hanging around.

Every ruled ribbon intersection takes place at a sharp angle, the brutal grids highlighting a squillion gleaming windows in the setting sun. Wow, I'm totally unprepared for Manhattan's unique beauty – the mad but principled architecture of the place.

Dusk is fast approaching as the long car purrs to a halt at 165 West End Avenue, Sally-Ann and Dennis dutifully despatched. No shops, no buzz or hustle here – a near total absence of activity on the streets in this quiet residential part of town; the unbroken street wall entirely made of handsome nineteenth-century residences around twelve storeys tall. As I unlock the front door of my tenth floor apartment, a wild haze of mauve and ochre streams across the hallway, hues of a setting sun on the twinkling Hudson below. A quick recce reveals that every room offers this sensational uninterrupted view and as I step onto the terrace I can smell the deep, dark water.

Dumping my case in the hall I begin to feel strange – out of my depth in this huge, lush Manhattan apartment.

Alone.

I long to hear a familiar, pragmatic, down-to-earth voice. It's time to call Bill in London.

'Look, babe,' he says, 'you're the first one to arrive so take the end bedroom with the en-suite. They might be noisy girls and you definitely need a bit of privacy and proper sleep. The Beach Boys are playing in New York – I'll ask Mike Love to give you a ring to cheer you up.'

Dear lovable, logical, Bill.

He knows the Beach Boys' singer will help out. An hour later Mike duly rings and makes me laugh, as always. We hang out with him whenever he's in London where he never stays at the Park Lane Hilton with the rest of the band, but in some low-key Kensington hotel where he can be 'more himself', and usually has a 'future wife' in tow. We've met quite a few of them now. I adore Mike Love; with a name like that who wouldn't?

Still no sign of my two sharers by morning, and breakfast beckons before I front up at the Ford Agency. A huge pack of Coco Pops sits on the kitchen worktop, longing to be noticed, but there's a bold sign printed on one side: '*WARNING*: Adding whole milk will add 160 calories to this product.' Hmmm . . . what *is* milk if it isn't whole, I wonder, and what the hell are calories? No other sugary stuff in the cupboards. I'm not fanatical about what I eat. If it's there to tempt me, I'll probably scoff it.

For me, staying in shape isn't about cutting out certain foods, but about eating well-tasty grub I enjoy, that truly satisfies me psychologically, as well as physically. Modelling has taught me to stand up for myself – and if the garment doesn't fit, it's no big deal. And it's no big deal to tell your agent either. They usually just laugh and say, 'No chocolate today for you, my girl!' And despite the vivid horror stories, none of the models I encounter diet drastically before every designer collection runway appearance. In fact, they eat more nourishing food than ever to keep up their energy levels. When you've experienced the back-stage scramble of changing an entire outfit and hair in just eight seconds, and doing this at least ten times in one show – or been photographed for six hours in the snowy Scottish Highlands wearing nothing but a wispy chiffon evening dress – you'll know it can't be done regularly on an empty stomach.

My London dinner with Eileen and Jerry Ford seems a lifetime away as I approach the Ford Agency's four-storey red-brick building at 344 East 59th Street. It's throbbing with activity when I arrive at nine on this late-October 1970 morning. A deep breath and I queasily remind myself that this $6 million-a-year business is the most successful model agency ever, besieged by hundreds of trembling hopefuls every week. I can hear the roar of oncoming traffic over the Queensboro Bridge as I climb to the second floor, to the heart of the agency, the booking room, where around forty people appear to be working at a feverish pace to ensure that each model's life is as lucrative and untroubled as possible. I later discover that over fifty phones handle several thousand calls a day, and all telephone transactions with clients are tape-recorded so there's no possible misunderstanding as to place, time or any other condition of the job.

Phones screech to be answered and, if they jangle more than once, Eileen's voice can be heard from her office: 'Answer that Goddam phone!' Walls of moving charts contain info about model activities, each one assigned her own booker according to her category; several for the teenage market, others for high-fashion models, and a separate department for television jobs.

This is seriously daunting; my mouth is dry.

Eileen beckons me into her office for our 'first-day chat', the famous speech given to every new girl on her books. 'Your rate will be $75 an hour. This is a high rate of pay because New York models work twice as hard, twice as fast and are twice as prepared for their jobs when they report for work. You must take care of your looks, your wardrobe, and get enough sleep. Before you leave each job you present your voucher book for signature by the client. These will be presented by you to us once a week and paid a week later. And please remember that this job does not depend on looks alone; many more intangibles make a top model. Be distinctive! It's how well you project your personality and character that counts. And know how to interpret a designer's creations to make them come alive! Jane Fonda, Candice Bergen, Ali MacGraw and Camilla Sparv were all highly successful models with this agency and Ruth Derujinsky, whose apartment you are renting, is a leading advertising agency executive and also a former Ford model.'

No pressure then.

'On Monday,' she continues, 'you will begin your castings and go-sees, showing your portfolio to potential clients, and leaving your composite. Modelling here is everything it's cracked up to be, though it is a Spartan life. The most beautiful girls in the world can be found sitting alone by their television sets on Saturday nights, but every successful model I know seems to love her work and thrive on it. Are you a Capricorn? What a pity. Most top models are Capricorn – they're noted for their patience, perseverance and drive for success.'

It's brutally clear that the Fords do not take prisoners, but the industry won't take a model seriously until she's lived and worked in New York.

'Thank you, Eileen. I'll do my very best.'

'The two girls sharing your apartment will arrive sometime over the weekend. One last thing, a friend of mine is giving a small party tonight if you'd like to go along. It should be fun.' A wide maternal smile ends the new girl first-day chat as she hands me a scribbled note with a recommended bank, and an accountancy firm for tax called . . . Blonder and Seymour!

En route to my very first social evening in New York, I stop off at a tiny, neon-drenched bar for a quick bevvy, but when I slide onto the bar stool polished by a thousand previous backsides and down a large one, the cocktail waiter eyes me up suspiciously. And my glow doesn't last long. The second I walk into the party I know I'm way out of my comfort zone. The blow-dried brigade of assembled women (hours and small fortunes ploughed into scorching hair into gleaming helmets) have good bags, nice shoes, complete outfits, masked make-up, perfect nails and not much noticeable imagination.

They stare at my insouciant thatch as if I've just reversed out of a bramble bush and their conversations all appear to be punctuated by a constant stream of strange self-analysis that I've never encountered before.

'. . . I'm feeling *SO* positive at the moment . . . '

'Yeah, me too, I'm in such a calm place and fully embracing it.'

'Well, I've just bought herbal remedies that are really doing their work and my kinetic balance is perfect.'

'. . . and my energy levels are excellent right now too. I'm in such a good space . . .'

Great! Fancy a glass or two of wine then, in-between yoga and seeing your therapist?

No, perhaps not.

Next to me, a tortoise-necked man with bulging waistline and receding hairline talks briskly and bluntly with much evading, but sadly no evoking, eliciting or elucidating. He looks at me blankly before shoulder-surfing someone less weird to talk to, and I focus on his snake-like slitherings of hair brushed forward to disguise the bald bits. Mind you, I've always found receding hairlines very attractive if accompanied by Clive James-esque humour. (He once told me, 'My hair needs to be cut close to my head if it's not to look like a hard-boiled egg being squeezed into an astrakhan glove.')

But this is a room where charm, whimsy and irony are unknown, or considered 'quaint' qualities often mistaken for stupidity. And it's pretty obvious that this is not a town where the creatively uninformed survive. Everyone's hell-bent on which movies to view, the books to devour, what art to see, who is currently *hot*.

Focus, Culture, Work, Success. It's the only game in town.

I try to lighten up and tell a no-fail joke. But there are no belly laughs, just forced smiles.

'Oh, that's so funny,' repeat my listeners. But no one really laughs. 'Did you know bangs are in this fall,' whispers the woman next to me, trying to bond. What? Oh, hair – not guns!

A couple of drinks later I make my excuses and leave. I've planned some sightseeing for tomorrow which could reveal a much needed touch of pure wholesome soul. The Harlem Apollo launched the careers of James Brown, Marvin Gaye, Aretha Franklin and many more of my musical heroes. I want to see this hallowed ground.

Not altogether unaware that the traditionally African-American neighbourhood has fallen into decline and some white folk are scared to visit, I hail a cab on a cold, cloudy Sunday and the cabbie looks shocked. Should he wait for me?

'No thanks, I'll be fine.'

After paying my respects to the grand old building which displays an impressive row of bullet holes, I naturally decide to walk home. During our teenage years in Yorkshire, my best pal Andrea and I walked and hitch-hiked everywhere. It provided more than free travel: it propelled us into a series of arbitrary encounters with people we would otherwise never meet, a bit like walking a dog. Andrea and I got so adept at it that we found ourselves tutting if an old truck stopped beside our thumb . . . nothing but an Aston Martin, thanks.

Harlem appears to be cool but tough – its signature tune the constant squeal of car alarms combined with loud bursts of soul music at every traffic light. Emerging briskly from a subterranean corridor at the end of a long, poorly lit street, I'm made abruptly aware that four chunky black guys have formed a horseshoe around me, barring my exit.

'Wadya doin' here, Ma'am?' drawls the biggest guy.

I tell him I'm English, here to work with the Ford Agency, that I love blues and soul music and wanted to see the Apollo. The small gang run their eyes over my ebony Biba trench coat and large-brimmed fedora and nod.

Forming a huddle with his boys, the leader scribbles on a piece of paper and hands it to me. 'Lady, this can be a very dangerous place to wander the streets and you need to take more care. If you ever get trouble of any kind during your stay here, you dial this number and we can make sure you're safe. Good day, Ma'am.'

It's not long before I'm in familiar territory again and drop into a deli to buy food for supper. Relieved to find a place open late, I ask the bustling owner what time he closes. 'Twenty-four seven, lady. You have a nice day now.' Have a nice day? It's eight at night! I might have been to five funerals for all he knows. This weird desire for others to be happy, slotted into a brief commercial transaction, is another new one on me.

Turning the key in the apartment door, I nearly jump out of my skin when a tall shadow steps into the hallway. 'Hello, my name's Jane and I see you bagged the best room.' No irony and a slight trace of contempt. Model Jane has just arrived from London and introduces me to Margie, no Ford model, but her best friend. Hmmm, this is going to be fun.

'Hi, I'm Sherry, your head booker, and you will start your go-sees today by seeing New York's leading photographers so that we can get a reaction from the top. Your composites have arrived, so take a pile with you and leave one at each studio. Your composite is . . . well, very unusual, and we just hope it works for you.'

The high-gloss, super-indulgent eight-pager cost me more to print than the price of a brand-new Mini.

When I'd presented my unique layout and robust choice of pics to London agent Jill, she was somewhat concerned. 'You've got to have at least one laughing shot. This is for America, not Iceland.' It's true, I'll never be considered for Pasadena cheerleader with a pink Sobranie dripping from my lips. But Eileen wanted 'different'.

Richard Avedon's studio is on the top floor of 110 East 58th Street, an unremarkable, characterless building, neither old nor new. In the joyless foyer, solid stairs curve generously around a wire-caged elevator, its ancient heavy trellises and outer door reminding the user it's a bit slow and wobbly, takes two at the most, and there's a precipitous drop if things go wrong. But I don't expect this. Inside the lift a tramp has passed out. He's probably just trying to keep warm; it's cold outside. When I gently step over him, he barely moves.

The lift judders upwards and opens directly into a spanking white reception.

An elegant redhead, 'Hi, I'm Jenny,' flashes a razor smile from behind her desk before vigorously assessing my composite and portfolio.

Several handsome young photographic assistants dash in and out of the studio behind her and she asks one of them to take a quick flick through my photo folio.

171

Looking him directly in the eye, she says, 'I hope it doesn't rain today?'

I later discover this is the code for 'I think we should forget this girl.' But if it's 'What a wonderful day today' it means she's 'a winner' and is allowed to meet the man himself – the legendary Richard Avedon, considered the greatest fashion photographer in the world.

I'm the rainy type, apparently.

While I wait for the lift down and ponder if it still contains the tramp, a bearded assistant with wild flowing locks and beaming assurance appears by my side. He looks English. He is English. His name is Peter and he's Avedon's first assistant, which means the most important one. Would I like a drink sometime? We exchange numbers.

Next, it's Irving Penn, elder brother of Arthur Penn, who directed *Bonnie & Clyde*. Hmmm, I probably won't be meeting him either. But the door to the small, unprepossessing studio is quietly opened by a slight, balding man with a kind, sensitive face. No one else appears to be around. Probably in his late fifties, but looking older, he has a gentle nature, the type of man who prefers to notice than be noticed.

It is *indeed* Mr Penn, the photographer's photographer – as self-effacing as his Rolleiflex. Revered for the pure quality of his work, his fashion images have a cool, glacial, detached yet erotically charged atmosphere. Looking slowly through my portfolio as though choosing something from a menu that doesn't quite agree with him, he finally stares directly into my eyes and says, 'Thank you, Miss Nixon' and 'Goodbye.'

172

Now it's Hiro who, along with Richard Avedon and Irving Penn, is regarded as the snapper who has redefined American fashion photography in the Sixties. Studio after studio, on it goes.

'Are you by chance related to . . .?'

'NO! No relation at all.'

'Your mother isn't called Pat, is she?'

'Well, yes she is. But my father was not called Dick . . .!' making the point, time and time again, that the current loathed President 'Tricky Dicky' Nixon has not produced a tricky Vikki Nixon.

It feels unnatural and odd to be so constantly, ruthlessly, physically assessed but the modelling template here dictates that absolutely nothing counts beyond the face and body once-over. Does anyone give a remote damn if I have a mind, a brain, a soul, a heart?

Eileen calls me into her office the next morning. 'Your composite is frightening people – they want something softer, sweeter, less confrontational . . . and less black and weird dressing. We've also had comments about the gap in your two front teeth; you must get them fixed as soon as possible because we Americans like perfect teeth. And those shots in your composite with cigarettes are not to their liking.'

Oh come on, Eileen! This country marketed cigarettes like no other. America was the pioneer of understanding that the key to selling a product isn't the quality of the product, but the quality of the idea of the product. Make the brand as visible as possible – on buildings, on ashtrays, on bumper stickers – so that it becomes part of the all-American experience. Cigarettes and Coca-Cola are the great American legacy!

True, but out of context. The American dream is always a flashing Macleans smile.

I step forlornly from Eileen's office and make my way over to Sherry's booking desk, and hear a voice: '*This* is the best composite I've ever seen.' A slight, fine-boned female, mid-twenties, with a navy knitted beanie pulled down over her ears, Levi's and donkey jacket, is holding a composite and looking in my direction. 'Is this yours?' I nod and Sherry says, 'Oh Vikki, this is Lauren Hutton, one of our very top models.'

Lauren's face is exquisite, but she doesn't dress like the other absurdly glamorous models I've met in the agency. She looks normal, ultra casual, more like a postgraduate art student. Recognising from my expression that I've had an Eileen talking-to, she suggests coffee. 'You need cheering up.'

Lauren couldn't be kinder, friendlier or more down-to-earth as we sip our brew in a diner opposite the agency. 'Don't be too concerned,' she says; 'agencies are just secretarial services really. They're certainly your partners, but don't think they'll ever make you – you have to go after that yourself. A lot of modelling is how much crap you can take.'

'What about this gap between my two front teeth?' I ask. She smiles. Five years older than me, centuries wiser and currently America's top model, I can see she has an even wider gap than mine. 'At my very first interview Eileen said 'Your teeth and nose need fixing!' But I didn't. I simply slip this on.' She shows me her device, tells me how it slips into the gap, and as we saunter back to the agency, she teaches me how to whistle. 'Push your two fingers inside your mouth to fold back your tongue – and blow . . . hard! Essential for hailing cabs from the far side of Central Park – and impossible without a gap.'

Discovering our mutual, passionate love of travel, Lauren reveals to her rapt fan that she saves every penny she earns in order to take off for a couple of months to roam the world, trekking from the Himalayas to Africa to South America, the Amazon jungle . . . wherever takes her fancy. 'No make-up, no mirrors, no tourism, just companions wearing leaves and filed teeth in hunter-gatherer groups that only explorers and anthropologists know about.' I'm speechless. What a woman, inner beauty, decent human values, unimaginable courage and a complete lack of vanity!

Lauren had always broken the rules. When 'real' *Vogue* models didn't 'do' catalogue work, she upped her rate and did it. Three years after our chat Lauren would become the first model in history to land an exclusive advertising contract, self-engineered by refusing all cosmetic ads until she got a contract.

Jerry Ford negotiated this ground-breaking deal for the '73–'83 Revlon Ultima campaign, worth millions, which catapulted Lauren into the history books as the first ever genuine supermodel. That blueprint for an exclusive contract with a major cosmetics company changed the modelling business for ever and proved that a grounded, unaffected woman can be the ultimate financial success story in this invulnerable, unarguable city.

'Ask your booker to make an appointment to see Diana Vreeland at *Vogue*,' Lauren suggests before we leave. 'She discovered me and she's always on the look-out for new, different models. And she *loves* rebels.'

A day later, and this rebel is on the nineteenth floor of the Condé Nast building at 420 Lexington, side-stepping cubicles of editors, assistants, copy-writers, rails of clothes, rooms full of shoes, hats, furs, gloves, jewellery and beauty products, before turning into Diana Vreeland's *Vogue* office. Vivid scarlet varnished walls and a leopard-skin carpet hint at what lies ahead.

I stand awkwardly, trying to look relaxed and cool, waiting for this grande dame with a fearless eye who changed American *Vogue* for ever when she took up its helm in 1963 at sixty years old, having previously fashion-edited *Harper's Bazaar*, then *Vogue*'s only (and at that time, more chic) rival.

Known for her singular vision, creative mind and razor wit and for championing the unexpected and outlandish – coining the word 'Youthquake' in 1965 to celebrate the freedom of American youth inspired by pop's British invasion, she'd detested untouchable, snooty beauty. And society ladies in white gloves were no more. Celebrating what makes people unique, she loves translating the zeitgeist of the times and, notably fascinated by 'Swinging London', was the perfect editor to document the decade unfolding around her, quickly highlighting Mick Jagger and embracing the first batch of European models to arrive in the States – wide-eyed Jean Shrimpton and ethereal Sandra Paul, who had two *Vogue* covers in a row, unheard of, even for American girls. Then it was Twiggy and now in 1970 it's Veruschka.

But, oh God, what will she make of the 'Don't Mess With Me' scowler from Barnsley?

Suddenly she bursts through the door and I'm almost flattened by her imperious presence. I've rarely seen such energy. And her cheeks have five times more rouge than Anna Piaggi's! Even her ears are rouged, framing yanked-back, blue-black hair and an ultra forthright nose. Her tiny eyes fix pointedly on me.

'Take your hat off, girl! You should *never* wear hats. You don't have the right-shaped face!'

Flicking through my composite she declares, 'A Rubartelli shot! Very rare. He normally only works with Veruschka.'

Franco Rubartelli and girlfriend Veruschka are the current photographer and model hotties, constantly booked for Vreeland's every issue. Producing trippy spreads that often involve more creative body paint than clothes, this six-footer German countess with size 13 feet is a welcome contrast to the startle-eyed cutie pies still emulating Jean Shrimpton and Twiggy.

'Divine! I like you. Stay in town. We'll use you,' and with that Ms Vreeland snaps my portfolio shut. But would her actions speak louder than her words?

Lying on my bed contemplating my Vreeland fate and half-listening to Jane and Margie discussing 'tomorrow's groceries', I hear the apartment phone ring, then a yell through my door. 'It's someone called Peter – for you!'

'Hi,' he says. 'I met you at Avedon's studio and thought

you might like to come out for a bite to eat this evening. I could collect you in an hour.'

Blimey, things are perking up in all directions.

When Peter turns up he immediately charms the grocery gatherers – no easy task, I can tell you. He's bright, funny, vibrant and not bad looking either. I like Avedon's persistent assistant.

'I thought you might enjoy the food at a Deep South soul restaurant I know,' he suggests.

When we get there a waiter smiles as he plonks a plate in front of me. I've not the foggiest idea what it is, but here goes. Oh no, this is not the moment to have a flaccid sausage in my mouth; one mouthful brings back memories of something I'd rather forget. Peter picks up on my tooth-clogging torture. 'Try it with some hot sauce.'

With every glass of Californian Red, Peter becomes even more attractive. He appears to have a handle on New York that has so far eluded me and when he suggests rocking on to the Village Gate to hear Larry Coryell, I nearly propose to him on the spot. Coryell always tops my 'great guitarists list' with his seamless fusion of rock and jazz with eastern influences. I'd long hankered to hear him play live and he doesn't disappoint. Neither does Pete. When he suggests meeting tomorrow evening at Avedon's studio, I'm up for it.

The next morning the girls are nicer to me. They like Pete.

No sign of the tramp in the rickety lift as it precariously travels up to Avedon's studio. Juddering to a halt at the top-floor reception, the door opens onto an unexpected huddle of men sharing after-work tales. Pete steps forward and, with a clannish insouciance, introduces a small, elegant, complex-looking man with lively, deep brown eyes and an easy laugh. It's Richard Avedon.

'Ah, the lovely Brit who thinks the sidewalk steam is people sweating in the subway. Got to be the funniest thing I've heard,' he says, before kissing my hand and informing me his name is Dick. Hiro's new English assistant Neil also steps forward to be introduced, and finally Claude Picasso, Avedon's second assistant, who looks slightly lost and somewhat bogged down by the weight of his surname.

Pete confides to me, as he packs away Dick's tripod-mounted Hasselblad, that Claude and sister Paloma are currently being dragged though a complicated court case with their astute, tough mother Françoise Gilot, a former art student and the only mistress ever to walk out on Picasso Senior. She began proceedings in Paris a year ago over the financial distribution of the Picasso estate as French law prohibits 'children of adultery' from inheriting. It's apparently taken its toll on Claude and working for Avedon keeps him 'normal' and busy – but on first impressions I can't help thinking that he doesn't appear tough enough to handle great wealth anyway, as he seems more the sensitive, creative type.

How wrong that assessment would prove to be!

Pete is taking me this evening to Max's Kansas City, 'the most important café since Moulin Rouge' according to the *New York Times*. Sure enough, when we arrive around nine it has a winning, lived-in vibe with tables so close together it looks like everyone's sitting on the same one. We waft

179

through to the back room and Pete ushers me to a banquette. I slide neatly in, next to a man with fine white-blond hair, a pale face and a collar far too big for his neck.

Fuck! It's Andy Warhol and our knees are touching!

Pete whispers that Max's is now Andy's local because the Factory is directly opposite in Union Square. Around ten of his Factory entourage are at the table, but they all look eerily narcissistic and, frankly, a bit tacky. Andy doesn't look remotely pleased with himself, or tacky. Like most celebrities in real life, he simply looks like a smaller version of himself. But he does appear bored and strangely vacuous; doesn't move or say much and when he does, it's mostly to answer, 'Gee, I don't know . . .' in a reedy, deadpan voice, uttered so quietly that I can barely hear.

As the weeks go by, Pete and I regularly eat at Max's, the burgers *are* good, and sitting next to Andy gradually becomes less weird. I learn that the only way to get a verbal reaction from him is to ask direct questions, such as . . . How? What? Where? But never 'Do you believe that . . .?' 'No' . . . 'Is there something you . . .? 'Er. No' . . . 'Will you be . . .?' 'Gee. No.'

It takes time to discover that Andy is not as superficial as he appears, and is even somewhat religious, attending Catholic church virtually every Sunday and also helping out at soup kitchens. After being shot and seriously injured three years ago his work began to take on a darker imagery, a fascination with death in all its guises: fatal car accidents, the electric chair, symbols of skeletons, suicides. It's easy to think he doesn't possess a grain of irony about death but when a friend tells him he's contemplating suicide, Andy asks, 'Can I have your watch?'

Even during this 'macabre' era everything he creates is thought-provoking and engaging. He opens my eyes to what can be a subject for art (anything) and for making New York a place where art recognises that horror, revulsion and repetition can have beauty if it's honest and big-city tough.

One evening Andy invites us back to the silver-wrapped Factory – his cold, bony hand sliding into mine as we cross the square. But my imagined glimpses of half-finished canvasses in his star-studded studio are quickly shattered by the jaded reality of rumpled drag queens lounging around in a bleak, cold emptiness. It's almost beyond satire.

Yet dear Andy would have the last laugh. The first artist to ever believe that 'Making money is art, and working is art, and good business is the best art,' one of his works would one day fetch over a hundred million dollars, almost outselling Picasso as the most expensive painting ever. Not daft, our Andy.

However, not all creative works have such success. A gentle call from my mother makes me aware that Nick's troubles are resurfacing. His kind friend Philip Trevelyan tries to help. Nick featured in one of Philip's broadcast documentaries after they'd both attended the same Newcastle Fine Art course, and when Nick lands a job at a college in East Sussex, Philip's mother, Ursula, suggests Nick and his family live in a house she owns nearby. But Nick is becoming reckless in his business dealings with the furniture he's designing despite bespoke commissions from design high-flyers and Boss approaching to mass manufacture his designs, Heal's proposing stocking them and revered artist and ICA founder Sir Roland Penrose convinced he can build Nick's furniture into an international brand.

But Nick can't wait. He wants immediate high-profile recognition for Babylon Designs, not in two years' time. His contained academic world has inhibited his understanding that the process of efficient merchandising takes time; he can't get that it isn't enough in itself to be highly creative, that products have to be marketed well. They're not there to dream about, they are there to be sold.

He hates paperwork, dealing with firms, and having financial complications, and is now often spending copious amounts of money, disappearing from home for days on end and alcohol is becoming the vessel for his unachieved dreams. What the hell is happening to my savvy brother that's making him behave like this? The strong exciting one who taught me how to fly a kite, read a map, ride a bike, pitch a tent, make a catapult, and to whistle all our favourite tunes.

All that former bounce and gusto now seemingly replaced by a strange reserve and secrecy – as if he's always tending to some inner flame and trying to rebalance his brain. His 100 per cent supportive wife deals with this bravely. She's kind and cross with him in all the right ways; she's someone he can honestly talk to, accompanies him on trips to doctors, and always encourages him in his work. She's steered him positively while handling the organisational side of their life, looking after their two adorable young children, now aged five and four, and being a productive artist herself. But fearful the children are becoming seriously affected by Nick's erratic behaviour, she's now taken them elsewhere, which she believes is best for all their sakes. Nick never sees them again.

My mother convinces me to stay on in New York. She's getting strong support from her pals, she says, and 'You're not to worry, darling. Make the most of being in New York and concentrate on your work.' I try my best.

Big brother chauffeurs his little sis – Devon, 1951

Lauren Hutton's wise advice is to test-shoot with up-and-coming photographers when not on bookings, go-sees or castings. The most original of these is a young chap called Arthur Elgort who always wears a jaunty black beret, smokes a pipe, loves jazz and plays the trumpet. His approach to fashion photography is refreshingly, totally different – unposed, ad-hoc, impromptu, and always with natural light, nothing forced or artificial; the only snapper I've ever worked with who insists I remove every scrap of make-up before a shoot. Not an easy one, but his relaxed snapshot style is a breath of fresh air in a world where ultra-composed studio shots are the norm.

I adore Arthur – at last an all-American male with a healthy, self-deprecating wit and good sense of irony, and even our birthdays are on the same day. Sadly for me, he's off to Europe next week to try and catch a break because they simply don't get him here yet. But they'll love him there, I just know it.

Work is slowly picking up – confirmed bookings for *Cosmopolitan*, *Ladies' Home Journal*, the *New York Times* and a lucrative Dupont ad campaign, but not The Big One. It's proving elusive. But, a week later: 'Hi Vikki, this is Sherry from Ford. You have a fabulous booking.'

I brace myself, here it comes . . . *AVEDON, VREELAND* and *VOGUE*!

'You've been confirmed for *Harper's Bazaar* with Hiro!'

Oh no! If *Bazaar* books you first when you're new in town, Vreeland doesn't use you.

Well, at least the composite isn't terrifying everyone. The *Bazaar* booking (a studio shoot with three other models) has us all leaping through the air showing big white teeth behind blasts of blonde candyfloss hair. My gap tooth device gets its first outing and the shoot goes according to plan with nothing too weird or European or out-to-lunch: fresh, clean-cut and wholesome. You get the picture.

The British look now appears to be over in New York. The only major female prototype in modern history never to have been professionally manufactured has had her day. Americans wanted us for our style and individualism, but are now trying to change us to fit the mainstream. The unkempt look reigns no more. American girls had tried to copy it but looked too fit and laughed too much. They couldn't do *cool* – thought it meant standing around looking blank when, of course, it meant always giving the impression of movement while standing still.

So now it's a return to the immaculate beaming cheer-leaders and Eileen gradually has fewer and fewer British girls on her books . . . 'They come very strangely put together, like groupies, even the best of them. They aren't tidy, if anything rather messy, and they don't understand pure chic,' she told one journalist. She was right. We did style, not fashion.

I miss home and Bill, who often rings, but being in New York is becoming strangely compulsive. Sure it's tough and serious, but I'm starting to 'get' it and making a thousand dollars a day helps 'get it'. And if I keep this up I can soon afford to buy that lovely home for Mum, and help Nick and his family. Not quite time to return to London yet. And I'm enjoying seeing Pete.

We meet up for a drink at his place on West 19th Street, a slightly unloved arty outback near the Chelsea Hotel where Valerie Solanas took that gun from her bag and shot Andy Warhol 'because I just wanted him to pay attention to me.' A long list of creative types have made their final exits here, including poor old Dylan Thomas who drank eighteen glasses of whisky in quick succession in his room before crashing into a coma and dying in nearby St Vincent's Hospital.

Pete's apartment is compact and functional. It makes me

smile that nobody actually 'lives in' in Manhattan, so living quarters are the *only* things in town not twice as big as they need be. It's the view that counts, and every room in Pete's place has startling, in-your-face uninterrupted views of the Empire State Building.

'Fancy going to the Sanctuary on West 43rd?' he asks casually.

'Yeah, why not!'

I'm quite blasé about clubs. They always come in two categories – the queue-outside, swirl-and-sweat, bop-till-you-drop type, or the ones dripping in élan, panache and classy hedonism.

But the Sanctuary experience is something else. Located in an old German Baptist church (legal maximum capacity 346; illegal reality 1,000 a night), this first, totally uninhibited, gay disco in America has billionaires dancing with bent cops, trannies swopping beauty tips with bankers, and a strange array of ordinary people displaying extreme looks and dance moves to get them noticed. I spy more laydees in the powder room than on the dance floor and watch, utterly fazed, as three hunky showgals gyrate on top of the altar. Somewhat predictably, the Sanctuary lasts for only three years before morphing into a Methadone clinic, paving the way, several years down the line, for uptown, celeb-strewn Studio 54.

When I get back to my apartment a letter and a postcard are waiting for me. The card's from Arthur Elgort in Paris and, somewhat confusingly, has a photo of me leaving his studio in Manhattan on the front.

'Hello dear Vikki,' he writes, 'Paris is good and I've taken some nice things here. I have lots more work so I'm not sure when I'll be back. Hope you're doing fine. A large kiss for you Vikki from me, Love Arthur.'

Dear Arthur. I knew he was a winner. He still is. Thirty *Vogue* covers and counting.

The letter is from my mother. I usually giggle before opening her wonderful weekly reads, so alive and busy, so spicy with her parochial adventures.

Arthur's postcard from Paris.   Photo: Arthur Elgort

But not this time.

'Darling, I'm so sorry I didn't get a letter to you sooner, but there has been a drama here. The police rang in the middle of the night to say that Nick had taken an overdose and is in hospital. He's okay, so please don't worry.'

I book an immediate flight to London.

*

Returning to the familiarity of Barnsley after his marriage breakdown, Nick has been living in a room in Mum's house, which is also let to local students after she acquired her live-in bursar's job. It's here he was found by his local best friend Roger who smashed the door down to see him barely breathing on the floor, dragged him to his car, and drove him to the nearest casualty department.

Now out of hospital, Nick is staying with friends in London and being 'medically monitored' with a cross-section of pills. He has a manual job to keep fit and focused but I'm deeply concerned about his frame of mind. He's never appeared to me to be addicted to any substances; he just takes things to extremes.

Treatments for 'mind' conditions are still controversial because they're so difficult to define. The psychiatric route has still barely opened a chink of light on addictions, depression and schizophrenia. Patients struggle on with pills and therapists, or a combination of both. Doctors are bludgeoned with drugs from the happiness-pushing pharmaceutical companies who make billions coming to the rescue of doctors unsure of what to do with a depressed patient – when the talking cure of warmth and sympathetic understanding would possibly work better.

But it's hard. No one sufferer has the same experiences and there is no one solution. How do you know if someone's unable to cope in a temporary crisis or is destructing in a long-term way? And how do you know when someone has recovered?

*

Back in London, Nick and I arrange to meet as soon as possible. I'm standing outside the Maida Vale flat I still share with Bill as I watch Nick's lofty frame lope down the street in his familiar Levi 501s, blond desert boots and sandy-hued suede jacket thrown over a denim shirt. He's still as nonchalantly handsome as ever. Finally spotting my madly flapping hands, his face – his entire being – breaks into an enormous smile.

'So good to see you, Vic,' he beams as I rush towards him. How I love those enigmatic eyes and that beautiful, mellifluous voice, honed by regular daily packs of untipped Player's Navy Cut. He lifts me off the ground in his familiar protective embrace – my treasured big brother, seven years older, always looking out for his little 'tadpole'. I can almost smell our childhood home – the Nescafe and nicotine, the freshly cooked scrambled eggs, a waft of Cussons Imperial Leather, and the faintest whiff of Gordon's gin. I want to help Nick, to mend the brokenness, to stop this self-sabotage, to try to find answers for the chaos in his life. Whatever happened to the gregarious life explorer who bought a glossy Paul Klee art book for his twelve-year-old sister to help her understand that 'there are as many ways of looking as there are of seeing'?

I watch him light a cigarette with his silver Zippo lighter, and smoke it à la Humphrey Bogart as we sit on my terrace, close and comfortable, effortlessly wallowing in family memories, habits and jokes. I begin to feel that I know what he's thinking simply by looking at his face. We arrange to meet two days later.

189

The world of fashion feels especially frivolous and somewhat fatuous now, but is a financial must and the automatic cachet of working in New York has produced confirmed European bookings for months ahead: *Vogue* and the Paris collections, a Martini commercial on location in Malta, the Burberry campaign, a Revlon ad, an Oscar cigarette commercial for Greece and White Horse whisky. Rags, fags, booze and slap.

It's the phone again.

'Hello darling, Jill here. Can you be at the *Vogue* studio at four sharp tomorrow? Parks wants to see you for a job next week.'

Norman Parkinson, one of the few high-profile photographers I've yet to work with. And I'm ten minutes late for our meeting, caught up chatting to Lady Rendlesham who opened the Yves Saint Laurent boutique in Bond Street and who so terrorises her customers that most of them wait until they know she's gone out before shopping there. But I find her formidable spikiness good fun, and it's endearing that she always allows her two beloved dogs to curl up and snooze on Yves' latest ensembles after they've been so artfully and painstakingly displayed in the window.

Parks is furious with me. He's of that generation where punctuality doesn't simply count, it's sacrosanct. Standing six feet five with a proud moustache, he's elegantly attired in an Indian tunic and embroidered Kashmiri cap, but still remains quintessentially old-school British. After giving me a robust ticking off he dismisses me and rings the agency to complain. But I get the job – a prestigious ad campaign to be shot on a boat off the Kent coast with a male model called Tinker Paterson.

Making sure I get a good night's sleep, I wake refreshed and perky. Taking a tingling cold shower I hear the shrill ring of the phone. It won't stop ringing . . . it's probably Mum or Bill, who's currently in Berlin, or is it Frankfurt? But it's Nick. Can I meet him at King's Cross station in an hour?

'Why, what's wrong?'

'I'm thinking of throwing myself on the track.'

He sounds rational and terrifyingly composed. I try to stay calm but my heart shatters. I simply do not understand the thread of thought that brings him to this state. I want to run to him, but something inside tells me it's the wrong thing to do.

'I *will* meet you, Nick, but later. There'll be more time to help you. I'll meet you at seven at our usual spot on Primrose Hill.'

The drive to Kent with Norman Parkinson, the ad agency creatives and Tinker Paterson, passes in a surreal state of frozen tension. What if I've wrongly assessed the situation with Nick?

I try not to think.

To just be.

The shoot goes well and we finish on time. Before returning to London, Parks wants to try an experimental *Vogue* test shot, with me standing 'mascot-style' at the helm of a tiny speedboat as it races through the water. Finally it's a wrap.

'You're very brave,' says Parks. 'I don't know many girls who would have done that without flinching.'

But the danger wasn't remotely assessed. I simply want to finish the job and dash to my brother on Primrose Hill. In the car, returning to London, I don't pray for an easy time. I pray for the strength to endure a most difficult one.

Nick is nowhere to be seen. I run to a phone box and ring my mother. Has she heard from him? Yes, he rang to say he's working overtime tonight. My knees buckle with relief and I drag myself home. In the next few days Nick is admitted to Bethlem Royal, a psychiatric hospital that deals with extreme cases of mental illness.

On my first visit to Bethlem Royal I'm surprised and relieved by how normal the place is. The patients are mostly subdued, not ranting and raving. No rattling doors, no groping through grilled windows – one man simply stands and gazes into the far distance. A woman in a dressing gown talks to herself and another sings quite loudly, but is oblivious to everyone but her. There's a distant piano playing, and now and then a moan or a laugh. It isn't scary and is nothing like the original Bedlam, a giant asylum which housed the criminally insane. Now it has billiard tables and cavernous armchairs. In fact it's quite calm.

Tranquil, even.

No, that's not quite the right word.

Tranquillised.

Eventually I reach the end of an ancient corridor, turn right and spy Nick chatting to a fellow inmate and looking happy and relaxed. Mentally he appears to be fine, and we both smile knowingly when a silver-haired man pushes us apart shouting 'Make way for the Sergeant Major' as he goose-steps round the room in his striped, fleecy pyjamas.

Nick is encouraged to be creatively active as the hospital has recently opened a small on-site museum specialising in work by artistic patients suffering mental problems. A good opportunity for Nick to focus his attention on what he loves doing. He's designing an exciting 'floating' table that has a stainless-steel frame and Perspex top with an indent filled with Klein-blue powder. It appears to be a floating swimming pool. Mum and I are funding the production costs which include externally handmade, hand-polished screws and fixings, each taking a day to produce.

Lulled into a London-based work and home schedule, I'm staggered and stunned when Pete turns up from the States. I'd moved in with him before I left New York; our happiness progressed to an affair, and we had such fun. But he knew about Bill, and it was acknowledged that what occurred in New York stayed in New York.

Now here he is, wanting us to be seriously together and live in Manhattan. This is more than confusing. I don't want to hurt Bill or Pete, but knowing who or what I really want isn't top priority right now. And working again in New York? Well, I didn't exactly 'take Manhattan' last time round. 'A new composite could be the answer,' says Pete. 'Please consider it.' He suggests a meeting with Nick, and isn't remotely fazed by Nick's 'illness' or the Bethlem Royal surroundings. He's also very taken with *Swimming Pool* and snaps it from every possible angle, as is his way.

Two weeks later and back in Manhattan, Pete rings to say he's shown the shots to Dick Avedon who is intrigued and has a plan to help. Avedon suggests air-freighting *Swimming Pool* to his Manhattan studio and he, under contract to *Vogue*, will snap it for the arts and culture section of the magazine. 'Well-heeled readers will fight each other to acquire from this exclusive limited edition,' Pete says, and Nick will get the kudos he craves – and the bucks and confidence to approach his beloved wife and children for a new life together.

When I break this news to Nick he inhales deeply, calmly, and focuses on finishing his artwork. Three months later Bethlem Royal's medical team declare him fit for purpose and due for release, no nearer to confirming his exact diagnosis or his long-term prognosis. There appears to be no problem with his plan to travel to New York to promote the prototype – as long as he's accompanied and supported.

It is late November when we board an economic charter flight bound for New York packed with drained young Brits searching for the new after too much self-gratification, their cultural life-force vastly diminished. The Swinging Sixties high-octane days of mind-opening drugs and revolution are over and those who've had the best time want to suffer the most. 'Excuse me while I touch the sky' has become 'Show me a cloud with a silver lining.'

Even for the homing young Americans the on-board atmosphere is sombre with mass disillusionment – Jimi Hendrix, Janis Joplin and Jim Morrison have all died this summer in squalid heroin-related circumstances, Vietnam drags on and Nixon is heading for meltdown.

But these two Nixons remain buoyant with expectation – and on arrival Nick instantly embraces New York and our friends Nelson, Neil, Edie and Claude Picasso. When Pete leaves for work each morning, Nick and I sprawl around our host's cosy kitchen, sipping endless coffee and chatting for hours. Most conversations are about his children. Will he ever see them again? Will they grow up to be creative, intelligent, beautiful, capable and happy? How much he dearly loves them; they are his hope of happiness, and pieces of his dreams. The downstairs coffee shop becomes accustomed to Nick dropping in to buy cigarettes, wearing the tweed jacket that at five and sixpence had caught his eye on a second-hand stall in Barnsley Market a year ago because it was so *cool*. He'd proudly paraded it in front of Mum and me, and we'd both said it looked vaguely familiar. When Nick did the perfect three-point-turn while checking out the inside pocket, out fell a torn piece of paper full of scribbled numbers and the word *Monday*.

It was in my father's handwriting.

For several days we stay in and around the apartment awaiting the freight company's confirmation of *Swimming Pool*'s safe arrival.

Then a phone call.

They've lost track of it.

More days go by.

Elation melts away.

Deadlines pass.

It turns up. But the container has been accidentally

smashed in transit and there's a procedure to go through before it's released – airport trips to examine the item and its broken container for insurance purposes. This process will take time, quite some time, we're informed. Now there's no time for Richard Avedon to photograph it as planned, before he leaves Manhattan for the Christmas vacation. Nick, Peter and I assemble his treasure trove in Avedon's studio to check it survived its precarious journey unscathed.

After Peter photographs it against a stark white background we celebrate its pure form and unscarred beauty. But the crucial moment has passed and New York closes down for the holidays. His mission unaccomplished means Nick wants to stay in New York for Christmas, but our mother's planning to travel from Barnsley to London to spend it with us at my flat in Maida Vale. Pete's also returning to London to see his family.

'Come on, Nick, we'll come back in January. It's not far away.'

But he's adamant. Our pal Nelson steps in. He would consider it an honour if Nick guested with him over the Christmas period until we return. Nelson is lively, bright, stable and kind. Nick jumps at his generous invitation.

Peter heads off to London on a pre-booked scheduled flight, and a biting wind enfolds Nick and me as we hug each other goodbye at the coach terminal. 'I'll phone you as soon as I land in London,' I yell, boarding the coach and flopping into the left window seat directly behind the driver. Nick leans his tall frame against the near-side of the exit tunnel, collar turned up against the sudden downpour – his beaming face and slow, regal waves becoming a succession

196

of smudged cameos against the driver's windscreen until he's out of vision.

Nick in Richard Avedon's studio – New York, 1971.

The weather deteriorates fast on the airport expressway. At the charter flight check-in an angry crowd has gathered, then a man stands on his suitcase to inform us that the charter-flight company has gone bust. There will be no flight to London. Passengers shout and cry. It's two days before Christmas for God's sake and all scheduled flights have been booked-out for months. We stand there motionless, waiting for news. Finally an announcement – another charter company has agreed to take us to London. We pack like sardines into an already overloaded plane and race down the runway for take-off.

It fails.

'Ladies and gentlemen,' the captain announces, 'we are too heavy. The plane's weight is making it dangerous to take off and wind conditions are making it worse. I will try again to get our plane airborne, but those of you who may not have the stomach for this are invited to leave the aircraft now and return to the lounge.'

No one moves.

When the second attempt fails there is no talk or laughter, only the chaotic scramble to tear open our duty-free alcohol. Panic is not blind. It sees all too clearly. The third time we make it. But there are few jokes and any mirth is nervous and jittery throughout the eight-hour flight to Heathrow.

It's all been worth it when I see my mother's face on Christmas Day and Bill and I take both our mums to the Savoy Hotel for Christmas lunch.

Bill heads off to Germany on business a few days later and, post-phone-call from Pete, I'm in the hall of his parents' house in West Hampstead about to be introduced to his mother. But she completely ignores me and thrusts a slip of paper into Peter's hand.

'There's been an urgent call. This is the number.'

Nelson's number.

'When . . . Where . . . How?' Peter whispers.

I only have to look at his face to know.

It comes in waves, stinging my pupils, tightening my throat, pounding my stomach, leaving me gasping; then a piercing, searing, stifling pain. My eyes fix on the tunnel and over and over again I see his smiling, waving face. And the plane . . . fate . . . a toss of the coin . . . me or him . . . him or me? It could have been me.

Why wasn't it me?

I force a veil of numbness to wrap itself around me, allowing me to cope but not to feel, preparing me for the most difficult journey of my life. My mother opens the door to my London flat. As always, her achingly lovely face lights up whenever she sees me. I open my mouth . . . but no sound comes out. It is Peter who is forced to break the news that her only son has taken his life. Ten years after her husband took his.

Peter and I make our way to the Pathological Building on 29th Street which houses the official mortuary for New York County, where I'm to formally identify my brother's body. Walking through the door of Bellevue Morgue, we're plunged into a sea of tragic faces, all turning to look at the newcomers. Mostly black and Hispanic, they're all wailing loudly and clutching one another, or perching on the edge of benches, their tortured heads shaking in their hands.

Peter and I don't speak; we focus on the drab, peeling paintwork, the metal window frames, the torn patches on seats and our own thoughts. At a desk in the centre of the room a middle-aged woman in a pale blue shirt beckons me to approach her, and asks the name of the deceased. She hands me a numbered ticket and tells me to wait until my number is called.

A raffle ticket.

And the prize is my dead brother.

We wait and wait, then glance at a leaflet which informs us:

Around 20,000 bodies a year pass through the morgue, 8,500 of which are never claimed. All unclaimed bodies are photographed and a docket is entered for them at the Police Dept's Bureau of Missing Persons. After reposing for two weeks in the morgue's refrigerated vaults, some of the cadavers are given to private embalming schools whose students practice in a room adjoining the vaults, and a number are allotted to medical schools for dissection. The remainder, about 170 a week, are placed in plain wooden coffins and carried on a large barge, up the East River to Potter's Field on Hart's Island . . .

This does not belong in my reality. I catch the eye of a woman sitting opposite who's wearing an elegant green sari. Her face has a resigned yet troubled expression, something between a smile and a grimace, and we mentally connect to share our pain. Excruciating sounds fill the air, only quietening when a number is called.

Then the massive force of darkness comes down like a blind. He can't be gone. It's not possible. He's barely thirty.

As it is happening, I know I will remember this moment as long as I live.

I've been here before. Nothing will be the same. Ever. Ever. Again.

A sob cuts through my thoughts as my number is called and we are led into a small room. No one tells us what to expect. Suddenly there are trembles and a huge metal tray groans upwards in a steel lift, like an unsteady dumb-waiter delivering a meal. It stops at viewing level and a uniformed man casually pulls out a long trolley. A body wrapped and swathed in white gauze lies in front of me, with only face and feet uncovered.

I see his feet first.

His long, delicate feet, sticking up so pitifully and pointlessly.

A bullet goes off in my head.

I turn to run leaving Peter to fill in the forms.

A day later, Nick's body is released by the coroner and is lying in an undertaker's Midtown chapel of rest awaiting instructions. Peter is working with Dick Avedon on a shoot. I must face this alone.

I don't want to see my brother's lifeless body.

The male undertaker leads me through the hallway to a large open-plan room with several corpses laid out on trestles. They all look dead with their parchment skin and sunken lips. There is nothing – absolutely nothing – like the silence of death to feel still alive.

But nothing has prepared me for seeing Nick.

For a while all I can do is stand and stare, too full of fear to move forward. His face is white and wax-like, as handsome as ever, hair brushed back, his hands resting on his chest. He looks so peaceful. No pain now. Just lying there. His head on a pillow. I want to hug him but can't bring myself to do it, knowing how icy cold his skin will be.

Oh Nick, my glorious brother. I love you more than life itself . . . I feel so . . .

My mind begins to race out of control into waves of despair and panic. I simply have to get out of here, to run, to keep on running. I can't stop running . . . running over roads, along sidewalks, through traffic, brakes, horns and wailing sirens, half-dodging people, ducking, leaping, swerving, startling people, scattering families, feet crashing through puddles . . . running, panting, gasping.

I stop breathless in a shop doorway. I can't run any more. A tap on my hunched shoulder makes me turn to see a sad, exhausted black woman staring at me. She slowly unwinds her long, grey woollen scarf to show me her neck. A knife wound. Across her entire neck. She holds out her hand for money.

This is not a world I understand any more. I must keep on running . . . running for hours, running for miles, heart pounding, people everywhere, hundreds of people . . . *nobody cares*.

And then I recognise a street in Greenwich Village where our friends Neil and Edie live. I run to their entrance and press the bell.

'Who is it?' a female voice asks from behind the secure door.

'Oh Edie, it's me. Please let me in, I need to talk to you about Nick.'

Silence.

'Let me in . . . let me come in Edie, please.'

'Neil isn't here and you won't get any sympathy from me. You shouldn't have left him. *It's all your fault.*'

Nelson is sobbing as he recalls every detail leading to the most shocking event of his life. Nick was, he thought, on good form as he set off for Peter's apartment to pick up some clothes, but when he didn't return Nelson arrived to find the door firmly locked from the inside. The police broke it down and found Nick's body.

'It's so touching,' sobs Nelson, 'that the cops kept referring to Nick as "the English gentleman".'

A post-mortem reveals that Nick washed down a quantity of barbiturate sleeping tablets with Californian wine. He left no goodbye, no note, only the enduring agony of not knowing if he meant it or not. It's not easy to kill yourself outright with wine and pills; taking the right amount of each is paramount.

Did he mean to do it?

Surely not.

His passions. His convictions. His caring. His love.

Maybe he didn't want to take his life – he just wanted to change the life he had.

My immediate acute grief is so absolute that it becomes abstract. This is it then, this everything, this nothing. A new life promised . . . so full of promise . . . and now . . . *nothing*. All done, all finished.

I have no recall of anyone handing me Nick's watch or

his clothes, or if his body was repatriated to England, or of a funeral. No recall of what happened to him from that moment on and too distraught ever to discuss it with my mother. Nelson flew over to see her and *Swimming Pool* was later safely returned to the UK, and stored for his children.

No more happy shrieks of reunion, only the agonising, crashing waves of regret. I grieve for the life that has not been lived, that he isn't here to see the remarkable, high-achieving lives of his daughter and son, five and four when he last saw them.

I imagine the music we'd have played at his funeral to honour his brief enjoyment of life: his favourites, Charlie Parker, Dizzy Gillespie, Miles Davis, early Beach Boys and the 'Everybody's Talkin' theme sung by Harry Nilsson from 1969's *Midnight Cowboy*: 'I'm going where the sun is shining through the pouring rain . . . only the echoes of my mind' – the last movie we ever saw together.

The lack of finality in confronting both family suicides kept both events surreal and made me believe that I'd dreamt it all – no proof, so it never really happened. The pain was so paramount, so deeply embedded inside me that I just froze everything for forty years until I opened that trunk in the attic.

One thing I do know. For Nick's honour I will not have him blamed. It was his life and it may have become impossible for him. It could have been a spur-of-the-moment action, or a conclusion of something suffered long-term or an accidental combination of alcohol and medication. Whatever really happened, he is always, always remembered with supreme love and honour.

Two days after Nick's death I ring his closest friend Roger Walton, still living in Barnsley, to break the news. A long silence is followed by a strangled cough that can only be described as a suppressed scream. And then Roger's pragmatic Yorkshire voice: 'He thought he could beat death, you know. He didn't want to die. It was a kind of bizarre game of how far he could push it. He wanted to see whether he would live or die – playing Russian roulette with his life. He's the most wonderful bloke I ever met in my life. A true genius. A one-off. That was our Nick.' Roger names his son Nicholas the following year, in honour of his best friend.

Nicholas Nixon, 1941–1971. Photo: Peter Waldman

10

SNAPPED IN ZURICH

'Life is a daring adventure or nothing at all'
Helen Keller

Eileen Ford could be compassionate, but not that often.
Nick's suicide in New York provokes a sensitive and kind-
hearted approach. 'You must continue to work, but in a
gentler environment, dear.' I know she's right, but all I crave
is silence and deep midnight darkness.

This unreal living from a suitcase, rushing out at the crack
of dawn for whirlwind fashion shoots in diverse locations,
multi smiles in multi countries, holds little attraction now.

But I'm gently assured that it is no good thing to continue
to live each day in 'if onlys', recurring images, and the
constant search for explanations. A call from Eileen to a
Zurich model agency guarantees a month's bookings before I
arrive. And that is judged to be that.

Boyfriend Bill and New York Peter, both kind, caring and
sensitive men, are still mega-supportive but gently step back

and allow me to rebuild the life around me in my own good time. They continue to be astonishingly kind to my mother, keeping a close eye on her well-being. She, as selfless as ever, also encourages me to continue to model.

Having worked in Switzerland before, jetting in for quick bookings, I'm aware that its people do not all live under mountains, yodelling softly while milking their cows. Yet it is not unlike Corbusier's definition of a house; 'a machine for living in', a place where heads rule hearts, the dull clichés all true: more banks than dentists, stonkingly punctual trains, smooth chocolate, good watches and uninviting meals of melted cheese.

But not this time. When I arrive in Zurich there's a strangely infectious aura of calm and courtesy. It's as though I'm breathing through a different set of lungs – no sweating bodies rising from the subway, no screeching taxis, no angry cops. There's a fresh air of hope, a new-start place to renounce trauma and unpredictability and push on with my life; the ghosts of the past still chasing me, but not catching me yet.

Side-stepping the hoovering chambermaids in my spotless hotel, a quick recce of this medieval town draped around the neck of a slender lake reveals it to be Paris in reverse – the left bank is upmarket shopping territory corralled by the curving ritzy Bahnhofstrasse; the right bank a busy little tangle of bars, tiny shops and restaurants in narrow streets and passages, so utterly unspoilt that their pasts jump out from every corner.

At the end of a pebbled walkway I stumble across a

towering man, frozen to the spot, holding a map and staring open-mouthed at a corner building, muttering 'Dada'. Before I can hobble off murmuring 'Bonkers' he turns to me and says, 'Look, it's the site of Cabaret Voltaire where the Dada art movement began!' I can almost hear Nick gasp with delight as I stare at Europe's first anarchic club where Wassily Kandinsky, Paul Klee and Max Ernst hung out, exhibiting their often chaotic and brutal art (mirroring World War One raging around Europe) that regularly caused audiences to attack the stage. Holy cuckoo clocks! Who'd have thought it? Naughty Zurich!

Close to the model agency where my cheekbones will make their jutting, jittery appearance tomorrow morning, another building, Café Odeon, catches my eye and sultrily beckons me through its heavy revolving doors into a series of high-ceilinged art nouveau rooms with a long bar glowing with fine bottles and glasses. Below dusty chandeliers, vast windows and peach marble walls I sit on a stool at the bar and order a glass of champagne in the ear-splitting silence of this Sunday afternoon. The barman tinkers with a bottle of Dom Perignon.

'Er . . . I'd prefer something a little less expensive please.'

'No charge,' he smiles. He's bored and wants to pass some time.

By pure fluke I've chosen another Dadaist hang-out that also attracted Lenin, Trotsky, James Joyce, Hermann Hesse, Mata Hari and Somerset Maugham. What a knees-up that would have been – 'and Einstein gave lectures here when it opened in 1911' – the barman tells me in a high-pitched, breathless voice. I leave him a mega tip. He'd figured I would.

My first booking in Zurich is an underwhelming raincoat ad. Afterwards the stunning Shrimpton look-alike model Jan Ward and I head off for coffee. It's a revelation to discover that Jan, from Ohio, is that relatively rare thing – a well-read, wise, highly intelligent and sensitive model. With the comfort of a new friend's ear, I begin to pour forth about my family suicides. Jan is not remotely fazed as we focus on the fine line often tragically walked between genius and madness and the endless questions relating to both: does nature load the gun and the environment pull the trigger . . .?

What drives seemingly okay people to take their own lives without warning? It's a violent act that resounds across generations and for those left behind, the wounds never heal. Did Keith Moon mean to die forty years ago when he returned to his flat in Curzon Street after a night out with Paul and Linda McCartney and took thirty sedatives? That wild, dazzling and excessive brilliance of The Who's great drummer, who knew both the bright and dark sides of the Moon – only he knows which side beamed down on him that night. Did Jimi Hendrix want to die when he overdosed on barbiturates? Did Janis Joplin plan her heroin overdose?

We will never know.

Jan quotes Sylvia Plath, who killed herself at thirty as did my brother, and we question how this tormented American would feel about being buried in a remote graveyard on top of the rugged Yorkshire moors. We finally both agree that the suicidal need to feel loved and understood, not hectored or given highbrow rationales for living.

Friendships are intense and brief in this transient world of modelling and the following day Jan leaves town for yet another snap-happy city on the international treadmill of the life we've both chosen. A week later I receive a package from her containing *The Colossus and Other Poems*; *Ariel*; *Winter Trees*, and *The Bell Jar*, all penned by Sylvia Plath.

Dear Jan had activated my ability to cope, but I never see her again. I often imagined that she'd marry an urbane French philosopher and live on left-bank Paris. In fact she married Justin de Villeneuve, aka Nigel Davies, Twiggy's former boyfriend and manager, and lived in Peckham.

Back at the model agency I can barely believe my eyes. Jackie Kennedy's younger, more dewy 'sister' has arrived in town – the beautiful Jackie look-alike model Linda Morand, whom I briefly worked with on a *Vogue* shoot in Paris, is here to work too. I need to have some fun. She's the one – and tomorrow we're working together. Bring it on!

The door to the apartment is opened by an exquisite-looking butler, a black man in white jacket and gloves. His pale chestnut eyes usher us into a huge, exotic entrance hall. This hallowed abode belongs to a zillionaire proprietor of Switzerland's newspaper and magazine industry and our mission is to shoot a glittering cocktail-frock story for one of his publications.

We can't stop giggling – the male snapper, feisty fashion editor, top model Linda, and me. We've all seen glitzy places in our time, but this one takes some beating. You could fit two Toblerones into each of our mouths as we gaze at the continually revolving rooms with low-key organ music and subdued, sensual lighting.

Everything and everywhere purrs with exquisite taste, including the gallons of vintage bubbly that the butler constantly proffers on silver trays. Floating in the centre of the main revolving room is an almighty swimming pool – don't even ask how it was technically possible – but it teasingly beckons us all. Seconds after the snapper's last shot, I raise my left eyebrow, Linda nods, and with a mutual compulsion, we clasp hands and leap in – billowing evening frocks, full make-up, flailing hairpieces et al., followed by photographer, fashion editor and . . . No, the butler stays put. He's seen it all before.

'Café Odeon?' I suggest to Linda. She beams her approval and, still giddy with Dom Pom and pool play, we slide through the revolving doors to embrace the Parisian-type buzz of the lively bar and low-lit tables, now packed with musicians, philosophers, students, beautiful girls, and not a banker in sight.

Then I see him. At seven in the evening, standing by the bar, a glass of something in his hand, relating a tale to a cluster of rapt faces. He looks ridiculous, like a time-warp hippie with shoulder-length hair, embroidered waistcoat, tight, tight jeans and calf-length Afghan coat. Oh, and a hat. One of those idiotic leather hats from a Clint Eastwood western. In the role of drug-addled, Woodstock relic cum raconteur, he was unbeatable.

He looked dangerously provocative, unsuitable, different, extreme.

And I wanted him, desperately. Head over heels at first sight. It could have been a classic *coup de foudre*, but he isn't playing.

I persuade Linda to return with me the following evening. And there he is. Alone this time. He slowly makes his way across the room and the only noise I hear is my beating heart drowned by my suppressed giggles. His fleshy, beckoning lips, partly obscured by a winding, floaty scarf, are framed by sexy stubble.

He looks me in the eye, his lips part and, in soft Swiss-accented English, he says, 'You're beautiful. You must have been told this many times before, no?'

'No! Never! You're the first!'

Linda discreetly vanishes and here I am in a state of half ecstasy, half dread with a complete stranger. 'My name is Heinrich, but everyone calls me Heini.' What a daft name, I think, fixing my gaze on his hand-tooled cowboy boots. But I don't care. Would I like to go to dinner? Yeah. I'd never been out with a guy who wears paisley hipsters.

The Kronenhalle restaurant is unlike any restaurant I've ever eaten in before, its bottle-green leather walls casually hung with Miró, Picasso and Matisse originals donated by the artists who ate here, paying for their meals with their work. And as we make our way to the cosy table for two, Heini nonchalantly murmurs that the tables, with their red speckled marble tops and spindly legs, were designed by Giacometti.

A linguistic tussle ensues. My heart-throb's grasp of English is distinctly limited. I speak no German, even less of the Swiss-German dialect, and we resort to speaking in halting French when pushed. I just stare at him, bewitched by his magnificent aura, the spell only broken by a culinary confusion over 'raising the steaks' and a jaw-dropping moment when he leans towards me and whispers, '*Scheiterhaufen?*' Luckily this turns out to be a bread and butter pudding with calvados.

'I bet you're a drugs dealer,' I laugh, staring at his black-painted fingernails and the cowboy hat imprint still visible on his flattened hair. 'No one looks like you any more.'

Heini looks hurt. 'I attend the Jung Institute of Analytical Psychotherapy in Küsnacht.'

To prove the point he launches into a complex diatribe about the difference between Jung and Freud. Jung thought spiritual experience was essential to our well-being, and Freud didn't, I think is the essence. Oh God, now he's ranting on about the ink blot test by that other Swiss shrink Hermann Rorschach, tricky enough to understand in one language, let alone four.

I'd spotted the Jung Institute the day before, an imposing white house overlooking Lake Zurich, where Jung lived and practised before founding his institute for the training and analytical researching of psychology and psychotherapy. Most of its graduates specialised in psychiatry. What perfect timing! My very own shrink – just when I need one.

Heini delivers me back to my hotel with a kiss on the forehead and his phone number. 'I don't want to put you on a peddle stool, but I am on tender hooks hoping you will ring.'

I'd never heard it put so well.

214

I knew then that Heini was somehow going to turn the key that would open my heart. He was different to any guy I'd ever met. Not particularly funny or smart, just different.

He was the first man I could look at and watch with continuing pleasure. He had a slow smile which promised everything.

I had always been the one to do the leaving, never the more loving one, and had never been hurt and then hardened. Not by a boyfriend anyway. It was as though I'd separated myself from the rest of the world with a piece of glass – perhaps because of being spat out of the safety pocket of cosy family life after Dad's suicide, or possibly to do with the ever transient life of being a model. Everything had become pared down in my life.

Even emotions. Especially emotions.

But I also knew how it worked. That it all went wrong if you loved someone more than yourself. That men like and respect women who are somehow out of reach, self-sufficient and possess a certain fire, but are also kind and warm. That they *hate* women who continually need to be validated and who drive them mad with demands of 'Tell me you love me.'

My first boyfriend's parents had little time for me. I was teasingly coquettish with their son but curious about the world – not an engagement ring – always itching to discover what lay beyond, not knowing where this strange ambition came from or where it would lead. And this dear first boyfriend, practical and clear-sighted, had a serious life plan to be embarked upon at eighteen, wanting marriage when I was just sixteen. Subsequent boyfriends also wanted marriage but

215

that's because they did the choosing. I'd always been attracted to men because they were attracted to me. Until now.

Here, at last, was the man I had originally invented for myself.

After Heini and I made love in my hotel room we lay there for hours, side by side, not touching, not moving, utterly still. It was as though a mighty door had opened inside my head which this man had enigmatically guided me through. I didn't hesitate. I was totally in love.

Big changes were taking place in Zurich. A few months earlier Switzerland had been the last country in Europe to give women the vote. Now, shaking off its image of prim reserve, it was condoning an open drug scene. The liberal Swiss drug policies were attracting addicts from all over Europe and the Café Odeon began to lose its cool Parisian appeal, becoming tense and edgy.

I was still terrified of mind-expanding drugs; travelling outside my own head, unable to control my thoughts, held no appeal. I knew there was no safety net if things got weird, but I was a little curious about acid and had always envied people who had Dalí-esque dreams. Mine were mainly a rehash of the previous day's mundane events. I often wondered what kind of images acid would reveal. I'd quite like to be distracted by a rabbit leapfrogging over a mushroom which turns into a boat boarded by a squirrel with a lace face and orange eyes. As long as I didn't get sucked down a cave and into a tunnel guarded by two feathered bears and an octopus with writhing tentacles.

One winter evening, Heini persuaded me to drop some acid with him in my hotel room. It was good stuff, he said, and would not give me unwanted side effects involving demonic visitations and private clinics. This was to be my moment of blinding sensory enhancement, of hearing colours and smelling the stars and seeing profound truths in cracks in the pavement. And the man who'd invented the stuff was Swiss, a chemist called Albert Hofmann. I was somewhat nervous about discovering the boundless possibilities of the entire universe in a single raindrop.

But alas, I had no imaginings whatsoever. No marmalade skies for me, only a need to pee, and taking three hours to reach the loo two metres away. Oh, and seeing the back of my own head in detailed close-up as it swivelled around my neck; the real intensified to such a degree that it didn't seem remotely real.

Work continued in abundance, as did my love life with Heini, but on a cold March evening several weeks later, he leaned towards me in our favourite bar and said, 'I'm leaving Zurich for two months in the mountains, and to attend important meetings at the Jung hospital in Arosa.'

My heart missed a beat.

'I hope you will come with me? You could travel back here for bookings.' On that very day, a postcard arrives from Eileen Ford, asking if I'd like to return to Manhattan for work. Oh what it is to be Jung(ish) in Switzerland when New York's calling.

One last booking, a poster campaign for Castrol (I can

never resist posing with a vintage sports car), before embarking on the mountain adventure of a lifetime.

After a two-hour journey to Chur, we board a compact red train that narrowly weaves its way up endless twisting valleys. Past sheer granite cliffs decked with tall pines and streams crashing down crevices, we stop only at tiny stations marked by weathered wooden huts. All around us, stupendous mountains and soaring slopes are so close we can touch them as we head up to our eighteen-hundred-metre-high destination.

Finally the landscape flattens out and we chug into the last station on the line, nestled into the most beautiful valley of them all. Here on the cusp of Austria at the edge of two glacial jade lakes, and overlooked by the mighty Weisshorn mountain, is Arosa.

Built around those two picture-postcard lakes, and once Arthur Conan Doyle's favourite resort, no one ever came to Arosa to see and be seen. No bars, clubs, shops, hotels and ski-lifts clinging to the sides of mountains. No cross old trouts in furs, or shops bursting with Bogner ski jackets or corks popping and crystal tinkling. Just a sense of real mountain life.

I watch Heini unlock the door to our rented chalet, his hair flying and mauve scarf whipping in the icy breeze. Savouring the distant whiff of bygone log fires and unopened drawers, we gaze at the magnificent Weisshorn that towers and overpowers our bedroom window, projecting its pale unearthly light onto the ceiling and cornices. In bed, in the early morning hours, Heini stirs and turns over, pulling me with him. I stroke his hair and drift back to sleep, my face buried in the nape of his neck, hoping to never wake.

When the promise of spring warms the sharp chilly air we stop slipping, sliding and stumbling in snow and begin our walks in the mountains, first through cobbled streets past four-hundred-year-old buildings, proper shops, tiny schools and neat domestic woodpiles. Then higher, where the air is as crisp as linen and it's so hushed you can hear the silence.

Summer in the Swiss Alps is far more beautiful than with the white stuff. We stroll, hand in hand, through vast sunny meadows knee deep in delicate alpine flowers, past fields of purple lupins and by tiny streams frothing over boulders. Up through the pine forest awash with small red squirrels – which will stay all day if we give them nuts – and way above Arosa to the cows with bells and the wild Ibex goats with large horns, and thick carpets of pastel-blue scabious plants and swaying harebells.

I'm living inside the ultimate picture postcard.

True happiness is a strange thing. How many times in our lives do we say 'Right now I'm at my absolute peak of happiness'? Very rarely, if ever, is it recognised in the moment. Happiness is mostly an accepted and subconscious contentment, and our perception of true happiness mostly retrospective. Our memories are of a happy weekend, good party, great night out, and often it wasn't, although the overall memory is fine.

But one fresh morning as I run down the mountain to the village shops to buy food to cook that evening, I experience my unique, ecstatic moment. Hearing the sound of cow bells tinkling across the valleys, seeing the horizon scored by serrated peaks and lakes glinting in the sunlight beneath me, I yell to the world 'I am so fucking happy!' utterly convinced that I'm Heidi and that if I run a little faster, I will take off and fly. Oh, God, I'm so happy! The passionate love, the space, the air, the food, the strong morning coffee, the wine in the evening, the taste of his skin, the sound of his harmonica as he sits on the edge of our bed, the sight of his toothbrush drying in the late afternoon sun. For the first time ever I have fallen desperately, hopelessly in love.

Or, have I fallen in love only to discover it is ever desperate and hopeless?

I came across the passport while washing his clothes, revealing that he is twenty, three years younger than me. No problem with that – he's well-worldly. But in Switzerland a year's National Military Service is compulsory for males aged nineteen to twenty. Strange when the Swiss have never ever been to war, but possibly this small country with four spoken languages is held together by a military desire to stay united. There are few exceptions to this imperative call-up, and those are mainly to do with illness.

Then Heini's behaviour begins to change, as though he's being slowly plucked out of an unrewarding dream. He won't discuss his research course any more and becomes moody and detached. And odd people start to arrive at our chalet; a young man with a bag of brown crystals that look like cat litter. And then another, who speaks in whispers and also brings stuff I'm not supposed to see. This isn't the behaviour of a psychologist. It's weird, intense and secretive. What the hell is going on?

The time has come for confrontation. Finally, I discover the devastating truth.

Heini does indeed attend the Jung Institute in Zurich and its experimental drug addiction therapy hospital in Arosa, with their international training programmes in Jungian theory and method for researchers and teachers. But he does not attend as a Jung-trained psychologist. He attends as a 'research' patient with a drug 'affiliation' – because the institute also provides therapy for 'those persons in crisis'.

It had started with opium, long before I met him, and ended in heroin. This Queen of Denial is utterly unaware that he's been in its grip. And still sometimes dealing the stuff. I had no idea. How dumb is that?

He tries to explain that heroin is a subtle thing that grabs you slowly.

He doesn't often mainline into veins, he says, because it gives too strong a flash, and I guess the game is up with visible tracks. Much safer, he says, to 'chase the dragon' by using aluminium foil to warm the heroin and breathe in its fumes. I can't quite believe what I'm hearing.

He stands in front of me, those cushion lips pounding, a cigarette in one hand, its packet clutched in the other.

'When I first tried heroin . . .'

'Yes, what . . . ? What the fuck does it do . . .?'

'. . . It dulled my pain so much that I knew I wanted to

feel that painlessness for ever. I – loved – it,' he gasps, and a large glistening tear runs slowly down his cheek.

Now it all comes out. There were loads of drugs around, but in the back of his mind there was always heroin. Long before he came across it, heroin was always there. To him it wasn't a dirty street drug, it was the magic potion he'd read about. It was Oscar Wilde, and Kubla Khan – an aspect of their world, that world, that appealed to him. In those early years for him it wasn't heroin; it was opium pure from the poppy as heroin is refined, more potent, a quicker rush.

I don't get it. I don't see it. Why hadn't I seen it? Why had he taken drugs to this degree? His childhood was trauma-free. What has happened in his life that caused him to take this road? Or was he . . . is he . . . just treading that familiar ultra-thin line between self-discovery and self-destruction?

This is getting horribly familiar. But I can't let go.

We stumble back to Zurich and stagger on, while I work around Europe making enough money to support us both. His sister watches over him when I'm away. I'm stupid and blind enough to believe that if I love him enough, he'll have the strength to change for good, and if I can just help him to change, he'll be perfect.

But how does an addict give up drugs?

Surely it begins with the matter of gaining insight that it *is* serious, that it's not just about having fun or a flirtation with death that occasionally goes too far. It's about acquiring a desire for a normal life, finding yourself instead of being eternally, hopelessly lost.

I'm resigned to the fact that his recovery will be a long, grindingly hard process, a daily struggle that requires his total application, discipline and self-belief – and that takes massive maturity. It can't be rushed. The real test will be when he leaves the peaceful surroundings of recovery and returns to the grittier reality of life in the city.

Only then can he say he is recovered.

But he's not.

In the summer of '73 he takes a near fatal dose of heroin and is hospitalised for a week. In October, he's arrested for dealing five and a half kilos of hash and sent for trial in Zurich.

After he's jailed, I return to London, and the following week a note arrives from the Swiss prison, written on the back of crumpled silver cigarette paper:

I am alone. I don't want to be alone but I know I will always be alone. There's no world that my eyes see. My mind is all I have and a lot of good memories. Alone day after day after day, my mind and me in this little cell. Waiting for the day my woman and me will be together again. Maybe never. I don't know how long. They haven't said. I don't care. I am dead. The only peace you'll ever find is when you die.

I love him desperately, but feel so helpless. This isn't how it was meant to be.

Friends try to help. Release, the British ground-breaking drugs charity organisation founded by the beautiful feminist painter Caroline Coon, strides in and, staggeringly, his sentence is reduced to six months on condition that he takes a job with Release in London after his own release in Zurich.

Back in London the nightmare is far from over. There are meetings to be had. I can't string along Bill and Peter any more. It isn't fair. The game is up. I love someone else who's about to land here when he gets out of jail.

I still adore Bill, but more in a younger sister kind of way. I'm sure he feels this too. The age difference impacted some time ago. 'Let's go to the Isle of Wight rock festival – Bob Dylan's appearing live,' I'll say, and he'll respond: 'I've booked a helicopter and a good hotel, so that we don't have to be anywhere near those smelly old hippies.' Hang on, Bill, I was looking forward to hanging out with a few existential minds rather than Dave Dee.

The huge flat in Maida Vale is still the London roof over my head, but Bill and I now have separate bedrooms. He's even kind enough to welcome my mother to live there when she gets a job in London, but our relationship has definitely gone from 'Let's go out tonight and have some fun' to 'Yes okay, but if you get home first, leave the light on in the hall.'

I know I'm going to miss his strong, reassuring presence in my life, but I also know that he means it when he says, 'I'll always be here for you.' We remain friends for years.

It's clear to see that Bill has realised something within me changed after Nick's death. My guilt has produced a subconscious mission to rescue extreme, self-destructive men.

It's also given me a kind of essential loneliness that nestles deep inside me, separating me.

Bill marries his secretary, and has his own grim-reaper close call in 1982 when Gary Numan is flying his single-engine Cessna Centurion back from the Cannes Music Festival with his father and Bill, still at WEA, on board. The plane develops a fuel gauge fault, quickly loses height and has to make a terrifying forced landing. It crashes into a field, bounces across into the busy A3051 in Hampshire and narrowly misses fast-moving traffic. Miraculously they all survive.

Now I must also tell Peter that our love is over, but can we remain best friends? No way. He instantly returns to New York and proclaims me a heartless bitch. I have to agree. I've hurt him badly, smashing his hopes, caring nothing for his feelings, too entrenched in my own pain. Why the hell am I turning my back on kind, loving, well-balanced guys to love and support a man on a mission of self-destruction?

I write to Heini in jail twice a week, counting the hours until I see the love of my life again, while my modelling work across Europe continues (yet more German shampoo ads with Herr Brosche). But on arrival at Heathrow he's stopped, searched and held in a detention centre – to be deported on the next possible flight. A single ticket, just £20 in his wallet, and falsely stating he's recently completed a psychology course leads Customs to find prison release papers in his jacket pocket. What now? I ring my proactive local MP who says he can possibly get a stay of deportation on compassionate grounds. Just seconds before

Heini is boarded on a plane back to Zurich, the injunction's lifted, on condition that we marry immediately. Heathrow releases his passport for one day only, and we do it!

I buy a will-o'-the-wisp chiffon dress. No time to look for shoes that match, the purple boots will do. He wears black leather jeans, a sleeveless vest and my most expensive belt. A snapper friend kindly offers to take photos, and a few stalwarts, including my mother, turn up at the local register office – as do two Customs Officers – before we launch off to a reception at the Roof Gardens restaurant above Biba, with its flocks of wing-clipped flamingos sauntering from table to table. A low-key affair but our happiness is complete.

Best man Trevor Myles, super-cool owner of the zebra-striped Mustang and Mr Freedom boutique, presents Heini with a bottle of Taittinger with the words, 'My gift for you.' New husband stares at him and utters, 'Very funny!' Well, Trevor didn't know that '*das Gift*' is German for poison.

Two weeks later, in June 1974, a letter arrives from Roy Jenkins at the Home Office stating that Heini has permission to stay for twelve months and is able to work. Impossible to imagine that happening today, but Roy Jenkins *was* the pioneering architect of legislation on censorship, divorce, abortion and homosexuality that changed a nation.

But eleven months later, Heini is back in that Swiss prison again. His job as a hip salesman in a King's Road boutique, organised by Trevor, didn't last long. My new husband became mean and extra moody, went off without telling me why or where, and was finally drawn back to Zurich, and jail. His problem is bigger than both of us.

I want to feel nothing, just a numbness that blocks the pain of getting it all so wrong. I don't want to probe my emotions – to feel degraded, to admit failure to myself. I don't want to ponder the hurt and betrayal of feeling ripped apart, the stupidity of trying to help someone who doesn't want to help himself. I want to be swallowed up by this loneliness that nestles deep inside me – a kind of nun-like seclusion.

The attraction to the tall graceful Swiss to whom I succumbed was overpowering. That pure carnality; I could never resist that visceral pull. His sombre, seductive glow took me to a new level of emotional and sensual understanding. As Quentin Crisp noted, charisma is the ability to influence without logic.

When I finally allow myself to feel, to define the pain, it is for our loss of potential – the time on our roller-coaster measured in those early precious moments, but largely characterised by extremes and disintegration. It's that death of hope, of the myriad of tiny dreams we'd embroidered around the promise of new love, of where it would go, what it would mean, the things we would do, the places we would go, the times we would share.

Love is a drug. Or as the great Carl Jung would put it: We were attracted to our perception of each other – not to each other's true selves. Jung called this 'projecting your animus'. I guess I'd projected most other parts I possessed, so why not my animus.

A postcard from Casablanca arrived three years later. 'I have been looking for you in every bar. But I never found you. Goodbye, my love.' He gave his contact address as that of another institute in Zurich. Was he an inmate or a teacher? He could have been either.

Perhaps by now he was both. Goodbye, my love.

11

BONDED IN BLIGHTY

'You never know how strong you are until being strong
is your only choice'
Bob Marley

The end of summer 1974, and my caring English model agent
Jill now keeps a close eye on me in London, making sure I
continue to work rather than wallow in the dismal failure of
my short marriage. A fashion spread, for *The Lady* sporting
timeless classic frocks with appropriate brooches and pearls,
finds me suitably summoned for a job in Antigua, the latest
up-and-coming Caribbean hideaway resort.

I'm to be the 'upmarket' brochure prop, lounging with
entitlement in the foreground of exquisite locations in order
to attract the 'right kind' of punter. The resort's promoter, Bill
Shand-Kydd, a jocular and charming bon viveur, confirms
the booking. We meet again to discuss the job's logistics in
more detail over a Chelsea drink.

Approaching the wine bar, I suddenly remember where
I've heard Shand-Kydd's name before.

Photo: Alec Murray

Playing it straight for The Lady *magazine*

Lord Lucan.

Every newspaper is pounding with the latest. After being accused of trying to murder his wife with a lead pipe and 'mistakenly' bludgeoning the nanny to death, Lord Lucan has vanished. The last two letters the 7th Earl wrote before disappearing – for what turns out to be for ever – were sent to Bill Shand-Kydd, who is married to Christina, Lucan's wife's sister – and possibly the very last person to talk to him alive. The police have interviewed all Lucan's friends who've closed ranks to protect him by consistently ducking questions and interviews. This naturally gives birth to endless conspiracy theories. He's thrown himself off a ferry and drowned in the Channel . . . he's become a hippie folk singer in Goa . . . he was killed by a hit-man . . . he's secretly living as a professional gambler in Botswana's Holiday Inn . . . a butcher in Brisbane . . . propping up a bar in some far-flung outpost of the former Empire . . . and even eaten by a tiger at John Aspinall's private zoo in Kent. But why do you mysteriously disappear if you are innocent?

Whatever happens, I must NOT mention any of this to Bill. Sometimes I do probe deeper faster than I should, but that's because I'm just so hopeless at the '. . . and have you come far?' small talk. Yet I can't stop thinking about what really did happen on that recent November night. How could Lucan have possibly mistaken the nanny for his wife? And why has everyone closed ranks so rigidly, to protect him?

Oh, God! Another drink later, and I feel compelled to ask.

'I would love to tell you more but I can't. Please don't ask again,' says Bill.

But I do. I'm wrong and grossly insensitive to push it. And now I'm looking at an icy stranger. You could rip the silence with an under-sharpened knife. The job is cancelled before I finish my drink and another 'lovely' is booked to fly out and cut the ribbon.

Trust me to forget that apart from the required features for modelling, other golden necessities prevail. To never have your head turned, to be ultra discreet and diplomatic and to never have an opinion more forthright than people believe your looks can handle. Perhaps it's time to move on from

231

modelling, and do a job where I'm allowed to ask questions and/or have an opinion.

The temptation for a model to branch out into acting is strong, a chance to prove she's more than a one-trick pony. Unexpectedly, opportunity soon knocks. London's most respected casting agent, Maud Spector, is looking for talent for an upcoming film. She's dignified, charming and very old school and briskly flicks through my portfolio. 'You've got a very mobile, interesting face, dear.'

Well it's good to know that gurning's an option if all else fails.

'I'd like you to take some acting lessons as soon as possible.'

Maud's choice of voice coach is Helen Goss, who works from her bright Draycott Place basement flat in Chelsea. A character actress in numerous British films from the Forties, she later became a drama teacher for Rank Studios. I adore her, and each week she gives me a long, famous speech to learn by heart to recite back to her. Then one day: 'You actually read that better than Diana Rigg! I'll ring Maud tomorrow as I know she wants you to screen test for the new Bond film *The Man With The Golden Gun*.

Ah ha! This must be that seminal epiphanic career change moment when I decide to give up modelling and give acting my all. What perfect timing! The stills camera will forever respond best to fresh dewy skin and hopeful eyes, and I want to officially quit modelling before it quits me. I believe that a good model should be a reflection of her time and not be

Out on the town in my favourite frock by Zandra Rhodes. I still have it. Shame about the shoes.

Ozzie Clarke Designs, 1969, V&A Permanent Collection   Photo: Jim Lee

That special moment on a ground-breaking shoot.

... hält die Muskeln Ihres Motors jung

Castrol GTX

Castrol poster for Germany and Switzerland, 1972

Always ready to lounge on a vintage sports car.

American composite, front and back covers, 1970

Photos: Albert Watson

When cigarettes are cool and essential accessories.

New York, 1972

Photo: Arthur Elgort

Capturing the future with ad-hoc honesty.

'I see the sad past in your eyes, and that interests me,' says photographer Terence Donovan when I arrive early for a booking. He was the last person in the world who anyone thought would take his own life. But he did.

Take your shoes off.

Stagger down the street.

Empty bottle over head.

19 magazine, 1974

Photos: Gian Barberis

Dull macs, two bottles of champagne and a raw, undone model thrust into this real-life landscape. Never a boring shoot for *19* magazine.

Observer magazine, 1975   Photo: John Bishop

Last ever UK booking, and who's the fresher face
on the left? It's Marie Helvin!

Sri Lanka, 1976   Photo: Felix Bader

When a deadly green pit viper lunges at my
ankle in the jungle, it's time to dump Vikki
and discover Victoria.

Melbourne, Australia, 1977

John McEnroe and the new scriptwriter.

Los Angeles, USA, to see Helmut Newton, 1978

Won't somebody please invent a mobile phone?

Model
BEHAVIOUR

Paris, New York, Milan, deli... Former top model Victoria Nixon tells LORRAINE CRIGHTON-SMITH how she made her transition from the catwalk to the kitchen

Photo: Boyarde Messenger

My deli in 1994 – first UK food shop to use revolutionary eco-friendly packaging: biodegradable limestone cutlery, palm husk containers and acid-free paper bags. No plastic!

Never too late to get it right.

persuaded back for those photographic and runway 'worn-well' appearances, when 'well-worn' is what judgemental eyes really think.

It's different with acting. If there's talent, a lovely starlet can morph into a respected lifetime actress. A model, it is thought, can rarely bring more to a fashion photo with age, so is expected to do a graceful, grateful exit, and get a life with more meaningful focus.

But strangely, I have little desire to pace up and down a stage or set with a nervous squeaky voice and racing pulse. Deep inside, I know I don't have it, my heart isn't in it and I've seen enough of myself in front of cameras, still or moving, to last a lifetime. The two essential 'talents' couldn't be more different. The stills camera makes everything freeze, the movie one zings it alive.

Models can do 'the necessary look' but most know bugger all about creating a convincing performance. And frankly, many actors I've met are a bit of a pain – boringly clichéd and predictable parodies of themselves. 'That's why we're actors, darling, we're so boring.' To which I always want to respond, 'Yeah, and isn't it extraordinary that Shirley Temple could act at the age of four.'

Turning down the opportunity to screen test for the Bond part, I later hear that producer Cubby Broccoli had already made up his mind. Maud Adams got the part, and rightly so. Roger Moore also wanted her. Months later, sitting in the West End first night audience and preparing to feel gentle hostility towards my 'rival', I can't find fault with her divine looks and convincing, if uncomplicated, performance.

At this delicate point, James Bond does enter my life – albeit briefly – and flirts!

Accompanying a film producer friend to the BAFTA awards ceremony at the Grosvenor House Hotel ballroom, I accidentally collide with Sean Connery, my ultimate James Bond, on the halfway landing of the ballroom stairs. 'You're very tall!' he snaps; this from a man known to love diminutive women, and who is unaccompanied by his petite and delicate French wife. 'Yes, I'm probably the only woman who has ever looked you in the eye,' I say, spurred on by a glass or two of bubbly. He smiles, more stirred than shaken, then laughs and we hug awkwardly before going about the tedious business of relocating our seats. Later when the clatter of cutlery and the uncorking of bottles ceases and the lights begin to fade in the glittering room signalling the 'And the winner is . . .' moment, he raises his glass and blows me a kiss. Such a shame that many a tight nut has been loosened by a small wench.

My other dream of becoming a famous poet stalls when I can't find a word that rhymes with silver. Still can't. And so it's back to modelling. It's what I know, I'm grateful for the work and travel, and diminishing returns are not distinctly threatening my career just yet. This morning's casting is at David Bailey's house/studio in Primrose Hill. It's for Martell Brandy and looks vaguely promising because the turn-out is poor – and the ad agency art director is desperate to shoot the campaign quickly. Somewhat grumpily, Bailey finally agrees to use me for the job. I'm not his type at all.

When I arrive on set the music's good. Lead Belly, I think, and there's a male model with a somewhat lobotomised stare waiting for his cue. Bailey makes no secret of his irritation with male models even before we start. I'm wearing a floor-length scarlet evening gown with platform shoes and Bailey is wearing a face like thunder. He walks across the studio like a dominant, stroppy badger.

'Fuck me, you're a big 'un!'

I fight the urge to pat the top of his head murmuring, 'It depends at which angle of your sweet five-foot-eight frame you're observing me from.'

Instead I simper a little giggle. I hate myself.

Bailey stands alertly by the camera and as the lights blaze I gaze into the lens. The male model hunkers down beside me and we engage with the product. 'Could be worse,' he whispers, 'could be dog food.' Bailey's right hand clutches the remote control while his assistant is behind the camera checking the focus. '*Now!*' Flash, click. '*Now!*' Flash, click.

When Bailey snaps his fingers his assistant passes him the Polaroid and Bailey repositions the male model to face me and shrieks, 'Stay like *that*.' By the third roll he's yelling so hard he sounds deranged. 'Magic! C'mon, that's not magic . . . Let's have some fuckin' magic here! *Come on* – more, more, yeah, good, come on, concentrate, that's nice, more like that. *That's it!* One more like that and you can both fuck off.'

I'd met Bailey once before at a Paris post-collections party in a rambling, gracious second-floor apartment near the Bois de Boulogne. Oak-panelled walls and regal double doors connected the massive rooms which all contained super-rich smiles and towering beauties, schmoozing and chattering under the glistening chandeliers.

Helmut Berger, The Most Beautiful Man In The World – so called since appearing in Visconti's *The Damned* – was holding court to an ecstatic throng of bee-stung lips, explaining that his latest film, Oscar Wilde's *Dorian Gray*, had a different ending to the novel. Instead of slicing the painting with a knife, thereby inadvertently killing himself, Dorian does this act deliberately. Neither of these gruesome films appeared to have dimmed Berger's startling joie de vivre. Oh, the memory of that evening . . .

Around twenty of us are ushered into a bronze dining room by two waiters in tailcoats. Helmut Berger immediately leaps to the head of the long, narrow table, and I'm placed on his right. Luckily Veruschka, positioned at the far end, is without her photographer boyfriend Franco Rubartelli, and I am mightily relieved, to say the least. He'd once sent me an airline ticket to meet up privately after we'd worked together in Rome and after he and Veruschka had briefly split up.

As the evening wears on, Herr Berger's frivolous antics grow wilder and wilder and when a cut-glass container containing chocolate mousse is placed in front of him to be passed around the table, he slowly leans forward and submerges his entire head in it. Gasps galore, and 'the most beautiful man in the world' spends the rest of the evening looking like a deranged Mars Bar. Against all odds he's still with us and now has the lived-in face he deserves, which probably makes him feel a hell of a lot more comfortable.

Leaving the party, I squish into the tiny lift with David Bailey and his girlfriend Penelope Tree – beautiful, calm and interesting-looking. I nod my approval and smile at Bailey – that familiar, cosy smile of recognition the English tend to do to each other abroad.

'Are you Swedish, missy?' he asks, coldly assessing me with those black, wide-set eyes through a thick, dark fringe. 'No laddie, I'm from Barnsley!'

I turn to catch his expression of utter contempt before adding, 'You can always tell a Yorkshire girl. But you can't tell her much!'

I get on loads better with Bailey's pals Brian Duffy and Terence Donovan, who make up the feted three famous for steamrollering the 'gazing wistfully at a long-stemmed rose' of the Cecil Beaton era and introducing a 'raw, heterosexual working-class grittiness to a new liberal decade'. Or so the press would have us believe.

But Brian Duffy doesn't fit the template of the aggressive, pulsating sex machine, wielding his lens astride an abandoned model. Duffy is a kind, bright humanitarian, a family man – slight and balding with just a few sandy curls left to frame his warm, open face, though very partial to a nice leather jacket with jeans. 'You're a Gemini, aren't you?' he guesses correctly on a difficult advertising shoot with lots of models on set. I've ended up with the worst outfit, truly awful, which the other girls have outright rejected. But someone has to wear it. 'How did you guess?' I ask him after the shoot. 'Because I'm Gemini too, and you handled that situation exactly as I would have.'

Terence Donovan has redefined fashion photography by placing his models in run-down streets and industrial landscapes, the locations previously only ever used in social documentaries. As with Brian, he doesn't remotely resemble the raucous working-class snapper he's caricatured to be – doesn't smoke, drink or take drugs, is a judo black belt, and later becomes a committed Buddhist. He has beautiful manners and a terrific sense of fun, and when I mistakenly arrive way too early for a booking, he takes endless shots of me in the garb I've turned up in because 'I can see your sad past in your eyes and that interests me.' Later he presents two huge prints, signed and stamped. Somehow he caught my punctured heart in his lens. I still treasure the photos to remind me of his genius talent, sparkling humour, warmth and perception.

He is the last person in the world that I ever imagined would take his own life. But years later he does. His family and legion of friends are beyond devastated, all agreeing that anyone else in the world would do this before Donovan; he was so controlled, so balanced, so philosophical, he made us models laugh until our sides ached – the very obverse, supposedly, of a suicide. We all search for an answer. He was taking steroids for eczema at the time which made him depressed. Could that have been it? As ever, we'll never ever know. Suicide is rarely about only one thing. It's a murder in which the killer is also the victim, and the motive and reason dies with the act.

One of Donovan's favourite models from the early Sixties is Grace Coddington, who became a close friend and often approached him for wise advice. He encouraged her to take up the prestigious fashion editor's job at English *Vogue*.

Grace and I never work together as models – different eras – but after she progresses from starring in shoots, to creating them, she books me for a job.

By now a narrative force in the fashion room at *Vogue*, she's soon to marry dashing young photographer and old Etonian, Willie Christie. Today's shoot is at Willie's rather grand town house in Chelsea's Gunter Grove.

Grace is known for never letting anything interfere with her pursuit of the perfect picture. She's polite, firm and detached. Willie is kind, handsome and slightly confused. And I am, well, how can I put this . . . it's one of the most difficult shoots of my life.

What Grace wants is a fresh ingénue she can mould into the story in her head. But Willie and I don't know what's going on in her head. I'm over the hill and Willie's under it. The 'had-enough' and the 'wannabe' simply can't deliver the goods.

After the job, I meet up with a pal in a nearby pub. He suggests dinner at the local Indian restaurant where we order a much-needed bottle of Côtes du Rhône. As we take our first gulps, a couple at the far end of the room get up to leave. Sweeping past our table, the woman's handbag accidently knocks over our bottle of red, ensuring a sad, short life for my white linen shirt.

The explosion of copper hair turns and I'm sure recognises the drenched victim, and promptly makes for the exit. It's Grace. But I understand if she can't stop and apologise. I haven't delivered. I've let her down.

It's a tricky job being a fashion editor, constantly striving to invent fashion narratives that make readers believe they are expressing their individual selves, while simply purchasing the same clothes as thousands of others. Norma Moriceau, *19* magazine's fashion editor, who later becomes costume designer for the *Mad Max* movies, always gets it right.

Turning up for a London location shoot on a cold, grim afternoon, I'm presented with six dull macs in various shades of sludge and two bottles of champagne. Norma's 'story' is a post-party crawl home featuring a worse-for-wear model wearing raincoats that wear well.

I'm to look completely wrecked as I guzzle champagne from one bottle and pour the other over my head – the very antithesis of selling the dream.

No hovering shadow waiting to brush translucent lilac powder onto my forehead and cheeks, no sultry smile, no slightly pouting lips peeping out from beneath an exquisitely coiffed mane.

Just dishevelled clothes, wet tangled hair and a raw, undone woman. Thrust me into an offbeat landscape and make me the heroine, let me tell the story rather than being part of yet another vacuous montage of predictable outfits.

I've never enjoyed a shoot as much in my life.

But fashion narratives can go way too far. Oliviero Toscani's audacious advertising campaigns for Benetton featuring the duck coated in black oil, the newly born baby covered in blood, and the condemned murderers lost him the campaign and nearly ruined his reputation for good. More recently, *Vice* magazine went even further. A model posing as Sylvia Plath kneels in front of a gas oven wearing a dress by Suno. Another portrays the death of Virginia Woolf by wading into a stream in a Christian Siriano coat. The Beat poet Elise Cowen is depicted lying prostrate on the pavement after jumping out of a building where her parents lived. Taiwanese author Sanmao, who hanged herself with a pair of stockings in 1991, is also depicted – and the model's stockings are credited and priced!

To use the suicide of female authors as a fashion narrative is the most tasteless and insensitive concept I've ever seen in the name of fashion. Thankfully it also appalled the most die-hard fashion pack and these images-too-far were quickly wiped from view.

A morning booking for the *Sunday Times Magazine* and I'm dragging my battered tote, bursting with accessories, down the main stairs from my fourth-floor Maida Vale flat. The ground-floor tenant hears my expletives, opens his front door and offers to carry my kit to my local underground station. It's not the first time, and I'm ever grateful. He seems to love accompanying my baggage and its grumpy owner round the corner, up the street, into the station, through the barrier, down the steps – right to the tube doors when the train arrives. He's warm, friendly, gives good word-play and a total lack of pretension. I love his company but have no idea where or how, or if, he works. Sometimes he's around, sometimes not. After a few of these impromptu bondings I ask him why he appears to enjoy the tube station vibe so much. A moment's reflection, then a smile and a shrug. 'Ah, maybe it's because an underground station changed my life.' Uh oh . . . yawn . . . here comes the love-struck lowdown of how he first met his girlfriend/wife. I try to look interested, but glance sneakily over his shoulder to see when the next train is approaching.

'Yeah, I'd probably be an art teacher now if I hadn't walked ten yards further down the platform . . . or missed the train . . . or been in the next carriage . . .'

Come on, mate, get to the point.

'. . . because I wouldn't have met saxophonist Andy Mackay, joined Roxy Music and as a result, have my career in music.'

Blimey, these chance encounters are with Brian Eno, the most innovating producer of cool sounds in London. Musician, composer, record producer, singer and visual artist, he'd never given music a professional thought until that fateful meeting with Roxy's saxophonist. As a result, he toured as their synthesiser player until '73. Then, tired of endless gigs and conflicts with Brian Ferry, he ditched the Ferry and went on to supreme collaborations with every revered name in the business.

I've never met a celebrated musician with more ability to keep his fame in context. Not a hint of annoying flamboyance. When I mention this he says, 'Well, I don't play things well, I use them well.' I'd always hoped our mansion block held more promise behind closed doors than Dave Dee.

He's even kind to my mother.

'Darling, who is that delightful chap who lives in the ground-floor flat? He always helps me carry my case up all

242

the stairs when I come to stay, and even asked me if I was good at Scrabble which he says he loves.'

'He's a famous musician.'

'Oh really, he seems to have much more to him than that.'

'He has, Mum, he has.'

By mid-1974 I'm working away more often and bumping into Brian Eno less frequently, but when I do he appears slightly more distant and a little tense. I guess he probably has a new live-in girlfriend and doesn't want to seem too friendly with me. But I'm wrong. He's troubled. I learn of this in a dramatic way.

I'm with a pal in early January 1975, enjoying a drink at my local Maida Vale pub, when everything stops as a young guy dashes in to announce that a man has just walked in front of a moving taxi a hundred yards down the road. It's hit him badly, run over his legs and thrown his head against a parked car, leaving him with a suspected skull fracture.

The injured man is Brian, and it's his turning point. The taxi incident sorts out his troubled head once and for all.

The following year he's in Berlin working with David Bowie, a partnership made in heaven for the two most multi-talented, enigmatic guys in the business. He helps produce Bowie's next trilogy of albums – these twin souls floating above the world and deconstructing fame before anyone has ever really come to grips with the concept. Sadly, I never meet Bowie, but I doubt that conversation and empathy would have flagged. His dad was a Yorkshireman like mine and both our brothers, whom we hero-worshipped, ended their own lives – his brother slipping out of hospital to lie in front of a train. Heartbreaking.

I make my way to a cattle-market casting, which often involves hundreds of girls being coldly assessed for one fairly insignificant job. To be coolly rejected by the client, adman and snapper across the great dividing table never gets any easier. 'She'd be great for the job if it wasn't for *that*,' they all murmur in unison, pointing to a pic in the model's folio and assessing the real life version with cold, narrow eyes.

What . . .? Nose hair . . .? Bunions . . .? Filthy fingernails . . .? Saggy kneecaps . . .? Entire head and body . . .?

We girls often turn up in pairs for moral support, swiftly appraising the assembled hopefuls and size of turn-out. If it's 'No chance' at first glance, we 'About turn' and scuttle off for coffee. There's no actual bitching or animosity between the models, but if the casting's for a hair ad which needs a thick, lustrous, glossy thatch, and one girl stands out as having the best barnet in the room, those of us with thin, stringy strands realise it's a given that the game's up even before we're tress-assessed, and make for the door. Our qualifications for the job aren't like others. It's initially based simply on whether someone likes your look for the gig.

No illusions now, at twenty-five, about what I have left to offer. Models have a window in high fashion, and the window closes a little bit more every day. But it stays ajar for certain campaigns like booze, cigarettes and catalogues, where looking real is more important than glossy glamour puss. Good news indeed. I'm finally buying my mother a house and need a healthy, consistent income.

Mum is currently sharing my rented Maida Vale flat. She sold her Barnsley house because she wanted to live and work nearer to me in London. But having let it to students when she was the live-in bursar of a Yorkshire drama college, the sale price reflected its dire need for a total refurb, and will barely buy a garden hut down south, let alone a house.

She hasn't stopped working since my father's death, facing life with a determined strength that never dilutes her huge-hearted warmth and humour. And now she's about to become a fledgling Mary Quant cosmetics consultant, having applied for the job at the grand age of sixty! Go Mum!

On her first day in the smart Regent Street store, I secretly spy on her from the luggage department. A young man approaches wearing an expensive sports jacket and navy cords.

'Can I help, sir?'

'Oh, yes please. My wife has asked me to get her Starkers.'

'I'm sorry about that sir, but what's that got to do with me?'

'Starkers foundation . . . do you have it?'

Oh, Mum! Blush Baby blusher, Jeepers Peepers eye-shadow, Bring Back the Lash mascara and Starkers – all Mary Quant best-sellers.

The rest of her sales team, all dewy girls in mini-skirts, immediately adore her – and initially she loves every unfolding minute.

But soon the nine-hour days, packed rush-hour tube journeys and the climb up four flights of stairs to the Maida Vale flat begin to take their toll. It is time for her to take it easy, and a comfortable retirement is the answer. We search for a home for her in Surrey, where she has good friends, and find a cottage she loves near Guildford town centre so she can walk to the shops. A house-warming party ensures she makes more friends quickly and her close ones keep an eye on her. She encourages me to 'Travel the world, darling, it's still waiting for you, and don't ever worry about me, I'm fine and love my life.'

With my London rent and Mum's mortgage to support, I have no hesitation in saying 'Yes!' to a month's catalogue shoot. Accepting a bread-and-butter job means losing the cake, but we high-fashion models envy the close-knit clan of catalogue girls who consistently travel and work together – often in sunny foreign climes for weeks on end, the pace of the booking more holiday than hassle.

A villa in Portugal with jolly snapper Bob Belton, his boyfriend assistant, three female models and a stylist sounds, well, not entirely a brave new world of reckless hedonism, but certainly just the job.

Catalogue location shoots start mega-early and finish by midday when the brutally harsh overhead light creates unflattering shadows. These girls know the photographer isn't remotely interested in composing a ground-breaking shot – it's all about making a cheap frock look goddess gown in the least possible time. And only a true professional can make a grungy Crimplene tent look 'Buy-Me-Now!'

246

Simple body rules apply: make sure your knees aren't facing the camera or your legs will look short. If you must sit, perch, or your backside and thighs will look twice their width.

Never ever stand with your legs apart – cross one leg in front of the other. Turn one hip away from the camera, 45 degrees to the lens, and stand on your back foot. Avoid fizzy drinks and creamy cocktails; they'll give you a bloated tum. If you've over-indulged the night before: drink enough water to fill a bath, undo the bloody zip, breathe in and try not to vomit.

The catalogue girls – VN lower left

I share a room with Julie, a stunning, fun-loving blonde from Sydney who instantly becomes a friend for life. We whisper late into the night with glasses of wine tucked under our beds. Julie is married to Mike, a cuddly, engaging man who runs a film production company, and when I mention my financial need for a lodger she has 'just the guy' – a friend of

Mike's in advertising. A date is set for us all to meet at her flat on our return to London.

Hmmm, an adman as a lodger . . . could be interesting. I've been on a few dates since my marriage ended, but none to write home about. Rich self-made men inevitably appear from nowhere for lofty blonde models – they love having one on their arm to match their latest Rolex. But these types have simply never appealed to me.

I've often observed that highly successful businessmen never stop defining themselves through their work. Being good at it is what gives them most pleasure, makes them feel most alive, and gives them the most intellectual stimulation. They're rarely motivated purely by financial gains – but by the deal, by the excitement of making things happen, of utilising and demonstrating their potency. They don't need the cash – they just love the chase, that deal, proving they still have what it takes. It's far more fun at work for them than at home – it's where their status is most pure, their ego most soothed and gratified.

But that control freakery doesn't interest me – that constant addictive need to feel necessary and visionary; that nothing would work if they weren't driving it on. These guys never know when and where to stop. It's pathological vanity. I want to yell at them, 'Leave the world alone – or at least separate it from your bloody ego.'

I prefer a man with an interesting creative brain, who is funny and clever in a worldly-wise way . . . broadminded and capable of handling any situation, masculine but not butch, and kind and sensitive. A tall order? Not entirely out of the question, surely. There's only one guy who got anywhere near that in recent months. His name is Olivier Todd.

A model pal with a BBC reporter boyfriend phoned to ask if I was free to accompany 'French intellectual' Olivier to dinner. He was over from Paris to present BBC's *24 Hours*, having previously presented *Panorama* on French television, which I'd often watched when working there – amazed and staggered at his maverick stance of supporting the Paris student riots in '68. On air he looks dashing and is already well known as the 'thinking woman's crumpet'. This is too good to be true. Why invite me?

'Oh, he loves blondes, but he's much too old for you to be involved with, and I think he may still be married, so it's just a fun evening.'

It's true that he won a scholarship to Cambridge to read Philosophy the year I was born, but still . . . a date with Olivier Todd, no less! We meet in the familiar confines of a French restaurant in Knightsbridge, lit by candles and Tiffany lamps, and a tiny table for two ensures our knees touch before we've even ordered first drinks. I like his rugged good looks and elegant hands, and the way he leans forward in his chair. There's nothing stuffy about him despite his highbrow television work and endless books, including a cerebral biography of Albert Camus.

Quickly tipsy with the giddy pleasure of being complete strangers, we reveal far too much in no time at all. It's also evident that this all-engaging raconteur can't bear people who, as he puts it, 'sit on the fence or take offence'. He told Jean-Paul Sartre at their first meeting, 'I like your novels but I

249

can't take your philosophy.' They've since had around eighty lunches together. I love the way Olivier constructs a theory and uses it to examine the facts rather than the other way round. It's a fact that a clever man who can make people laugh can have any woman he wishes to have.

Oh, the power and allure of the brainiac. We never meet again, but Olivier Todd confirmed to me that an exciting brain is the sexiest organ a man can ever possess. He's the one who got away. And the only man I've ever met who preferred to discuss current affairs rather than have one.

Awaiting my potential new lodger in Aussie model Julie's snazzy flat, just off the Edgware Road, she tells me all she knows about her husband's colleague. Finally the two admen roll in from work two hours later than expected, having consumed a fair amount of 'product'. Barney, a dead ringer for David Essex, trips over the doormat and lands at my feet.

'Have you been drinking?'

'Yes, of course, but I'll take the room in your flat. Now where is it again?' He has a certain charm about him.

'About five minutes away from here. Would you like to come and see it?'

'No, no, no. I'll move in tomorrow.'

I have a lodger, an adman who works for one of London's prestigious ad agencies producing television commercials, and from that moment on the flat buzzes and blasts with ad-speak . . . brand strategies, pitching, tag lines, talent, extras, rushes . . .

Barney, my adman lodger

A Cadbury's Flake television commercial is a given, thanks to my new adman lodger. He convinces the casting director that I'm his first talent choice, and off we go. The two-day shoot in a punt on a river in Suffolk has sunlight capturing the ripples on a chocolate phallus as it explodes into my mouth – notwithstanding that actually swallowing five boxes of over-wrinkled brown logs is, quite possibly, the least erotic thing I've ever done in my life.

Barney has been sharing a house with The Who's drummer Keith Moon in Bywater Street, a pretty cul-de-sac of pastel-coloured cottages just off the King's Road, so we have to make some new domestic rules. No television sets to be thrown out of the window to prove they'll land at the same time as a feather, and no cars to be driven up the stairs.

Annoyed at my assumption that Moonie is always a loony, my lodger proceeds to explain their friendship. The house they lived in belonged to Mary-Rose, a childhood friend of Barney. He lived in the basement flat and her upper part was let to Keith when she buzzed off abroad. Barney got the call at work.

'Hello, Mr Moon here, I've just moved in and wish to invite you up for a drink this evening.'

Their mutual exuberance formed a trusting bond, and on the days that Barney spied the lilac Rolls-Royce parked outside, with its six speakers and vast drinks cabinet, he knew it wouldn't be long before Chalky, Keith's affable driver, would be on the phone. 'Mr Moon would like to invite you for a few lines upstairs followed by several pints at the Chelsea Potter.' Ah . . . nothing quite like a hook, line and sinker to end the day.

'How,' I enquire one morning as the adman dashes off to work, 'can a grown man earn a living by persuading me to buy Persil washing powder rather than Bold?'

'Because they're different, that's why.'

'Don't be silly, they're all the same.'

'No, they're not. They all have distinctive, individual personalities. Fairy – soft and delicate for fragile undies; Bold – powerful and brash for workman's overalls; Daz helps mums get stains out of grubby T-shirts and Ariel works because it's scientific. It's all in the name!'

British advertising sure is the most exciting in the world during the early Seventies. Thirty-second tales, well told, are often better received than the programmes they support. A true Brit ad voice has emerged that isn't mock-American and which engages and amuses a nation.

Barney's job as a 'TV creative' is to contribute big ideas and use the best directors to realise them. This is central, far more important than client handling, clever research and media planning and it isn't long before New York agencies want to copy these clever, smart, witty campaigns and hire British 'creatives' in droves to steal the excitement.

Most of the London action takes place in Soho, the heart of the film/post-production industry, and lunch isn't lunch unless it's at least a three-bottler, lasting well into the afternoon and all on mega-generous expenses. After work I occasionally meet Barney at the Colony, a nicotine-yellowed, alcohol-embalmed club up a flight of stairs in Dean Street, known to all as Muriel's and presided over by Muriel Belcher who has a staggeringly foul mouth and addresses everyone as Cunty. It's here that Barney introduces me to his American actor friend, Rip Torn – oh, the pleasure of meeting someone, anyone, called Rip Torn – and the rarely sober artist, Francis Bacon. I soon discover how fine is the line between the bon-vivant adman lunching at L'Etoile and L'Escargot and the afternoon drinker at Muriel's: 'large vodka and no ice . . .' who takes his hat off to be silently sick in it and makes a stylish exit.

It isn't long before Barney is off to Cannes to shoot a new campaign TV commercial for Cossack Hair Spray for Men. He's sold the client his concept of a pilot writing Cossack across the sky in smoke, with an end shot of the man's hair falling perfectly into place and the tag line, 'All it controls is your hair.' As I have three days without work, a rare occurrence, he suggests I join him and the production team in Cannes.

The talent is Neil Williams, the British aerobatic champion, and cameras are mounted on his plane's front, back, side and wing to capture all the action. The actual sky-writer is France's finest and a dead ringer for Barbara Castle, who's paid a fortune to fly up to four thousand feet in a crop duster plane and write the logo in smoke. But the smoke doesn't work, her engine stalls and the plane falls out of the sky. Miraculously, she safely crash-lands but the plane is a write-off. Enter Willy Van Damme, Holland's finest aerobatic star, summoned from Amsterdam, and whose capable aircraft will surely do the trick. But he takes off from Nice airport and ends up in the jet lane over Marseille having only written the letter C, which no one can see.

A sunset is necessary, essential, for the shot to work. And each evening Willy is sent up to sky-write Cossack, and every evening it fails. Screamingly over-budget and way over schedule, the crew admit defeat, so we pack our bags and fly out of Nice. Only to see Willy, in the far distance, writing the perfect 'Cossack' in the sky as he heads for home. The sensational in-the-can footage of Neil going through 6g forces – his hair standing perfectly on end before flopping back into place – doesn't count for anything without the crucial sky-write, and Barney is 'let go' from Young & Rubicam with the words: 'You're too much for us.' Now it wouldn't be too hard for a couple of astute design students to produce that same campaign online without ever leaving their seats, but that live action was unforgettable.

The *Mad Men* ad era is truly over.

12

REFLECTED IN BARCELONA

'I am not strange. I am just not normal'

Salvador Dalí

My August plan is for somewhere new, knowing my mother is settled, secure and happy in her home. I still need to work to pay the bills, and I think I've found the perfect place.

A palpable throb of previously forbidden 'glamour' has begun to embrace Spain after General Franco's death in 1975. It marks the transition to democracy which makes it a different place to work in, and model agencies pop up in Madrid and Barcelona to catch the fall-out. It's the perfect place, in fact, for this old hand to 'show 'em the way' while the ingénues are busy conquering Paris and Milan.

Madrid is the most exquisite, elegant city but it is coastal Barcelona that offers the best paid modelling work and most amenable conditions in this smoulderingly hot summer. The cool action is all along the Ramblas, a strollable, tree-lined boulevard with neat shops, outdoor cafés and my teeny hotel with its tiny roof for sunbathing between jobs – but avoiding that lobster glow Brits can never refuse. I'm up here when Barney phones.

'Can I come out to join you?'

Could I possibly refuse anyone 'let go' for failed sky-writing, who has a friend called Rip Torn? Besides, I'm becoming rather fond of my out-of-work lodger.

As soon as Barney arrives, my model agent offers us her holiday-escape apartment in Sitges, a picturesque fishing village just thirty-five kilometres south of Barcelona, where I can take the coastal train for bookings back in town. Off-the-map tiny Sitges transcends tourism, but is still throbbing with sunburnt foreigners all heading for the myriad bars in narrow cobbled streets the minute daylight ends. Revellers overflow onto late-night pavements and we soon discover that the best bar in town gives live impromptu performances by two blues singers who've met in Sitges this summer. The duo's soulful voices and heart-searing harmonica playing are creating a buzz around the coast and word has reached Salvador Dalí, who summons them to entertain at his house near Cadaqués.

The lodger and I spot the two singers – a tiny Brit and a lanky Yank, both called John – hiring a smart car for their Dalí soirée and they immediately suggest that we hop aboard too. It has not gone unnoticed how well schooled Barney is in the Keith Moon art of outlandish behaviour – thus ever-equipped to play court jester – and that I bear a fleeting physical resemblance to Amanda Lear, Dalí's lofty blonde muse.

The coastal drive from Sitges to Cadaqués is a giddy nail-biter on roads that curve around sheer cliffs with staggering views and possible catastrophic drops in all directions. Our priority topic of conversation, 'Has Dalí sold out?' involves much emphatic swivelling of heads, compounding the dizzying hurtle along lofty roads that disappear into spooky, dark tunnels cut high into the mountain sides.

Having had a dear brother who studied and taught Fine Art at Newcastle University during its Pop Art era, I've been programmed to think of Dalí as a bit of a con artist. The creator of two of the world's most surrealistic images, the soft watch and lobster telephone, appears continually to embrace cheap fame and money, promoting his art to the point where he's barely able to function without a daily dose of worship. Back then we'd dismissed him as a charlatan showman and diverted our interest to the more subtle and obscure Paul Klee.

'Yeah, but you can't deny his early paintings dazzle in technique and imagination – and his imagery has been constantly hijacked into the world of pop and advertising,' says Barney.

'And, let's not forget,' adds Little John, 'how perceptive it was of Dalí – years before Andy Warhol – to realise the importance of celebrity to an artistic career.'

Yeah, we all concur that Dalí is okay after all.

Now American John is staring at my wrist. 'Your watch! Your watch! It's the *Persistence of Memory* watch. Oh my God, Dalí will love it!'

Indeed, my much loved, curved-face antique Cartier time-piece curls into its wearer's wrist, precisely resembling Dalí's melting image. Damn, why hadn't I realised that!

En route to Salvador Dalí's house in Cadaqués

But what lies ahead?

Parties and alleged orgies at the house, if the rumours are true, with Dalí watching and his wife Gala participating! We all concur we're old enough to look after ourselves and that Dalí, now in his early seventies, is old enough to know better. It's more fun to discuss the latest rumour that Dalí and Gala have recently built up a celebrated poo collection gathered from unsuspecting guests and displayed in delicate glass jars. A taverna pit stop en route ensures fewer possible resources to increase this particular 'artwork'.

Yet another tight corner and there, directly below us and nestling in the tiniest harbour I've ever seen, is the dazzling Dalí residence. The unmistakable whitewashed fortress is built from a warren of connected fishermen's cottages and topped with terracotta roofs and three gigantic alabaster eggs.

As we approach the bay the house looms more and more imposingly behind its high white walls surrounded by pointy tall cypress trees. All conversation stops as we park the car; only the sound of waves splashing against the rocks as we walk the few steps to the heavy mahogany front door. A white jacket immediately appears. Arturo will inform Señor Dalí of our arrival.

The small, cramped, silent hallway smells of rotting seaweed – not party time. Our only companion is an enormous stuffed bear festooned with weighty necklaces and holding a lamp in its paw. An umbrella stand, overflowing with a cacophony of canes in all shapes and sizes, covers the bear's feet. We all giggle nervously.

Arturo reappears to announce that Señor Dalí awaits us in the summer dining room. The boys wave me forward to 'front the cavalry' and I follow Arturo down two winding passages leading to a narrow, compact room dominated by a horseshoe-shaped slate table. Salvador Dalí half rises from his chair to greet us, supported by an elaborate wooden cane, and a rhino head hanging over the window behind makes him look fleetingly like a two-headed monster.

Dalí is how I imagined him to be, but slightly less so, as though he's been lightly rinsed in bleach. His sun-mottled forehead melts into long, thinning, unkempt hair and the

260

trademark moustache is not quite as perky as it appears in pics. He's wearing an embroidered off-white American-style denim shirt, linen trousers and locally made leather sandals. Perfectly fake New York teeth flash fleetingly when he smiles. He shakes our hands, introduces Gala at the far side of the table, and a French couple almost hidden in the corner; the man, Pierre, is Dalí's current agent, accompanied by his wife.

With his wobbly cane, Dalí gestures for me to sit beside him and instructs Arturo, in a strange patois of English, French and Spanish, to bring more champagne and glasses. The two Johns squeeze around the table but there's no chair for Barney, and Arturo is despatched yet again. At that moment Gala begins to bob up and down like a hyperactive child and girlishly beckons Barney to her side of the table, finally tugging him across it to sit on her knee.

Gala's coquettish effervescence and super-dyed black hair – rolled into a bob and adorned with huge black velvet bow – make her look infinitely younger than her years and she sports rather racy, fitted Capri pants. Her random costume jewellery jangles madly as she grabs one of several bottles of the blood-red champagne and proceeds to hit Barney over the head with it. In a friendly way of course.

The lodger looks charmed and amused. His newly delivered chair is ignored and he and Gala stay entwined. Dalí appears enchanted with their behaviour and as we watch them pouring champagne for each other and over each other, he gives me a 'look at the naughty children' smile and confides that Gala's hot and cold manner is because she's very shy.

This playful, cosy side of Dalí and Gala seems strangely at odds with their profligate and decadent image. I'd been forewarned that Gala's usual pattern of behaviour is to criticise, disengage or compete with other women, but when she observes that I don't mind her hijacking Barney, she slightly warms to me too. Flaunting young men in front of Dalí has long been one of Gala's games. But they've been together for over forty years and he appears to adore her. It obviously works. So does their fond bickering.

As if by the wave of an invisible flag, the real evening's entertainment begins. Both Johns leap up and, with a tap of their toes and a '1-2-3', their heart-wrenching harmonicas encase the tiny chamber, followed by a haunting blues song that needs no other accompaniment. Three more songs follow before the duo receives a standing ovation.

'I prefer classic, Wagner and so on, but this I like too,' Dalí whispers in my left ear. At least I think that's what he said. He rolls his *r's* and murmurs in an almost incomprehensible mixture of English, Spanish and French with Catalan thrown in to further confuse. But it could be me and the endless bottles of champagne Arturo has produced. I'm beginning to feel somewhat overly refreshed. Prolonged bibulous sessions tend to make me introspective rather than passion-filled and tempest-tossed – and Dalí seems to like this.

'Are you hungry, Victorrrhoea?' alarmingly rhyming with diarrhoea. 'What do you like to eat? Chocolate?'

Through my grapeful haze I have sudden unexpected clarity. Devouring calorific goodies on a new friend's terrace in Sitges, she'd mentioned that the word for chocolate and floor tile is the same in Catalan.

'Yes, I love chocolate, but not when it's too hard,' I say, gesturing towards the slated floor. Dalí's grey-green eyes look puzzled.

'*Rajoles*,' I whisper in his ear. It takes five seconds before his eyes light up, his moustache ends twitch and he bounces forward.

'Bravo, Victorrrrrrrrrrrrrrrrrrrrrhoea. And now I have a surprise.'

With the help of his old cane and my left shoulder he purposefully rises from his chair, gently takes my arm for support, and ushers me onto a wide whitewashed terrace bordered with flowering rosemary and tiny silvery green olive trees. Beyond the terrace it's just possible to see a garden sloping down to the minuscule secluded bay.

Tightly squeezed into the rocky terrain to our right is a narrow, vaguely phallic-shaped swimming pool with various child-like objects floating in it including three toy ducks. At the far end of the pool, on a covered stage is a colossal stuffed lion groping a nun and several plump assorted cushions on two battered old thrones. Frankly it all looks a bit tatty.

Waiting for the others to join us, Dalí asks 'Where are you from – New York?'

'No, Barnsley. You must know it?'

Dalí's never heard of Barnsley let alone been there. Mildly disappointed – I'm sure he'd love it – I don't let it spoil the evening.

Now all assembled on the terrace, Pierre gestures for

us to gather closer and announces, 'In return for your entertainment, Dalí will make the moon appear.' Barney and I catch each other's eye, half hoping that Keith might suddenly pop out from behind a lavender bush and drive his car into the pool.

Dalí slowly raises his arm and there, miles above us, the sky lights up and, silhouetted in the heavens, is a full beaming moon. It slowly passes behind a cloud.

Has Arturo spiked our drinks?

Dalí laughs at our reaction, and when we move closer we see that it's a wash-stand attached to the high concrete wall overlooking the terrace, which has a neon fluorescent light behind it – glowing exactly like moonlight. Tickled by his invention, Dalí informs us that he found the wash-stand in a second-hand shop in nearby Figueres.

Anti-climax is neatly bypassed when Pierre announces that we are all invited for dinner at a Cadaqués restaurant, just across the peninsula, and we are to follow in our car. When I ask 'Where's the loo?' the boys smirk . . . 'wait till we hit the restaurant or you might be sorry.' Arturo ushers Gala, Dalí and his two French guests into an ancient, enormous black Cadillac and it's a snail's pace procession into nearby Cadaqués, where, only minutes later, we pull up at an unpretentious restaurant on the quay.

Waiters smile fondly as we enter the half-full eating house and bowing bodies direct us towards a central table. Dalí gestures to me to sit on his right and blood-red champagne appears immediately, but no menus. It is Gala, speaking directly to the head waiter, who orders our food.

The restaurant lighting is unflatteringly bright and as I stretch to guzzle yet another glass of bubbles, Dalí grabs my wrist and declares 'This is divine!'

Ah ha! He's noticed my watch!

Maybe now's the time to ask if *Persistence of Memory* was inspired by Einstein's Theory of Relativity as supposed, or a Camembert cheese that melted in the sun, as stated by him.

But no, he appears besotted by my vein-ridden, bony hand.

'I like very much the skeleton, the structure.'

He's virtually devouring my hovering hand, which does, sadly, resemble a quail carcass. 'You know it is the only thing that remains after you are dead. And this too I like.'

Now he's looking at my jawbone, the very same one photographer Clive Arrowsmith decreed could slice salami. Bang on cue our meal arrives – *Langostino a la Catalina* – a Spanish tomato-based version of Lobster Thermidor. *Que sorpresa!* . . . An edible crustacean, the external skeleton. Dalí enthusiastically chomps away and halfway through the meal Gala orders chocolatey puds all round. But before they arrive Dalí abruptly appears over-fatigued and Gala's dancing raisin eyes quickly focus on our waiter. Resigned to what appears to be a familiar situation, she requests the bill and Pierre whisperingly confides that wherever, whatever Dalí is doing he is always in bed by eleven. Gala pays for our meal in neat bundles of crisp notes, then '*Vamos!*' she cries – and they are gone.

How we laugh on the winding, perilous journey back to Sitges. High on the rocky coastal road we dissect the evening – the bow in Gala's hair, the scarlet champagne, the tacky swimming pool, the wash-basin in the sky. We've loved every second. And as we screech around the last hairpin bend into Sitges, the guys decide on a tardy nightcap at one of the ever-open bars. But I've had it . . . and make an unsteady descent home, looking forward to reliving the evening's extraordinary events with Sarah, an English model who is briefly staying in our apartment.

Gently pushing open the front door I instantly feel a prickle of ice-cold draught. A scribbled note addressed to me in cobweb capitals straddles the doormat: 'A phone call from England at 9 this evening – your mother is dying. You must fly home. So sorry, but please don't wake me to discuss. Need my beauty sleep – big booking tomorrow. Thanks, Sarah.'

I gasp in disbelief. Is this part of some strange dream sequence, a tragi-comic extension of the day's revelries? My precious adored mother wouldn't die. She couldn't die. This brave, beautiful woman who'd endured the self-inflicted deaths of her husband and only son and selflessly encouraged her only daughter to embrace life with exuberance.

A wave of unbearable pain electrifies my body and my knees start to fold. I'm doing that thing I thought people only did in movies as my body slowly slides down the door into the foetal position. My throat tightens and my eyes start to burn. Moments . . . hours . . . a lifetime later . . . I open my eyes and begin to focus. Through the tears I begin to see the unmistakably familiar image curved around my wrist.

It is Dalí's melting watch.

The surreal – now unbearably, agonisingly real.

*

Mum dies three days after my return, aged sixty-one, at 12.15 A.M. on 4 July. No coincidence for this courageous, adored woman to die on Independence Day. Seeing her lying there in hospital – her breathing loud and erratic in her thin chest, tubes dripping fluids in and taking fluids away, then finally squeezing the last drop of breath from her lungs as she finally gives up her struggle – is embedded in my soul. No words can ever describe the intensity of pain I feel. Her 'little friends' had finally become her unwitting enemies. For years, she'd chosen not to see cigarettes as the direct cause of her hacking cough, ongoing bronchitis, chronic emphysema and finally, the heart disease that killed her. From an era when smoking was glamorous and exciting, her days had long been defined by the pleasure of the appropriate puff – after coffee, the end of a meal, the sitting down with a drink, the telephone chat – 'Hang on, darling, I'll just get a ciggy.'

Essential displacement activities mercifully kick in to sideline my agony. Funeral directors and the vicar need to know if I want to have her cremated remains dispersed in the Garden of Remembrance or in a special urn, and what music the organist should play. Then I have the unbearable task of breaking this devastating news to her full address book of besotted friends.

I can hardly bear to think of her body being burnt to ashes. Yet as her physical remains leave through the vestry oak door for the crematorium, a white butterfly flutters in on a shaft of sunlight – that ultimate symbol of freedom, happiness and sunny days. To this very day, whenever I see a white butterfly, I always say, 'Hello, Mum.' It gives me strength and hope.

After the funeral I try to ready the Guildford house for sale. I can't be in it without her. Silence hangs like a cobweb in the shadows. Every square inch is a living memory. Surrounded by her possessions it is the mundane items – the final bills, newspapers and shopping lists written in her familiar scrawl – that suddenly take on a heart-wrenching poignancy. Her magazines piled up for future reading sessions; the last day's television programmes carefully selected and underlined for viewing, her favourite horses confidently circled with a fountain pen for the day's racing from York.

I can hear her beautiful voice, so warm and full of fun, as I climb the stairs to her bedroom – 'Oh darling, could you be a poppet and pass my cardie?' Her make-up and half-full bottle of scent on the kidney-shaped dressing table; her hairdressing appointment card makes me smile briefly. 'A cut and blow-job please,' I once heard her say on the phone. She wanted to know why I giggled.

But most painful of all, her rows of shoes waiting for her to slip into, so obviously *her* shoes, so shaped to her enormous, uniquely misshapen feet that no one else could possibly ever wear them. Huge feet, all of us – my mother, father, brother and me. Always the family joke.

It's almost too painful and lonely to do this alone, in my mid-twenties, and no family left now. No points of reference ever again. Who will I ring when I can't recall the name of the Devon hotel where we always spent our family summer holidays – the long walks along the cliffs, dressing for dinner, listening to a palm-court orchestra playing show tunes from before the war, and consommé or shrimp cocktail for starters? Or the year I had my tonsils out?

A bleakness and emptiness descends on me. Everything lost. No anchor to my life now. Nothing else can be taken from me. God, the world's a lonely place – cities without sentiment, a life in permanent transit and an ever-travelling, transient circus of friends dispersed across the world. And now a family not of this world.

Taking a deep breath I go on a ruthless clearance offensive. On the dining table is a half-smoked pack of Silk Cut – she'd put a stop to the full-tar fags. Laughing wheezily in her last few years of stubborn smoking, my mother would often announce that anyone who wanted to kill her should simply tell her three good jokes in a row. Always tremendous fun, my mum – she could sip one small sherry all evening and be the life and soul of the party without ever needing to take centre stage.

It's the foodstuffs in the kitchen cupboards next. Endless jars of Heinz sandwich spread and tins of mandarin oranges which always remind me of tiny goldfish. I place them next to the piled clothes and stacked furniture. Next, her bureau with glossy family photos cascading out of albums. Everyone happy and laughing – making it ever more baffling why uplifting, charismatic life-enhancers like my father and brother would take their own lives. Finally, every letter I have ever written to her.

I sink and huddle into her favourite chair remembering how she taught me self-belief as a teenager and to 'always laugh before you cry', to ' keep your word, never let people down', and to 'know when it's your turn to stop and listen'.

My lack of convention never jarred with my mother's pragmatic approach to life. A creature of the war generation, she'd held things together in the wake of unimaginable destruction but understood that Sixties children, with their Utopian dreams, were hell-bent on pulling it all apart. She always loved our music and listened with total engagement whenever I announced my need to embark on new adventures. She encouraged me, cheered me on with intelligence, selfless acknowledgement and pure delight.

Wedged down one side of the chair is a crumpled piece of paper. I recognise Mum's wonderfully chaotic handwriting. It's not another shopping list. It's a poem she was writing.

I hold it next to my heart.

My daughter

When you were born on a summer's day
It doesn't seem all that time away
I shall never forget the joy and pride
'It's a little girl,' someone cried

Please God make her beautiful I prayed
Peeping in the cot where you laid
But I never dreamt how lovely you would be
I wish Dad could just see his chickadee

Beauty, courage, fame, humour
Unbelievable kindness, what more can I add
So much, but I don't think I ought'er
Because really it's just that you are my beloved daughter

Crying like a baby, I leave a note for the estate agent, close the front door for the last time, and walk off into the evening stillness. I pray that Mum is happy and drinking a delicious cocktail with my father and brother. Her suffering is over. Can I possibly ever be happy again without her? No comfort zone now to which I can ever retreat and hide away.

Moving slowly forward, I start to experience something very strange. I begin to feel . . . that time is precious, that I must always live my life in the moment. The space my mother has left will never be filled, yet because it's still there it's not a void; it's hard-edged, chiselled by her into my life – ineradicable, measured by her worth and my continuous

271

memories and discussions of her. I have to live on – for her sake, and my brother's and my father's – to live for them all, as well as for myself.

In consolation my life has taken on a kind of lightness that can sweep up at any moment into adventure. I *can* get through life without a dark river of malaise coursing through it.

I *will* be as happy as I make up my mind to be. I'll just get on with it, feeling free, with no constraints. One final look at the house now swathed in pools of evening mist and I can hear my mother's voice: 'Be kind to yourself and others, darling – we grow through compassion. Accept your history with no shame, no blame, simply the profound awareness that love and grief co-exist and must be acknowledged.'

'Yes, Mum.'

'That's the spirit, darling! Now buck up, get on with it . . . and *never say die*!'

Cheers! Happy family in Devon, 1954

13

REVERSED IN MELBOURNE

'Human life is a balance of fate and self-determination'

London estate agent Roy Brooks is unique in a trade notorious for its optimistic camouflage in the Sixties and Seventies. He places outrageous ads in Sunday broadsheets about the properties he offers for sale. They amuse and inform house-hunters and readers alike. But rather than smile wryly, salute his honesty and turn to the following page of the *Sunday Times*, I sit bolt upright: 'Dilapidated terraced house for sale with posh address and grumpy sitting tenant on top floor. Truly grim but cheap.'

This one could be my sanctuary and I want it to be my home. And what's more I can afford it. In cash. It's the bargain of the century, just off the King's Road in Chelsea, and practically next door to my agent and close friend Jill. But a phoned request to view is met with this irritated response. 'That house went first thing this morning. We've had more response to this property than any ad we've ever placed. Goodbye.'

Developers had spotted the immediate potential of offering a grumpy sitting tenant a substantial sum of money to leave, and selling the done-up freehold for a huge profit. But I can't get this house out of my head and ring the Roy Brooks Agency two weeks later and can barely believe my ears. The sale hasn't gone through because the sitting tenant won't be bought out. But I don't mind a tenant, however grumpy. I just want to live there.

'What if I pay you the full asking price in cash? I can have it on your desk in an hour?'

My Regent Street bank manager is waiting at the bank's door when my taxi draws up and laughingly thrusts the cash through the cab window. It feels like the early days in Milan when I had to stuff my earnings down my pants at the airport. The readies are counted out in Roy Brooks' agency and I'm handed the keys to my new home.

A frail and skeletal Miss Jenkins is huddled in the far corner of her top-floor flat, just a bundle of bones draped in thin skin, in front of her one-bar electric fire. She's wearing a viscose housecoat, crumpled socks and slippers and a pair of woollen gloves with cut-off fingers, and keeps flicking at the Players No. 6 pack on the stool next to her, alongside her assortment of medicines and pills.

'What's going to happen to me, love? These men in suits keep coming here and offering me money to get out, but I don't want to live anywhere else. I've been here for seventy-five years. I was born in that room next door.'

'Don't worry, Miss Jenkins. I've bought the house and you can stay as long as you like, and the very first thing I'm going to do is to make your flat nice and warm.' She died in the place she knew – and loved – six months later.

When I'd moved in, Barney came too. He'd landed another prestigious ad agency job producing television commercials and his scribbled notes and improvised ashtrays began to clutter every surface. 'Shoot Mobil Oil inserts' . . . 'Cutting room and rushes for Embassy' . . . 'Director for Mars?' . . . 'Film this in gradient sequence.' His hard work pays off and the agency wins a Clio (adland's Oscar) in Cannes for his Dunlop commercial. Then a familiar scenario begins to unravel.

Barney wants to shoot a Lambert & Butler cigarette commercial in a real landscape that looks exactly like the pack. But there's only one place in the world where the sky and sand truly merge in a completely straight line, and that's next to the equator. The cost of transport alone would outweigh the entire budget. This is ominously shaping up to be Cossack all over again. And it isn't the only impending disaster. Freezing weather says it all about the current state of Britain.

Ford car workers are on strike, miners need a 40 per cent rise, tanker drivers go for 60 per cent and dustmen are refusing to collect all rubbish. All British Airways staff walk out, followed by sewage workers. Children are locked out of schools, 999 calls go unanswered and bin bags pile up on the streets. At Liverpool docks, half a million pounds' worth of tomatoes rot on the quayside, housewives are panic buying and train drivers threaten to strike any time now.

On the day that grave-diggers down tools – leaving 225 unburied corpses piled up in a disused factory while the Chief Medical Officer ponders whether to resort to burial at sea – Barney asks if he can borrow my purple maxi-coat for a job interview.

'I don't mean to be rude, but you'd look ridiculous in it.'

'That's the idea. If I get the job in spite of the coat I'll know they're broad-minded enough to work with me. The job's in Australia, an eighteen-month contract to launch their first indigenous car, the Commodore.'

When I return home around seven, post wine-bar drinks and bibulous banter with two model pals, I spy yet another scribbled note on the kitchen table, this one addressed to me: 'I got the Australian job. It's in Melbourne and I get a house and a decent car. It's a hot summer there right now. Why don't you come with me and fly on my magic carpet? We might soar for ever or we may crash-land – no guarantees!'

'Why the landlady? Give me five reasons?' I scribble before dashing out to dinner.

He's in bed by the time I get back and a doormat note reads:

'1) *Reasonable sense of humour* 2) *Not bad looking* 3) 4) & 5) *Happen to love you madly.*'

I grab the dice and roll on our future.

'*No worries, mate! It all sounds bonza to me.*'

How blind I'd been about the lodger, locking myself out of love, being remote and elusive, avoiding an emotional entanglement of possible loss, paring everything down after a disastrous marriage, divorce, and my family deaths. But now the time was right to stop separating myself from the rest of the world with that piece of tough glass. It was time to risk my heart again.

It's the tiny details that make you love someone. When I saw him gently rescue a daddy-long-legs wedged in the bath, taking such care not to break its long, delicate, fragile limbs, that was the moment that did it for me.

We decide to marry at Chelsea Town Hall before leaving for Melbourne. My openly gay Canadian friend Antony Clavet, arguably the world's leading make-up artist, is summoned to titivate – we'd shared rooms, jokes, and his cool appraising eye on numerous location shoots when he'd applied my make-up with an expert and indomitable hand. He's just finished working on *Just a Gigolo* with his idols Marlene Dietrich and David Bowie. But after two strong spliffs he forgets his canvas is not Marlene, and I emerge looking like a geriatric New York transvestite on a night out at the Sanctuary.

Signing the register, I notice that my husband's middle Christian name is Cripps.

'Yeah, it's because of Stafford Cripps, a close relation on my mother's side.'

Who'd have thought it? My bon vivant, devil-may-care, generous new husband is related to the most parsimonious politician ever to hold office.

'No, no, you've got him wrong,' says Barney, dodging the confetti raining down onto the town hall steps and continuing his theme at our reception lunch amid the fierce and feverish drinking. I learn that dear old Stafford was never afraid to 'bite the bullet and slash spending if it made economic sense'; a quality, I note, that has bypassed this particular young member of his family.

I'm further informed by my new husband that the year I was conceived was the 'worst winter in living memory', when a threadbare, bomb-damaged Britain with a savage currency crisis saw Chancellor Stafford Cripps staring into the economic abyss. It would have been easy and popular to duck the challenge, being an aristocratic Marxist vegetarian, but he took tough decisions to raise taxes, force down consumption and devalue the pound, all designed to boost British industry and exports – particularly car exports.

'Yeah, and by the time he was out of office, Britain was on the brink of the biggest boom in history. Austerity was forgotten, and affluence was all the rage a few years later,' my new husband declares proudly.

'Perhaps you've chosen the wrong career. Britain needs *you* to Cripptify it *now*.'

But it falls on deaf ears and soon he is gone, to launch the General Motors Commodore car in Melbourne. I watch his plane roar through the sky, tail lights winking until it's a dot on the horizon. Sprucing up the house to let, before a down-under adventure, is my last chore.

Out of the blue, my Swiss model agent rings from Zurich. 'We have a client who is especially asking for you, it's for a week's advertising shoot on location for the chemicals giant ICI and the fee is superb.' I nearly drop the phone when she tells me the rate of pay, but don't quite catch the location, the line is poor . . . sounds like 'Sri Lanka', probably in southern Italy. Oh, God, why can't I ever resist a foreign adventure – that irrepressible urge to get on a plane, a boat, a horse, anything to dull the pain of losing my family. I always want another journey. Two weeks later at Heathrow airport it's the usual collect-the-ticket dash before the window-seat flop and a nice nap after lunch. I wake up in Karachi . . . finally arriving 'in Italy' fourteen hours later. Ceylon has recently changed its name to Sri Lanka. I vow to read more newspapers.

The snapper is an old hand I've worked with many times before. He's already in situ and after a welcoming drink he presents me with seven rolls of fabric and a raised eyebrow. 'But I thought this shoot was for Imperial Chemical Industries?' I murmur. He nods and informs me that ICI also make fabrics, the wrinkle-resistant polyesters Crimplene and Terylene were first, then Silk Look nylon, after acquiring Courtaulds. Our job, just him and me, is to make these sweaty materials come alive by styling them into instant desirable outfits that show their 'glamour and versatility'. So it is model, stylist, designer and seamstress on this trip rather than simply 'slip it on and smile'. Not surprising the fee was so inviting.

But this Indian Ocean island is a superb location, more 'old empire' than a primitive shock to the system, with a slightly dilapidated feelgood factor to the whole place – white Morris Oxfords parked outside tea shops and children scurrying around with cricket bats. Our old-time elegant hotel, on the tip of a lush jungle, has fine curries, freshly

279

picked papayas and tiny pink bananas which we eat in a coconut grove in the pungent sticky heat.

A cheeky toque macaque monkey steals my lunchtime sandwich, snatching it out of my hands, scampering off, and looks at me as he eats it. The shoot progresses well, hard work but fun, and the pics are surprisingly convincing.

Everything changes on the fifth morning when a coconut falls on a guest's head killing him stone dead. We're at the next table and it happens so fast we don't even have time to scream. This is beyond my understanding. It's beyond horrific. Wherever I go in the world, someone near me dies. I try to block it out. I have a sleepless night, constantly seeing the man's face in his last moments, so happy to be on holiday, leaning forward, laughing at his table.

The following day, posing in the jungle, I step on a large mottled log which leaps up and lunges. It's a green pit viper, camouflaged among the foliage, and one of the deadliest venomous snakes in the world. I just manage to jump to safety as it lunges for my ankle, but it could easily have been fatal. There is nothing, absolutely nothing, on earth that makes you feel more alive than being directly confronted by your own possible death.

These events are a clear strong sign that it's time for me to leave the party, to call it a day, to quit modelling for good. Time to dump Vikki and discover Victoria.

My last ever model booking is with a stunner who has many years work ahead of her before she calls it a day too. Yeah, it's Marie Helvin.

*

Clambering aboard the 747 leaving for Melbourne to join my new husband, it finally hits me. Banking on my looks for work is a finite game, and that game is up. It's time to face the truth and foster those qualities that grow rather than fade with the years. It's time to end that rush, that high, of *always* being in transit so that I won't have time to stop and feel and think about my future – and my past.

Modelling has been good for that. It's stopped me facing stuff. That's the beauty of it: a phone call, then a plane journey – always travelling but never arriving, even when I get there.

Now it's time to revive the one feature not often exposed in ten years of modelling – if indeed the grey matter between my ears still exists. A new success across the world will demand all the qualities my mother taught me: a steady nerve, courage, massive reserves of determination and no room whatsoever for self-doubt. And if I'm really lucky then opportunity, good fortune and skill may move into play and provide the perfect platform.

For now it's glass of Aussie Chardonnay and a super-long sleep.

The plane doors finally fly open and a blast of dry heat rushes into the cabin – tinged with a hint of air-con, sun oil and freshly brewed lager. Several masked men arrive on board and spray the entire plane with disinfectant, intent on destroying all foreign bodies.

Some of us survive and splutter down the steps to be greeted by a light so staggering, a brightness so powerful that any person wearing beige instantly disappears. This all-encompassing golden glow makes everyone's arrival here feel like a surreal mega holiday.

Melbourne appears to be an egalitarian, classless place but paradoxically the arrival hall has everyone dressed to the nines – the bandbox-fresh women all wearing hats, white gloves and elegant outfits, the men looking somewhat self-conscious in ultra-smart suits. There's a discernible excitement in the air. I leap into Barney's arms and we melt in exhausted exuberance.

'Why is everyone dressed like this? What's going on here?'

'It's to celebrate your arrival,' he laughs. For a nanosecond I believe him, but I've arrived on Melbourne Cup Day, the horse race that brings Australia to its knees – the smartest event of the year, and the one where Jean Shrimpton unwittingly showed the world how to look sensational in the first-ever mini, a white Orlon and silk frock she'd made herself.

The next morning Barney is catapulted into a seven-day shoot in the Northern Territory where he'll be hanging out of helicopters and shooting with a crew around the clock in a lavish high-budget production. Never have an ad agency and its man been better suited – horses for courses plus a stash of resources.

My first glimpse of Melbourne reveals stunning buildings erected from early gold wealth and generous, evocative Victorian houses with elegant cast-iron lacework verandas. Less orgasmic than the first sighting of Sydney's heart-stopping Harbour Bridge and Opera House, but also less brash – more like the London I used to know rather than the one I've left behind.

The sun, high in the sky as if it's always noon, makes me feel alive. I want to bin my washed-out pastels, blond cashmere and endless shades of biscuit, and unpack the linen only ever worn on holiday – here it's brights and whites that tone with fluorescent even teeth and engaging smiles, these golden people at ease with themselves, always light and content, no traumas concealed behind their healthy fresh faces.

It's the *sheilas* who impress the most – spirited, more forthright than the men but always utterly feminine. Not remotely judgemental about my modelling career, no snide remarks behind cupped hands, no questions, only interested in my here-and-now and my future in their country. They're not the only ones.

How will the grey matter get its initial workout?

The answer arrives sooner than I think. Two weeks on and my husband arrives home from work looking drained, slightly the worse for wear via too many Scotch and cokes. I'd expected him to be over the moon as he's shooting and producing a commercial tomorrow which has John McEnroe as talent – a milk ad for the Victorian dairy industry. But something's up.

'John doesn't like the script! We've only got him for the next two days because he's also playing in tournaments, but he's not happy doing the commercial because of this script.' He throws it in my direction.

'But it's complete crap. You can't expect a hip young guy like McEnroe to say this stuff. It's an old person's take on what a young man might say and do. It's all too contrived.'

Barney pours himself another Scotch, looks me directly in the eyes and speaks very slowly. 'Listen to me. The only answer to this mess is that *you* rewrite it.'

'Oh, don't be ridiculous.'

'You're always saying you want to use your brain, well now's your chance. I know you can do it. When you've finished, take it round to John's hotel and explain to him how it works; he's expecting me . . . I mean you. It's a seven o'clock start in the morning. See you then.'

John McEnroe already has a reputation for throwing rackets at umpires, but more for his ability to hit a ball as if serving round the edge of an imaginary building. He deserves better than this script. The teenage target audience means the script needs a light, cajoling fresh approach. And so I make it 'a day in the life' of what John enjoys most and the precocious tag line becomes the background soundtrack.

The Old Melbourne Hotel is a strange labyrinth of passages, back staircases and narrow corridors. I wish I'd known. When John McEnroe says 'Hi, come on up,' it takes twenty minutes to find his room. Down three long corridors with no sign of his room number, then another corridor and I'm beginning to feel like the kid on the tricycle in Kubrick's *The Shining*. Through two more swing doors, left a bit, right a bit and suddenly, in the distance, I hear music. It gets deafening, and as I fall over a discarded tray strewn outside the last door of the last room of the last corridor, I'm pretty sure I've hit my target.

Two loud knocks before the music is turned down and the door flung open. Our hero is wearing a denim jacket over crumpled mauve T-shirt and well-worn jeans. Music cassettes, tennis gear, wooden rackets and loose change take up every conceivable surface of the spacious room though his bathroom shelf is surprisingly sparse – a well-used yellow toothbrush, a hairbrush, cheap Gillette hand razor and a small can of French shaving cream. No fancy aftershaves for our man John.

After greetings and hotel comfort assessments, his initial gaucheness melts away and we get down to the nitty gritty. The milk commercial is to be shot spasmodically over the next two days of his stay here, fitting all the necessary situations into his packed schedule of tournament games, duties and press conferences.

My fledgling script portrays John as a charismatic, laid-back sort, rather than the short-fuse tennis player who can be as charming as a dead mouse in a loaf of bread. There's a shaving sequence and John seems quite happy with that. In fact he uses it as an excuse not to shave for the next three days, causing many a cryptic remark from television commentators. 'You could get a shot of me having a massage before my next match,' he says and suggests several ideas and improvements to the script.

I haven't felt so wired for years. My life suddenly feels like a strange and twisted dream. I love this unexpected transition from target to shooter.

Filming begins the following morning in a milk-bar location, but incessant world travel makes John's sleeping patterns difficult. He can never go to bed before the early hours and it's more than anyone's life is worth to wake him before eleven. Bearing all this in mind, I call Mr McEnroe at 11.10 A.M. and ask him to head to the film director's house near our first location. 'Something to eat before we go?' our director asks when John shows up. This man's hobby is food, the walls of his hall framed with 'tried and tested' menus from Maxim's and Tour d'Argent in Paris. 'Got any bread without seeds in it?' asks John, shovelling the forthcoming huge sandwich into his mouth at such speed you can literally hear his stomach scream for mercy.

In the first milk-bar set-up John will exit drinking a carton of our product. But first he asks the owner for a disgusting-looking ice-cream cornet and insists on paying for it. Amy, who owns a Chinese restaurant across the road, wants him to eat there while in Melbourne. 'Yeah, sure,' says John, signing her menu, and as she scuttles back, he shouts, 'Hey let me look at that menu, Amy. Can you make me something to eat right now?' The tiny lady beams broadly and says, 'Yes, anything, *anything.*' He orders spring rolls and pork spare ribs. Amy dashes off and I tell John he's crazy – she'll never have pork ribs ready in five minutes and if she does, they'll be undercooked and he'll be ill.

'Ah well, you only live once,' he says.

Tonight we're filming at the Underground, a nightclub owned by Brian Goldsmith, Olivia Newton-John's brother-in-law. John loves this place and spends every night he's in town here with his pal Vitas Gerulaitis, the flamboyant, leonine player who is currently the most popular personality on the international tennis circuit. The two players are very

286

close, Vitas not remotely intimidated by John on or off court. They probably share the same relaxation props. Asked what he likes best, grass or hard court? John has been known to reply, 'I don't know, I've never smoked hard court.'

The club is packed and our director decides to shoot a scene with John lounging around the grand piano, the very same one Liza Minnelli and Peter Allen, her former Aussie husband, used for an impromptu singalong two weeks ago. The Friday night crowd, sensing some action, is heaving and I worry that John may get tricky; he lost an important match earlier in the day. But his defeat appears to have had little effect as he clowns around, taking a swig from the glass of milk placed nearby. Unfortunately it's the wrong glass. It's Barney's and has a large quantity of Scotch mixed in with the milk – a newly acquired habit.

The director wants to film McEnroe 'gyrating on the dance floor' and the crew disappear to set up the shot. John strides over and grabs my arm. 'Victoria, this dancing shot . . . I hate the idea of dancing with all these people watching. Can you talk to him? I'd really appreciate it.'

The shot is changed and later we relax at a table tucked away in the darkest corner of the dining room. A smiling face framed with a cloud of blond hair arrives. It's Vitas, who parks himself at the table and orders a gargantuan meal. One of his long lists of blondes also pulls up a chair and glugs down a glass of champagne. John seems relaxed and happy to be surrounded by friends.

Suddenly, with immaculately bad timing, a very drunk and aggressive woman arrives at our table and starts prodding John and delivering a torrent of abuse. The mood has been broken, but not for long. I revere Vitas almost as much as John does. He's like the Pied Piper. Everybody wants to be around Vitas. The ultimate party boy drives a shiny yellow Rolls-Royce and plays in a rock band called Just One Kiss. I've rarely met anyone more full of life, more charismatic than Vitas.

Sharing a secret joke with Vitas Gerulaitis

Several years later, however, his carefree life is interrupted when he's named in an alleged conspiracy to buy £20,000 worth of cocaine. Although not indicted, he knows his image is tarnished and senses it's the right moment to leave the tennis party.

A stunned public were quick to suspect and blame drugs after he was found dead at forty in a Long Island guest cottage belonging to a friend. But he'd put a stop to drug-taking after rehab and had become a successful tennis analyst for CBS. The autopsy disclosed that his blood contained lethally high levels of carbon monoxide, the deadly gas that killed my father. The police stated it came from a faulty air-conditioning system, which I hope is the truth.

The next day is our last with John and the most important day of the shoot, but he loses his match against low-ranking Eliot Teltscher, and walks off court tight-lipped, his boyish vulnerability now strikingly apparent. The crew wait outside his dressing room, quaking in their trainers. A terrifying smashing and bashing from within is followed by a minute of total silence.

The loser emerges, calm and collected, and saunters into the press conference next door leaving the tortured remnants of what was, minutes ago, a spanking new Dunlop tennis racket. Almost every string is broken, and the wooden frame completely ripped in half. His self-discipline admirably restored, McEnroe jumps into his hired Mazda sports car and drives fast to our last location, the Wentworth Hotel.

Not one of us mentions his defeat, the crew more concerned about not losing the available, but fast-fading, light. Our next set-up has John hopping into a bed for what will be the opening shot of the commercial. I'm getting quite blasé now. 'Take off your watch and place it on the bedside table,' I suggest.

'No way,' he snaps, looking at his solid gold Rolex Oyster. 'I had to buy this. Why the hell should I give them free advertising?'

The last shot is tricky. It has the most dialogue in the script and is the only vaguely 'hard sell' part of the commercial.

The audio recording boys thrust tape at him and, wired for sound, John plays around with the lines until he feels happy that they sound natural. The clapper slams, the director shouts 'Action' and the charged electric atmosphere shoots adrenalin around John's body.

'Speak up!' yells a sound operator. 'More energy!' demands the director. Fourteen takes later and John half-heartedly apologises to the crew. 'It's a hard life when you're on your own,' he half sings. 'You guys are a team . . . I'm just a one-man travelling entourage.' He turns to me. 'Did you get that one, Victoria? Not a bad quote.'

'Yeah, that hits a nerve with me too, John,' I say gently.

Trooping down in the lift, glasses of bubbly in hand – the last shot in the bag without a hitch – he puts his arm on mine and whispers, 'I'm concerned about Barney. He's drinking too much.'

'I know.'

I like and respect John. And the commercial is shortlisted for a Clio in Cannes!

I write a few more ads on a freelance basis, winning an industry award for one effort, but my real interest is in seeing commercials actually being produced. I've noticed a weakness on set. There's never any pre-production co-ordination between the casting agent, talent, hairdresser, make-up artist, stylist, or art director before the day of the shoot and if the film director doesn't like what he initially sees on set, the time wasted getting it right means a large crew hanging around, upping the budget massively.

So I form a pre-production company which co-ordinates the director's vision before the shoot. It's a first, and it works! My only disappointment is in turning down a new, stunning young model for a commercial because of her inexperience. Her name is Elle Macpherson.

Everyone I meet in Oz is friendly and approachable – all the men possess that unique, crazy sense of humour. Where else in the world would the word bastard be an endearment? 'You whinging pommie bastard' (regardless of gender) soon becomes 'you pommie bastard' (a mate) to just plain 'bastard' (a good mate) progressing, if you're really lucky, to being 'a dag' (a really good mate). A dag, for the uninitiated, is the dung-matted locks of wool that hang from a sheep's bottom. Only those who know why it's a compliment to be likened to what's sticking out of a sheep's arse will ever make it to be honorary Australians. And if you're ever told to 'Go to Buggery!' it's worth knowing that Buggery is a mountain located about sixteen kilometres east of Mount Buller, Victoria's ski resort, and its companion areas include The Bastard's Neck, Terrible Hollow, The Crosscut Saw and Mount Despair.

Approaching the Eighties, Oz is seeking cultural change to enhance its world recognition. The government has created tax deals to finance home-grown movies which they hope will impact overseas yet retain a true Aussie soul and essence, paving the way for that commercial cracker *Crocodile Dundee*. The bit's between my teeth now, but how to be part of the action? Film Victoria, a state corporation, invests in documentaries if significantly Oz in content or featuring Aussies who've become internationally famous.

I know not a single famous soul with an ounce of ocker heritage.

Half-heartedly flicking through a vintage *Vogue* while waiting for the barbie to sizzle, the page falls open at a Helmut Newton photograph.

That's it! I have my man! Born in Berlin in the twenties and the son of a wealthy Jewish industrialist, Helmut fled the country at eighteen, first to Singapore, then to Melbourne where he chose to settle for seventeen years, working as a photographer and marrying local girl June Browne in 1948.

But there is one small problem. The last time we worked together I'd sworn at him and stormed out of the *Vogue* studio in London. It doesn't bode well but I bash away on my typewriter. This is a hell of a lot more complex to develop than a thirty-second TV commercial, but I spread a gigantic jigsaw puzzle of research material on the floor and gradually piece it all together. Despite raised eyebrows from Barney, things begin to take shape.

My documentary will explore the evolution of Newton's style with special emphasis on the 'mysterious' Melbourne years, a place at odds with his passion for glamorous international locations. Little research material is available on this era of Newton's life and initial funds from Film Victoria will help explore this paradox in depth. In the film I'll bring Helmut back here, to see Melbourne through his eyes. Is it more glamorous now? And does he want it to be?

At last I'm on a roll. It's all shaping up in my head.

I'll contrast his traumatic early life in Germany to the glitzy world of his fantasies, and thoroughly explore his views of the women in his images – are they victims or heroines? I want to capture the irony of his strong, provocative images – grand hotels, swimming pools, castles, super-privileged places and people – with his witty, often cruel, observations of this *beau-monde*.

And I'll throw in his knack of using his craft to reflect the changing social and physical face of the female – for which I'm most grateful. When Yves Saint Laurent transformed the tailored tuxedo into high fashion for women, it was Newton who said '*Le Smoking* is exactly the way I wish my ideal woman to be dressed' and it was yours truly who helped launch the look.

Brutally loud musical activity in the studio above my office makes concentration tricky at times – for twenty-year-old producer/director Richard Lowenstein is putting together some movie called *Dogs in Space* featuring an unknown band called INXS. The lead singer, an amiable guy called Michael Hutchence, all set to play the lead role, never hesitates to drop in for a chat whenever he returns from grabbing a coffee.

At the end of three months, I've shown my treatment to no one; I don't dare to. But I finally bang it into Film Victoria for assessment and, staggeringly, it's green-lighted for funding by the Project Committee – on condition that I obtain the necessary rights clearances from the man himself and have access to his archives and memorabilia appropriate to the film's production.

Helmut sounds keen and flattered when we speak on the phone. Needless to say, I use my married surname. He sends a letter confirming his interest but the hard work has only just begun. He won't budge or sign anything until he's clapped eyes on the producer. Little does he know the producer is that stroppy model he discovered in London's Bond Street. Helmut has a reputation for having very little time for models. Even less, no doubt, for one who told him to fuck off.

His winter months are spent in Los Angeles, and my departure day arrives. A lawyer friend gives me a crash course in deal making and Film Victoria writes a strong, supportive letter. But an hour before leaving for the airport, the phone rings. It's Henry Talbot, Newton's close Australian friend who shared a studio with him in Melbourne all those years ago.

'Victoria, it's off, you must cancel everything.'

Helmut, he explains, has received my telex with arrival details, but has left my number at his home in Monte Carlo, and Henry just *has to find* me before I get on the flight. He can't explain why. 'Just stop her!'

I knew it. It's all been too easy. Pouring myself a strong drink I sit motionless in a chair for three hours, staring into space. Lesson number one is that nothing goes according to plan in film making. Just like the rest of my life. Anything could happen. It always has.

The next day a profusely apologetic Helmut Newton rings to explain. A film producer friend has contacted him to discuss a television project, and he can't possibly let me make the journey until he's discussed this one first. He'll call me.

I unpack, feeling physically sick, and throw the Newton paperwork across the room.

He rings forty-eight hours later. 'All clear, come out whenever you can!' I wait ten days.

The night before the flight, Barney presents me with a cuddly koala which unzips to reveal a bottle of vintage Bollinger 'to bring you good luck'. Touched by his kindness, I'm suddenly hit by an overwhelming sadness that I have no family left to share this excitement with.

'Sometimes I feel as if I've just landed from Mars,' I whisper, blinking back tears.

To Barney's eternal credit, he avoids the 'Poor you, it must be so painful, all your family dead, but you know I love you' routine.

Slowly turning to me, his kind eyes locking into mine, he says: 'Landed from Mars? You certainly did. And a most dignified landing it was too. Now you have another opportunity to make a successful entry into an impenetrable world. Go for it, Vic. I know you can do it.'

14

LIVENED IN LOS ANGELES

'The road to success is always under construction'

Arnold Palmer

As the taxi slides eastwards on Sunset the lushness of West Hollywood slowly evaporates into the sleazy scrub of old Hollywood with its forlorn sex shops, disparate gangs and anxious hookers eyeing up every passing car. Turning into the shabby forecourt of this once splendid but now dilapidated hotel, it's brutally obvious that it's long had its day.

How stupid of me to choose downtown simply because I've never stayed here before. On two previous modelling assignments both the assigned hotels were predictably and safely tucked behind Rodeo Drive. But curious to see other parts of Los Angeles, I quickly agreed when a Melbourne travel agent suggested the Ambassador Hotel.

Lying in bed in my seedy room with its dog-eared furniture and gurgling pipes, I wonder what that constant loud knocking is. Opportunity perhaps, or the tragic haunted echo of Robert Kennedy's assassination here nine years ago, which took place in the hotel's main kitchen after his brief victory speech in the Embassy ballroom.

I try to clear my head and focus on two vital points for tomorrow's meeting with Helmut Newton:

1) Do not appear lacking in judgement, knowledge or experience.

2) Never be recognised as the model he discovered in Bond Street.

The tamed hair, crow's feet and boring suit should do it, but it's not an easy look to pull off for a jeans and T-shirt gal. Drawing the tatty window blinds at bedtime, I notice a middle-aged man gazing up into my seventh-floor room. Sorry mate, it's definitely curtains for you – and for me too if Helmut twigs. Sleep does not come easily. Our past, last encounter leaps into focus, as clear as day . . .

Based in Paris in 1970, Helmut and I both needed to make our way to London for the booking with British *Vogue*; his flight is booked for the morning of the shoot, mine departing the evening before. But the latter is grounded by severe weather conditions and the next morning's flights are all fully booked. I ring Helmut from the airport. He is his usual charming self.

'How dare you do this to me! This is an important shoot. I don't care how you get to London, *but just get there*! And never let me down like this again!' He hangs up.

Seriously thrown, I stand next to a small gaggle of English businessmen who also have crucial London assignments. They suggest we join forces and travel by train to Calais and cross by ferry to Dover, so we dash to the Gare du Nord and leap on the last locomotive leaving for the coast, our crisis confirming instant camaraderie for its no-more-stranded souls. But when our sturdy ferry growls into motion and edges its way from the quay not one of us can imagine the danger in store. As we head towards the open sea the solid tank begins to creak and croak as it bashes and batters its way through the angry ocean and our faces take on horror-film gleams as we rip open our duty-free booze and consume every drop we can lay our hands on. If we're going down, we're going down giggling, or at the very least, gurgling.

Through a veil of early morning mist we finally spy the British coastline. Exhausted and bedraggled, I have barely enough time to catch the departing train to London and have a warm-up shower at home, before I hail a cab to Hanover Square and take the lift to *Vogue*'s top-floor studio.

'You're ten minutes late and you look like shit!' shouts Helmut, as I walk into the dressing room. I watch his pulsating neck sink slowly back into his ebony polo neck.

'I told you this was an important shoot! Look, I've invented *this machine*! Look! Look at it! It allows you to photograph yourself and I've persuaded *Vogue* to let me do this. And I chose *you* for the job!'

I stare at the contraption next to him which is hooked up to a motor-drive camera. The machine has a tilting mechanism that I can adjust, a mirror next to the camera with which I can check my pose and a strobe light connected to the magic box. Before each exposure a bell will ring and a warning light blinks.

'But why?' I ask.

'I designed it to keep the model on her toes and to keep her excited.'

Just my effing luck.

'The idea came to me because it makes me so mad how new young fashion photographers live with their favourite model and won't allow others to use her.' He lowers his voice. 'Magazines encourage this situation as it cuts down on hotel expenses when they go on location. But the models are always better at their job than their mechanical boyfriends. It shows in the pictures.'

'Yeah, right.' My head is pounding

'Okay, so it's up to you to control the whole sitting. *You* will decide when to stop. The entire responsibility is with *you*. The lighting has been set up and a cross marked on the floor where you must stand. You are totally alone in the studio and you can only call an assistant to change the film. *You completely control the sitting.*' He grins like a manic school boy. 'I do admit that by the end of the day you will be worn out – the responsibility will be too much for you!'

Bloody hell! This is a nightmare.

I give it my best shot for hours. Newton badgers me to continue. But I can't. Something inside me explodes. I can't stop it.

'*Oh fuck off, Helmut, I am NOT a brainless doll! Do you have any idea what I went through to get here? That's it from me!*'

Strangely, he appears to enjoy my outburst. It's as though an inert prop has suddenly come alive, forcing human emotion to burst through its seams. He tries to book me for a job two weeks later in Paris, but I notify my French and British model agents that I simply can't ever work with him again.

The sun is blazing, not a human in sight, as my taxi makes its customary way along Sunset Boulevard to the Chateau Marmont, where Helmut and his wife June spend the European winter months. You drive everywhere here. I smile as I remember a friend telling me that 'walking in L.A. implies simplicity of purpose'. Only stark rows of exhaust-fumed-out palm trees line the road until West Hollywood becomes glitzily familiar and the tall white castle peeps into view at the foot of the lush Hollywood Hills.

But the Chateau now looks like a tired shadow of its former semi-sumptuous self. Built as apartments before becoming a hotel, it once again has suites with kitchens and living rooms, and has acquired around nine cottages next door. Yet it's the hotel's glamorous yet tragic past, the corridors ever haunted by dead stars and has-beens, that undoubtedly makes it irresistibly appealing to Helmut Newton.

The male receptionist in the gothic-arched entrance informs the Newton apartment of my arrival as I wait on a shabby upholstered chair gazing at the once grand piano in the far corner. No action from the bar next door, no dining room whatsoever, and not the remotest sign of room service.

With a none-too-convincing swagger and a tightly held briefcase, I make my way along a scary external terrace to Helmut Newton's suite. The astounding sight of the entire city stretched out beneath me does nothing to distract my pounding heart.

Helmut flings open the door, looking not a day older than at our last meeting. He must be, what, around sixty now and is wearing a navy sweat-shirt tucked into white waist-high chinos. A pair of round glasses, pushed back on his forehead, peep out from under an attractive still thick head of hair.

'My dear, you look *divine*,' he bellows in perfectly enunciated English with a still definable German accent. I'm flattered until I later realise that this is his standard greeting to every female he meets. But thankfully he doesn't appear to recognise the 'fuck off' culprit.

June has twinkly eyes, a neat dark bob with fringe, deep crimson nails and a reassuring Melbourne accent which instantly puts me at ease. She scoots off to make coffee in the kitchenette and he ushers me through to a living room with queasy saffron walls and a smoke-grey carpet.

Helmut gets straight down to business. He talks affectionately about Australia and of proudly retaining his Oz citizenship. Reminiscing comes easily: 'They were funny times . . .' of his studio in Melbourne, meeting 'Junie', leaving Australia in 1957 and triumphantly driving into London in their white Porsche with red leather seats when British *Vogue* offered him a job, how he broke his contract when he found the Brits 'too stuck up', and became an immediate hit in French *Vogue*, and how commissions streamed in from both sides of the Atlantic.

Two hours later and 'Helmie' and 'Junie' are still going strong on memories. It's obvious they have a very snug relationship punctuated by low-voltage bickering. The only time his affable whine booms with indignation is when I ask June why she calls herself Alice Springs for work. He jumps in, his voice rising sharply: 'When June started work as a photographer, I couldn't risk her coming a cropper – that would have been too embarrassing. So we put a pin in a map of Australia and wherever it landed, that would be it.'

Lucky it wasn't Moonie Ponds, I think, but quickly change the subject. I ask which of his two homes he prefers, Hollywood or Monaco, where they'll return in summer. 'Well, L.A. is superficial, but then *I'm* superficial. And Monte Carlo, well, it's terrific how much better life is when you don't pay any tax. But I never go out when I'm there. June does. It was hard at first, a cold place, a bit like a living museum. But I did a strong exhibition and now I'm accepted – even friendly with the Grimaldis. Caroline is always saying, "Call me Caroline", but I just can't do it. The true answer to your question is that home is wherever Junie is.'

Helmie and Junie invite me to dinner that evening at Ma Maison; their lawyer Alan will also be there to grill me. Round one has been okay but it's not over yet. The elegant see-and-be-seen restaurant is bustling with activity and lively conversation when I spot Helmut at the bar. 'Make room for Victoria,' he says graciously. Then he does a double take.

'You know, I'm sure we've met before.'

'Oh, I look a bit like lots of people,' I say, trying to sound casual.

'No, there's something about you I recognise' he says.

'I'm often told that, Helmut. Tall blondes do look pretty similar. Would you like a drink?'

June's sturdy frame looks striking in a white jacket, strong jewellery and a V-necked black shirt and Helmut has thrown a sports jacket over his white pants. Alan is in serious business attire. We make our way to the table for four and when various friends approach our hosts for chats, Alan grills me on why I want to produce the film. I waffle through until he nods.

June and I bond further by discussing Clive James's latest book, which takes a tongue-in-cheek look at literary London from an Oz perspective. Helmut smiles approvingly, leans forward and says, 'Autumn is a good time for me to come to Melbourne, I don't want to be there when it's hot and I need to travel first class.' It's all going swimmingly until he begins to tell an amusing story of how June 'blew a show in Paris by telling everyone to fuck off' at which point Alan groans and suggests that June is becoming like Gala, Dalí's wife.

This offends her greatly and the mood changes; she stops being twinkly and fun, and her coiffured hair begins to sweep over her face. Slightly the worse for wear, she starts to get stroppy about Helmut's work. 'Avedon and Penn take pictures for themselves, but Helmut does it to shock people . . . his eye is cold and distant . . .' I detect a slight element of professional jealousy. Helmut may be pretty tyrannical, but June gives as good as she gets.

Alan is coolly dismissed and Helmut offers to drop me at my hotel, moderately shocked when I tell him which one. June flops in the back of the car and keeps up a non-stop blistering critique of Helmut's work. He catches my eye, shrugs and changes gear. 'I had a very cruel mother,' he says.

'Maybe that's why I married June.' With a gentle smile that precludes further immediate discussion on the subject, he gives me a hand out of the lofty vehicle and says, 'Always remember this, Victoria. Nobody has it perfect.'

We arrange to meet the following day near the Beverly Wilshire Hotel, at a gallery where his latest exhibition is showing. Back in my grubby hotel room, I plan an early morning visit to Disneyland in Anaheim to keep me surreally occupied and suppress my pre-meeting nerves.

Arriving before Helmut at the gallery allows me time to absorb the images, which all have a mysterious ingredient, a kind of haunting unease and uncertainty that somehow reflects in his personality. Life is never real in his pictures, never what it seems to be; it's enhanced, hyped, given an artificial visual buzz. His work is never spontaneous, as I can personally verify! It's choreographed with a Teutonic intensity.

Helmut's models are placed as an afterthought to complete the visual jigsaw, to add some spice to his landscape. They're projected as cold, lonely creatures only superficially swathed in glamour and it's not too surprising that he frequently upsets new feminists. Dare I broach this with him when he turns up? Well, why not?

'Are the constant accusations of misogyny well founded?' I venture. He hugely enjoys this. 'Well my models rarely understand what I'm doing in my pictures, and I don't bother to explain anything to them because they don't have much intelligence,' he says grinning sheepishly. I suppress my immediate desire to say 'fuck off' again.

A quick, nervous trip to Disneyland before meeting Helmut

He's difficult to read – a private, complicated man who constantly provokes confusion. 'Always judge a man by his character, not his personality,' advised my mother many years ago, but with Helmut it's hard to tell which is which, to separate the two. Whichever it is, I do like him. I shouldn't, but I do.

Especially when he admits his tyranny comes from personal insecurity which, he assures me, is mellowing with age.

At a late lunch in the buzzing Rodeo Drive restaurant, he certainly proves to be a talented raconteur with a wicked sense of humour. I can't remember laughing like this for years. To capture his energy and style I suggest we use the oral history technique for the documentary which means recording him at length using the initial taping session as a foundation – a first-person voiceover.

'From these tapes we'll finalise a shooting draft of the script, ensuring a combination of spontaneity with strong stylised visuals and the best of your photographs, some treated by modern video graphic techniques to generate visual impact. We'll cover you in some of your places of influence, including Paris and Monte Carlo. And put the record straight about your attitude to women!'

Helmut nods enthusiastically.

Blimey, this has been quite a journey. Here I am, sitting opposite a man directly responsible for launching my two careers . . . if only he knew.

At that moment, as we're tucking into our strawberry tarts with the last of our Napa Valley Cabernet, a tall, blonde model rushes over to our table. She's wearing a ridiculous hat – a rust straw bucket trimmed with a horsehair bow.

'Hi Helmut, I just *love* the photos you took of me in last month's *Vogue*.'

'You looked divine, my dear. My dear, you look *divine*!' He repeats the now-familiar two-liner while struggling to his feet. After a minute of inane chatter, the ingénue model leaves and Helmut flops back into his chair and mumbles, 'The next time I run into her, make sure I'm driving.'

'Oh come on, Helmut, she simply wanted to thank you.'

'Well, I prefer defiant types for work, and also girls who look like women – tall with broad shoulders and built like truck drivers. But I detest it when they're stupid. I mean, can you imagine what it must be like to be a model?'

'Well yeah, sometimes I can.'

'They don't know – and they don't want to know – anything about real life, just about shallow, meaningless glamour for its own sake . . . make-up and shoes . . .' He watches the model exit the restaurant: '. . . and stupid hats!'

'That's not fair,' I counter. 'And anyway, life can change completely at the drop of a hat.'

'Come on, Victoria. Has your life ever changed with the drop of a hat?'

'It has – always and radically – in the blink of an eye. But then, what could be worse than getting to the end of your life and realising you hadn't really lived it?'

'Ha Ha Ha! No, really, what were you doing before your television production job?'

'Oh, absolutely nothing that would remotely interest you, Helmut. Now where were we?'

Helmut never makes it back to Australia to appear in my programme. A triple heart bypass operation means he can't fly for several months, and when he's well enough, he wants me to plan an exhibition of his work at Sydney's National Portrait Gallery to coincide with his stay. But the female director of the gallery refuses my request because she finds his photographs mysogynistic . . . a certain irony here, but Helmut never does discover that I was the model who first reproached him for this two decades ago.

Fade to black and roll credits. But not quite yet . . .

The last photographer to capture Savador Dalí alive was Helmut Newton. They were friends and it is perhaps appropriate that Helmut died on the same day – 23 January – fifteen years later. He was exiting the Chateau Marmont driveway behind the wheel of his silver Cadillac when it unexpectedly accelerated, shot across the road and smashed into the opposite wall, clipping a Press Association photographer on the way.

Helmut is buried next to his friend Marlene Dietrich in a Berlin cemetery and I often imagine him smiling wryly that the manner of his death mirrored his work sublimely – a cruel outcome cutting through the elegance of a decadently glamorous setting and going, as always, that bit too far.

Today, as I write the final words of this chapter, I can't help noticing that the date is a decade to the day since Helmut's death – twenty-five years to the day after Dalí's. A strange coincidence. But no more than that.

Life isn't measured by the years or number of breaths we take – only by the moments that Take Our Breath Away.

Cue music – that one by Berlin will do nicely.

15

WIRED IN SYDNEY

'You can't stop the waves but you can learn to surf'

Jon Kabat-Zinn

It's now the Eighties and an avant-garde glossy magazine *POL* hits the Aussie media arena, and I'm its Melbourne editor. But Barney's advertising career demands a move to Sydney. And *this*, I soon discover, is where the real action is – due to a legendary hotel called the Sebel Townhouse, not a remotely lush building but the coolest place on earth. Any international high-profiler wanting to stay extra low but mega-cool knows to inhabit this small, insignificant-looking hotel near Kings Cross. It's more private club than hotel. Once you've checked in you never want to leave.

Staying here produces a rigorous desire in me to live life at full throttle, having recently discovered a drug I actually enjoy – and the Sebel is full of it – around the pool, in the bar, in the carpets, everywhere. Never seduced by the effects of Sixties drugs, of discovering my inner self to reveal hidden mystical truths, I find that I *am* interested in that icy rush of clarity and optimism from a good line of cocaine. One line of pure coke can get you high all night, and I need a break. I want to grab this life and know the iridescent highs and thrills of those no-brakes nights on the tiles. I feel safe here in Oz, invisible, twelve thousand miles from home. I want to let rip, and to know that it's doing me good.

'Hi, my name's Barney and I'm legless too'

When a friend from our Dalí days in Spain arrives in Sydney, Barney and I make a post-prandial zip to his harbourside hotel suite for a riotous catch-up, where we dance to remember and dance to forget. But our pal gets over-excited, grabs a fire hose from the hotel's top corridor and sets off the fire alarm. It's midnight, the police are promptly summoned, we're all arrested, released after making statements, and turn up at the Sebel Townhouse in a police paddy wagon.

Whoa – who on earth is this bloke wearing a lightbulb?

Michael, the manager, is standing outside looking intense.

'Oh God,' I whisper to Barney, 'here comes the ban for life.'

'I only have one thing to say to you guys,' says Michael sternly. 'As you are the first guests to ever arrive at my hotel in a police vehicle, I'd like to offer you a complimentary bottle of Dom Perignon and the entire penthouse suite is yours for the night!'

The problem with coke is that one line is never enough. Within ten minutes it feels like time for another. But the reality is that another doesn't get you any higher, and the comedown can be so intense you want to scratch off your skin.

It's getting too outrageous for me. No safety pocket. I want to feel great, but within reason. The 'within reason' is what counts.

I'm done with the fake glam pull of this reckless lifestyle. This is clearly not a sustainable life-choice for me. But I've learned a lot.

There's a concept forming in my head for a candid television series about the absurdity of fame, having observed in close-up that the longer and brighter your flame the further removed from reality you become. I've known those who can't live with it, those who can't live without it, the uncontrolled egos, the self-destructive urges, the meteoric rises followed by tragic demises. I want to tell the inside story, that the bonuses don't inevitably outweigh the drawbacks, that you trade your right for privacy for the hollow rewards of fame.

The timing is right: this is shaping up to be the last era before the cold hand of the PR industry begins to shut down access to people in the public eye for ever – before fame becomes a goal in itself rather than the by-product of artistic endeavour.

My best friend Rhonda, married to Fred Schepisi, currently Australia's foremost feature film director, helps, through Fred's contacts, to raise development funds. Another pal introduces me to a television producer prepared to support the project. Trevor Lucas is tall, angular, with flaming red hair, and appears to know more about the stark reality of fame than anyone I've met who lives permanently in Oz. 'Yeah,' says my intro pal, 'that's because he was in a band called Fairport Convention and married its lead singer Sandy Denny who was so incredibly talented but very tortured.'

Virtually unknown here in his homeland, even after Fairport's soar to folk-rock fame elsewhere, Trevor is mild-mannered, keeps to himself, and went through a tough

312

time being Sandy's co-band member, producer and eventual husband, especially towards the end of her life.

I learn from him that Robert Plant thought Sandy Denny the greatest British female singer ever, extolling her sad, intensely emotional voice; the only guest vocalist ever to record with Led Zeppelin. But she never made the super-big time. Her 'pure as a bell' voice was extraordinarily beautiful but she was plagued by insecurities, suppressed with drink and cocaine. The demons kicked in, her life became increasingly chaotic and she died at thirty-one of a brain haemorrhage after falling downstairs at her parents' home. Trevor returned to Australia with their one-year old daughter, began to produce albums and film scores and told me that from the moment they worked together, he knew and accepted that Sandy was always going to overshadow him; they had a tempestuous relationship, not unlike Sylvia Plath and Ted Hughes, but he adored her.

Trevor patiently shows me the ropes and spurs me on to ring ex-boyfriend Bill at WEA Records in London to run *The Price of Fame* concept by him. Almost before I know it, Paul Gambaccini is lined up as narrator/interviewer and we're off to Hollywood to interview fifteen celebrities at the height of their fame including David Cassidy, Sylvester Stallone, John Cleese, Ali MacGraw, Victoria Principal, Marianne Faithfull, Richard Harris, Richard Carpenter, Sonny Bono and Alan Parker.

The resulting footage is jaw-dropping thanks to Paul's exceptional interviewing skills and the utter raw honesty of our celebrity interviewees. A one-hour pilot is produced which is destined to be 'extraordinary viewing'.

But it isn't to be. Every Australian television network turns it down because what viewers want to see, they declare, is '*happy* celebrities'. But this is not a soap opera – it's a compelling factual programme with a timely theme, a strong important message, and it will make an unforgettable series.

But it's way ahead of its time.

The party is over in Oz for me.

And so is my second marriage.

Barney and I, having soared for years, don't crash-land. We just find ourselves at opposite ends of his magic carpet. We're still close friends and had some amazing times together, but didn't last the long-marriage distance. His 'bit of a drink problem' had become a full-scale concern. But while we two were in his alcoholic haze of denial, his advertising agency always knew of 'a very good place to dry out and repair . . . don't worry . . . we'll pick up the bill' whenever the pressure of a new ad campaign became too much. It was the accepted norm in advertising during this era that a drink problem was just a temporary glitch.

Those *Mad Men* storylines aren't that wide of the mark. Believe me!

Barney was dried out thirteen times before I realised this was another battle I couldn't win. My thoughts of starting a family during this time were tempered by the stark reality of suicides on my side and ongoing uncertainties on his. I didn't want to create another troubled life, knowing the most important thing of all is to be wanted and cared for by reasonably stable parents. And reproduction didn't feel primal or urgent.

It's long been medically recognised that people addicted to various substances frequently suffer from anxiety, depression and other mood disorders. But Barney was troubled by anxiety long before he became 'an alcoholic' and he used alcohol as a tranquilliser. 'If you rid me of anxiety, I'll stop drinking,' he told countless doctors. To which the standard refrain was always, 'You're anxious because you drink! Stop drinking and your anxiety will subside.'

After we divorced, Barney lived and worked in Amsterdam, having more wild times before he embraced Buddhism and found peace at last.

So, *Mad Men* scriptwriters, where exactly did you find your inspiration for Don Draper?

16

SHOPPED

'There are two kinds of fool. The ones who never climb
Mount Fujiyama. And the ones who do it twice'

Japanese proverb

What fate beholds me now, as I approach my forties? Am
I all set to totter into middle age in four-inch heels with a
twinkling designer bag and giggly toy boy on my arm? Not
a chance. What I crave now is peace – a life lived quietly, no
mess, no trouble, no agonising. Time to return to my house
in London and live alone.

I've never steered off course in my belief that the key to
freedom is economic independence – to always earn enough
to give myself an escape route if things go wrong – but it was
easier in the modelling days when big bucks came relatively
fast. Here in London the television industry is pulsating with
ambitious graduates queuing up to be part of the 'meedya' –
and this non-academic former model just back from Oz simply
won't cut it without a PhD in Advanced Dramatic Intentions.

I pass my local butcher's shop, just off Chelsea's King's Road, and wave to owner Dave – but avoid going in because I only ever see macabre parts of animals, not mouth-watering chop and steak presentations. It's been like that ever since my grandmother explained that the cows lining up outside our local abattoir were about to be killed so that we could have a delicious Sunday joint. I hadn't made the connection before and was horrified.

I can't kill anything, not even the tiniest ant. Yeah, it's an extreme perspective, but viewing close-up premature death so often has left a legacy of caring about life in all its forms. I want everyone and everything to have a good, long innings and I have a passionate belief that lives have equal value anywhere on the planet. Everything has as much right to be here as we do. I even see cut flowers as dying the second they enter a vase, so if you ever feel inclined, please be sure to make it a pot-plant instead.

Dave the butcher strides to the door of his shop. 'I'm selling up, love. Do you want to buy it cheap?' He wipes a bead of sweat, or is it a tear, from his cheek and tells me a new local supermarket has sent him under.

I decide to buy the place. My 'save everything and everyone' mantra has just saved my butcher! But the butchery itself has to go – I morph it into the delicious deli I always hoped to discover in London but never found, and it doesn't take long to produce mouth-watering goodies to lure in the neighbourhood. Not yet the over-the-top era of 'physalis salads with pomegranate molasses and edible rose petals', 'organic mangosteens harvested by moonlight', 'scallops cooked over juniper branches' and 'potatoes roasted in decomposed autumn leaves' but you get the picture – healthy, visually seductive, not too clever, let the flavours do the talking. The deli doors fly open, the locals pour in, and the press are most intrigued. 'Can you believe it – a former model selling food?'

Inventive drool fodder becomes the new rock'n'roll! Who'd have thought it? Certainly not my amazing mum who rarely made food for fun, always finding something more exciting to do than chop and whip and peel and snip. I often imagine her surprised, amused reaction followed by 'Well done, darling!' as she beams down on me from heaven.

I've simply found that gap in the marketplace, giving locals what doesn't already exist, and improving what does. My long-held belief in low-human-intervention food recognisable from its origins hits the mark. Not for me those supermarket meals with components made in up to sixty different countries purporting to be 'home-made' or the dipping of cut fresh fruit in antioxidant and chlorinated water to prevent browning and keep them looking 'fresh' for ever. My crusade is to sell healthy great value nosh without misleading food labels, harsh packaging, chemicals and dirty tricks. We're the first in England in 1992 to use revolutionary eco-friendly packaging – biodegradable limestone cutlery, palm-husk containers and acid-free paper bags. No plastic.

I work fourteen-hour days but it doesn't feel like work. A daily 5.30 A.M. delivery from Covent Garden ensures we have just-picked British fruit and vegetables. No cellophane-packed sweetcorn from Senegal, tired radishes from

Morocco, sour grapes from South Africa or spring onions from Egypt. Not for this deli. We grow herbs in our garden behind the kitchen and stock honey from a pal who keeps local bees.

Adding a café soon after opening while playing gobble funk sounds, the young staff and I whizz and bustle around the tiny kitchen concocting all manner of healthy food. We give each other spicy names. There's Cumin (good at welcoming newcomers), Nutmeg (nicely bonkers) and Ginger (the hair). I'm Cardamom, and always the one who has to spice up Hugh Grant's day because the others freeze in awe whenever he enters, and explode in ecstasy after he leaves.

My other favourite customer is fashion snapper Bob Carlos Clarke, sometimes labelled 'Britain's answer to Helmut Newton'. His studio's nearby, and he often appears with Beano on his shoulder, an Amazon parrot he rescued from a Brixton pet shop in 1970. We all love Bob and Beano, but it's Bob who always craves our undivided attention – and gets it. He's blessed with that dry wit and beguiling charm peculiar to the Irish. He has a thing about exotic animals, and when I mention my childhood pet alligator he tells me how he once convinced Jerry Hall to straddle a ten-foot alligator.

Over time I realise that Bob is more complex and extreme than he initially appears. I recognise the signs. His charismatic, soulful persona slowly changes over the next few months and he becomes a very loose cannon. Not long after entering the Priory rehab centre in Barnes, south-west London, he checks himself out, walks the short distance to a railway track and jumps in front of a train. My shop is in mourning for weeks. It's a shocking outcome for such a deeply loved customer. Beano the parrot is buried next to his owner in Brompton Cemetery, just up the road from the shop. He outlived Bob by ten years, dying at sixty-five. I think of them each time I pass there. God bless, dear Bob and Beano.

I wouldn't mind having a nice man around the place now. I don't fear time spent alone but could be up for a guy who's cheerful and not sexist. It doesn't take long for a customer to sniff out my cocooned fragility although his persistence makes me initially wary of his superficial charm. He stands too close and showers me with compliments. Against my better judgement I quickly succumb to his determined campaign. One day he turns up on the doorstep of my house nearby, says his wife has thrown him out and he has nowhere else to go. My insane rescuing complex kicks in again.

What's *wrong* with me! This permanent fixing . . . this trying to make others feel better . . . this overwhelming sense of responsibility for men – and lack of sympathy for myself. If people I like are in pain, how can I dare to feel pleasure?

He quickly moves in, and it takes no time to discover we have absolutely nothing in common. He's not a reader, we have no shared interests, and his taste in music is dire. After jacking in his part-time job, he offers to do the shop's accounts.

I'm about to be conned.

Big time.

With a profoundly cunning campaign he begins to isolate

me from my friends and the cruelty begins. His biting words stay in my head long after the physical assaults heal.

I'm too ashamed to confide in anyone. How the hell could I have let this happen? How can a strong, assertive woman have allowed herself to be set up like this? I thought I was wising up.

I've placed myself entirely with someone who I met only months ago and barely know. He doesn't want friendship, he wants ownership.

I begin to find it normal to live in a near-permanent state of emergency, always sensing something terrible is about to happen – poised and ready like an animal. Smiling convincingly with customers in my shop gets harder. The social interactions become surreal.

'Good morning, Mrs Smith, and how are you today?'

'God, I'm so stressed.'

'Oh, poor you, what's wrong?'

'It's this weather. It's really getting me down and now I think I've got a cold coming on.'

Try living with a mad, controlling fucker who beats you up.

'I'm seeing my doctor later to see if he can give me anything to cheer me up.'

'Ah, yes. I'm sure he'll prescribe something to help.'

Yes indeed. What would we do without the stress-management industry playing on the fear that we can't cope with life's demands without their addictive products – based on the promise that 'the sufferer' has a chemical imbalance of not having enough serotonin in his or her brain.

I've always thought and found that serotonin, that

feelgood factor, is brought about by light, exercise, friends and a healthy diet. Surely doctors would do more good by focusing on exactly what's causing a patient's depression rather than adding more medication to the bathroom shelf.

But it's not an easy one. Depression is serious and very real. Feeling alone and scared of appearing in any way mad can strike anyone, however highly educated, intelligent and thoughtful. Many of the greatest, toughest people of all time have suffered from depression. Words help. Comfort helps. Support helps. The act of talking is in itself a therapy. Understanding your thoughts so that you don't become them.

Since my father and brother took their own lives I've learnt that no tests or scans can diagnose or measure the progress of depression. So much depends on the skill and judgement of your doctor. Apart from diagnosis difficulties there's the hurdle of determining whether an antidepressant drug will help or hinder, and fears about addiction and side-effects. The confusion over the difference between tranquillisers, which are addictive, and antidepressants, which aren't but can have other complictions, contributes to the reluctance that many patients have when urged by their doctor to start medication.

I've seen that depressive illness is a collection of different disorders of mood and feeling, rather than a single entity. Some patients benefit from cognitive therapy with a skilled psychologist, in addition to medication, and a small group will need treatment for life – just as a diabetic needs insulin. The bottom line is that a supportive GP or psychiatrist can dispel medication myths, can strengthen confidence and treat them with wisdom to feel safe, supported, and up to facing their problems. Someone who's so well trained that they're prepared to break the rules.

Personal responsibility and courage – not blaming others for the way you feel – always helps. Life can be a bitch, but is it any worse than it was for past generations who've coped without medication? Grief, despair, heartbreak – these are all perennial themes, but the mind and body have a unique ability to deal with life's ups and downs. But who am I to talk? I can't even get my own life in order. When am I going to stop feeling everyone's pain – and face my own?

When I beg my abuser to leave on numerous occasions, he informs me that he's now legally entitled to half my house. He philanders with hookers, stays out all night, leaves threatening notes with kitchen knives – and when I discover he's stolen £25,000 from the business he attacks me with such force that I'm unable to show my face in the shop.

How can this be happening to me? I thought I'd seen it all.

A friend persuades me to inform the law; I drag myself to my local police station. They are superb. I feel listened to, respected and safe. Two days later, a Saturday morning, I get a call from them to attend the Royal Courts of Justice. A barrister friend accompanies me. I can barely look at the perpetrator, but I give my evidence, and he's jailed.

After his release he continues to leave his imprint on my life, bombarding me with malicious phone calls, stalking me around London, and attacking the premises. The police do their best, but he plays a clever game of escaping evidence. It doesn't stop until he dies from alcohol abuse two years later.

It's time to dig deep, to take stock. I have even lost my house. The bank has taken it to pay off debts incurred by him. My home has gone, the sanctuary I bought and made my own, with money I had earned. My proudest symbol of hard work and success, my lifeline, my anchor.

Gone.

For ever.

I thought I was wising up. But how the hell do you tell when someone has a genuine mental disorder – with a medical label for their extreme behaviour – or is simply a nasty piece of work? Where do the labels start and stop?

It will take another two decades before the law fully recognises that domestic violence is not just about physical violence. It's also about coercive control, patterned behaviour which is similar in almost every case, carried out to isolate a person from sources of support and deprive them of the means needed for independence. This includes controlling money, isolating a victim from family and friends, monitoring activities, threatening to harm and repeatedly putting the victim down. At last it's been recognised that domestic violence is not solely direct physical violence but can include psychological abuse and other forms of controlling coercive behaviour – the vile abuse that breaks spirits and robs victims of their sense of identity. That demands ownership not friendship.

Defining extreme behaviour is difficult, but I think that viewing alcoholism or heroin addiction as a disease doesn't really help the sufferer. Surely drink and drug abuse is an attempt to blot out distress; you choose to do it. It's an active decision; a botched attempt to deal with difficult personal problems. But isn't recovering all about taking responsibilty and realising you are the architect of your own misery? Addiction *is* devastating. It's destroyed many of the decent, brilliant, lovable people I've ever known. But I don't think we should pretend that it is something it's not.

Fifty years ago we were told that mental illness was caused by chemical imbalance, that we simply needed to readjust neuro-transmitters such as serotonin and dopamine with pills. But most of the scientific research into the benefits of pharmaceuticals was done by companies selling the drugs. It still is. But still no research to prove its claims!

And then there's suicide. I only have to hear the word 'suicide' in any context to scream silently. It is now the leading cause of death among men under the age of thirty-five. A million people a year kill themselves. Between ten and twenty million people a year try to.

I know the shock and pain of an unexplained suicide never leaves you. Here they are, living life, with a promising future . . . then one day . . . no note, not a clue left behind, just a gaping hole in the lives of all who knew them and devastation for those left behind who loved them. It's an unending absence. The only question is *why?*

Of all the people I've known who died by their own hand, only one left a note. When he died aged thirty-two in 1973, Michael Cooper, Keith Richards' close friend and the photographer on my 1967 *Nova* shoot, left this note addressed to his son Adam:

Don't believe the court when they say that I killed myself when the balance of my mind was disturbed. I just live in a disturbed world, and as the old poem says, 'I hear the sound of a different drum.' I come from what our generation will call the 'Half and Halfs'! A generation that made few changes, but had to experience too many other kinds of changes they had no control over, so some of us were bound to fall by the wayside. I'm one of those.

Michael's photography was known for its 100% total honesty. And so was his tragic, untimely death.

The act of suicide leaves those of us left behind living permanently in the moment, expecting anything to happen; what's the point of pension plans, insurance policies and all that stuff? The manner of my father and brother's deaths made me cut my life to the bone, to strip away all the padding.

I now know that suicide is three times more common among children whose parents died that way, but not as a direct result of genes – it's the manner of the death that plants the idea of repeating it, following the example of loved ones. There is strong evidence that suicide is contagious, that they 'give you permission' if they took their own life.

I've never seriously considered it. I am so grateful to be alive, and I love life. But things were different for my brother Nick. He was the one who found my father dying under a car, in a situation that could only have been a suicide. Prior to that, Nick had all the cheeky assurance and vivid bounce and gusto of a Fifties youth, but his stoicism and strength melted away and six months later he had also attempted suicide. The brilliant multi-scholarship university art student became a troubled young man in a psychiatric ward.

But then perhaps my brother *was* mentally ill. Mental health is so fiendishly difficult to define because minds go wrong in different ways, the pain is felt in different ways, to different degrees, and provokes different responses.

Perhaps he was schizophrenic; the average age onset is eighteen in men, which is around the time he first attempted to self-destruct. I used to think of schizophrenics as having wild, severely split personalities, but I know now that it's better described as being, to mental illness, what cancer is to physical ailments, and sufferers are far more likely to harm themselves than others. The suicide rate is high, but what causes schizophrenia? Some scientists believe there is no single cause, that it develops because it is genetically predisposed to do so; but genes alone are not responsible. Other forces, such as events in the life of the person at risk, determine its presence. And, indeed, a personal disaster – like the traumatic death of a relative – may bring on that onset.

Because of my personal experience with an abuser, I totally agree with eminent psychiatrist Hervey Cleckley who describes a psychopathic person (now called a sociopathic person) as 'outwardly, a perfect mimic of a normally functioning person'. They are seemingly sincere, intelligent, even charming in their external presentation, but internally do not have the ability to experience genuine emotion. The label 'psychopath', he says, has been wrongly embraced by popular culture because of movies such as *American Psycho* which suggests they are all serial killers and other violent criminals, irrespective of whether they qualify.

He's right. Would we all have rushed out to see *Chicken Pox'd*?

And Cleckley's clinical profile of the sixteen behavioural characteristics that make up the profile of a psychopath could apply to half the people I've met in my life!

Enough! My aim now is to wise up, to stop my immediate attraction to damaged souls who I always try to rescue from themselves. That's why I've created a guide that addresses the conflict between my heart and head. It may help you, too, or someone you know.

17

LESSONS IN LIFE

'Dear Past: Thank you for all the lessons. Dear Future: I'm ready'

- KNOW what you want. Choose a partner rather than allowing them to choose you. It's not about finding the right partner but avoiding the wrong one.
- Never ignore your gut feelings. Your intuition is the best guide you have. Does this person FEEL right for you?
- You may realise that what you deserve is better than you thought.
- If you're always 'helping' people, ask yourself if you do it to feel superior, thereby avoiding your own feelings of inadequacy.
- Realise the right person brings out the best in you. The wrong 'un brings out the absolute worst.
- Your childhood experiences make you choose certain partners in adult life. If you're unhappy with these choices, look back on your past to find out why.

- Learn to look at a partner's character rather than their personality.
- Be sure they're not looking for a mother or father figure.
- If they tell you they're a member of AA, make sure their focus is cars not bars.
- Don't choose a child if you really want a grown-up.
- Watch out if you see one of you as strong and the other as weak.
- Watch out if one of you always gets their own way.
- Make sure their support system is there for you as much as yours is there for them.
- Look very closely at the way they treat their family and friends, and how family and friends treat them.
- Never edit your thoughts, behaviour or habits to please them. Be honest to yourself.

IDENTIFYING NEGATIVE TRAITS . . .
- It won't work if you believe in your partner more than they believe in themselves.
- If you often feel sorry for your partner, always needing to comfort and encourage them, you're mistaking sympathy for love.
- Watch out if your partner makes it difficult for you to put across your point of view.
- Don't get involved with a drink or drug abuser. They've already found the love of their life. You'll never ever stand a chance of competing unless they seriously decide to stop.
- Never compromise your values and beliefs to avoid conflict.

- Don't stay with a partner long after you realise they're never going to get their act together. You're kidding yourself.
- Watch out if they're very similar to your last partner.
- If you always attract losers ask yourself whether you seek them to avoid commitment.
- Don't tolerate behaviour from your partner that you'd never put up with from a friend.
- Beware if you are constantly ambitious for them. You're living in hope not reality.
- You're not with the right person if you are unable to be yourself.
- Never say, 'If I just love them a bit more they'll change.' Their behaviour is never determined by how loving you are.

DANGER ZONE
- Watch out if you find yourself making excuses to your friends and family for your partner's problems.
- Watch out if disagreements make you feel scared or vulnerable.
- Watch out for the partner who doesn't like one or both of their parents.
- Beware if they never find solutions to their problems and are more comfortable feeling sorry for themselves than improving their life.
- Beware the 'charmers' who change once they've snared you. They'll charm and punish you systematically until they gain control.
- If they say 'Don't tie me down' they're not the one for you.

- Beware if their behaviour appears irrational or menacing after seemingly few alcoholic drinks or recreational drugs. They're either using more than you know about or have future addiction problems.
- Face the hard fact that no amount of your patience, understanding or love will make them stop if they have a drink or drug problem. Have enough love and respect for yourself to leave.
- Beware the one who heavily criticises their past partners. You may be the next one they blame.
- Watch out if they can't keep a job, have no savings, and say, 'What's yours is mine.'
- Stay clear of the one who says their partner doesn't understand them, they're not having sex, they're only staying for the children, they're leaving home soon.
- Watch out if you feel it's natural to be unhappy or bored with a long-term partner.
- Beware if your partner constantly labels you as selfish and greedy when you don't do what they want.
- Don't ever feel guilty about leaving a loser because you feel they won't be able to cope without you.
- Leave pronto if they ever excuse violent behaviour by saying, 'You provoked me!'

The fundamental essence of survival and self-respect is to be a realist, and to learn from the past when it comes to choices. Otherwise our guard goes down again and – thwack!

ALWAYS REMEMBER
- You can't change him/her into what you want them to be.
- You get what you believe you deserve.
- Never mistake drama and tension for true love.
- Never ignore a flaw from the start – it will only get worse.
- Never consider anyone who makes you remotely unhappy.
- Don't think you're in love when you're really in lust.
- The fewer the needs the greater the love.
- Do you like him/her as much as you love them?
- Are you intellectually attracted to them?
- The right one sees you as equal.
- The right one is honest and doesn't play games.
- The right one respects your feelings, your time, your belongings, your ambitions and your achievements.

18

RESOLUTION

'Love does not consist of gazing at each other but in
looking outward together in the same direction'

Antoine de Saint-Exupéry

The mid-Nineties, and I've wised up and set myself a new
standard of honesty. It's time to challenge fate and secure
some happiness. I'll surround myself with happy people
because happy people make things happen. They control
their moods, not the other way round. I'll stimulate the
happy part of my brain so no dark side gets a look-in. I'll
only see friends who make me laugh. I'll only go on dates
with upbeat men and be sure to keep an emotional chasm
between us until I know them.

This works a treat! Men like women who are fun, self-
contained and not too keen on them. Paradoxically it makes
me more of a challenge – my refusal to feel anything is
interpreted as cool, mysterious disdain. I go out with the
handsome son of a very senior vicar for a while. When

introduced to him, he turns to his son and asks, 'Are you sleeping with her? And if not, why not?'

I have a few dates with the screenwriter and author Jeremy Lloyd – Joanna Lumley's former husband – a lovely man, but not quite right for me. One day at lunch in Morton's he gives me a copy of his latest book and scribbles inside:

'To dearest Victoria, a heroine not in need of rescue.'

Proof perhaps that I'm finally on the road to rescuing myself rather than other people.

A friend invites me to her drinks party – lots of nice men there and one in particular who stands next to me as if he's known me for years. None of that 'Have you come far?', 'What do you do?' stuff. Side by side we covertly discuss the assembled throng as though both in MI6. I like his energy, his curiosity, that he segues from laughter and chatter to serious concern about subjects in a nanosecond. I love his sense of humour, his compassion, his worldly intelligence, his stunning good looks.

He takes my number. But never calls.

A year later I'm walking home when he pulls up alongside me on his bike.

'What took you so long?' I ask.

'I sensed you needed time.'

He was right. I did.

He never rode off.

That was twenty-four years ago. He ticked all the boxes. We shared an instant, complete connection that grew into love. Sometimes all we do is laugh. What about? I've no idea. Anything. Everything. We click, we fit, we complement each other perfectly. It just feels incredibly easy, not desperate and all-consuming.

Our first week together I asked a friend to check him out, to give me his thoughts – to make sure I'd got it right. Who better than my pragmatic Barnsley pal Michael Parkinson to judge a character in quick-fire close-up? Parky and I first met in Sydney when he was launching his Channel 10 television series there in the early Eighties. And when you meet someone from the same small Yorkshire mining town 12,000 miles away, you're best friends at the first 'Ay up'. He conducted the interview in my kitchen over cups of coffee.

'I like him. He's a good man.' That was enough for me. My heart was home.

What else makes my Mr Right? Well, he never flattens my spirit; he's a heart-lifter not a heart-sinker. He's not intimidated by my achievments and never tries to reduce me or wear me down. He has a touch that's tender, slow and provocative. He's not cynical about commitment, or my friends, or my desire to sometimes be alone. He cherishes his mother but doesn't want me to be her. He never asks, 'What are you thinking?' 'Where's my supper?' or 'How was it for you?' He's comfortable saying 'I love you'. He's a haven, a harbour from all the turbulence of the world. He makes me laugh even when I'm down. Especially if I'm down.

We pay a visit to Barnsley. I hadn't been back for years, the last visit way too painful on my own. But I feel strong enough now with Mr Right. There's no escaping it – this small, tough, northern town that deeply influenced my life, my character, my outlook, my determination to surivive.

I'd left it behind physically but never mentally. My beloved Barnsley hugely determined who I was, and am today.

Walking down the hill to my old family house, now completely dwarfed by the weeping willow planted by my father the year before he died, I stand and gaze, waiting for a breeze to whisper through the trees. I feel an electric shock pass through my body. I'd locked my story away for years and it all began here.

We pass my old grammar school, reincarnated as a sixth-form college since attended by Alex Turner to appease his teacher parents before forming the Arctic Monkeys. Its glorious playing fields – once surrounded by woods with hedgehogs, badgers and voles, where my brother and I watched bees sipping on lavender and scratched our bare arms on brambles – now long buried under identical rows of red-brick houses. Barnsley had not escaped the homogeneous housing and duplicated shopping malls; that all-abiding sameness that characterises contemporary life.

We drive past the proud Victorian building that housed the National Union of Mineworkers, where Arthur Scargill held court sitting on a purple throne. We look for the largest open market in England, created in 1249 by Royal Charter – its traders boasting they sold the freshest produce at the lowest margin prices in the north. But that had gone too. Ever since the District Council leader declared that all shoppers could catch meningitis from the open stalls!

Yet Barnsley still lays serious claim to two edible treasures of which it's always been proud – pork pies and rhubarb. Rhubarb is actually a strange vegetable that thinks it's a fruit – and one of the few things in life that is sweeter when forced. Kept in dark, warm temperatures, its shoots shoot upwards, creaking and cracking, searching for light and producing a particularly delicious flavour and tenderness. The vital gloom is always maintained and the crop is still picked at candlelight, though the special express trains from Barnsley station laid on every night to take the crop to London's Covent Garden are no more.

We have coffee in Pollyanna, the most unlikely shop in Barnsley, defying all convention by selling designer fashion since 1967 and since becoming one of the most successful independent shops outside London, stocking Issey Miyake, Commes des Garçons, Yohji Yamamoto, you name it. Not many people in the fashion business hail from Barnsley, but it does lay serious claim to one highly fashionable treasure. The most important and influential person in that world today has her roots in Barnsley. Behold . . . her name is Anna Wintour, the editor-in-chief of American *Vogue* since 1988.

Could the Devil who wears Prada *really* trace her heritage back to dear old Barnsley? Yes indeed. Anna's ancestors were from this fine region. The Revd Fitzgerald Thomas Wintour, born in 1830, is Anna's great-grandfather. He married in nearby Wakefield and became a church rector in a suburb of Barnsley for thirty-one years. He's buried here.

I've rarely worn Prada oversized sunglasses whatever the weather, or a pageboy haircut, but most certainly agree with Anna's pragmatic take on fashion – the first to truly democratise luxury by mixing low-end fashion items with more expensive pieces in her photo shoots. After initially becoming the editor of English *Vogue*, she told the London *Daily Telegraph* in 1986: 'I want the magazine to be pacy, sharp and sexy. I'm not interested in the super-rich or infinitely leisured. I want our readers to be energetic, executive women, with money of their own and a wide range of interests.' That's the spirit, lass!

Our like-minded great-grandfathers may have known each other. Mine was also a religious man, a strict evangelist after making his fortune with the sole right to work a French patent (a new technique for chemically scouring wool) which led to him manufacturing soap and oil. This allowed a life of luxury at Oakwood Hall. But that wasn't really him; he found his calling by writing 130 religious tracts.

On our last day in Barnsley I summon up enough courage to confront the building where my father took his own life – the car showroom on the corner of two busy shopping streets where I'd often played as a child. As we get closer, a memory comes flooding back. I'm sitting in Dad's car, holding a jam jar with my brother's dying goldfish floating on top. Lying sideways on top of the water, his one eye staring at me, Goldy seems a lost cause. My father's at the wheel and we're on a mission to save this beloved pet. Driving slowly we finally make it to the showroom were Dad summons a mechanic to bring a large cylinder of oxygen which is duly pumped into the jar. Goldy springs back to life.

How will I now react when I view these premises again? What were Dad's thoughts when he drove there for the last time? When he waited under that car for the chill of death to creep down his body until the poison reached his heart?

But it is gone – now just a pile of rubble with workmen digging frantically. 'Wasn't there a car showroom here?' I ask. 'Yes, love, we demolished it yesterday to build the relief road for the Town-End roundabout.'

A relief road.

The day before my visit.

God bless you, Dad.

Back in London, I welcome a young step-daughter into my life, and I love her and my brother's children as if they are my own. Of course my heart often aches when I pass a pram with a tiny smiling face, but I choose not to go down the panicking-forties path, wary it might change or threaten the status quo.

Perhaps sensing something within me, my other half arrives one day with a tiny Yorkshire Terrier which leaps into my arms and into all our hearts for the next sixteen years. Even the garbage men love Arthur, always dropping their bins to give him a gentle pat.

Husband Michael and I live a happy, privileged life. He designs breathtaking super-yachts and Formula One vehicles. I write books that are published, and the deli thrives deliciously. I have a glistening lifestyle – whisked off for passionate weekends in five-star hotels and glorious breaks in Venice, on private jets with friends, and to our magical midsummer marriage in the south of France.

But life goes deeper than the waves and rushes of golden endorsement. I sense we are losing touch with our reality, encased in this omnipresent luxury where hotel suite loo rolls always fold into origami points and fine-dining serves poke (the new ceviche which was the new sushi) and a chocolate meringue that faints when approached by its sauce. The honeymoon period has been sublime but 'life out there' is becoming detached as we constantly embrace the surreal bubble of privileged immunity where heads are easily turned and held by money and acclaim. We both want to stay real, to never develop that superior aura of entitlement.

On a chilly October evening in 2005, we are viewing devastating footage of the Kashmir earthquake on *Channel 4 News* – the intense coverage projects that raw feeling of utter futility which just makes you want to curl up and cry – when Michael turns to me and says: 'It's time to help these people.'

I know immediately these are not temporary words of news-driven sympathy.

I also know that he sincerely wants to make a difference. What I don't know is how.

But I was certain it would be very different to sending a donation, or seeking some kind of annoying sponsorship from friends – 'I'm cycling through the Serengeti on a bike with no seat, so please dig deep' – or involvement with some kind of celebrity 'fundraising' bash which misses the point.

The last one of those I'd attended was at the Savoy Hotel in London some years ago, when Naomi Campbell's mother Valerie addressed us halfway through our five-course meal as we sat in our finery. She came across as caring and compassionate, serious about the cause she supported. Behind her as she spoke were pictures of starving African children with huge stomachs and terrified eyes, their images fading in and out to remind us why we were there. But to her left was an overweight drunken slob holding court at his table and totally disregarding the speaker. That image stayed with me – that public display of immoderately rich self-satisfied do-gooders attending a charity function as an excuse for yet more self-indulgence – and I never attended another.

I hold nothing but true respect for high-profilers who possess raw, genuine, uncomplex compassion. But charity appeals inextricably linked to celebrities – always seen to be doing their bit for 'the destitute orphans whom I love' – can often leave me cold. I'm not impressed that they bravely take a few days out of their busy schedules to visit East Timor to be photographed with 'grateful' children.

Why not just quietly sell that spare house or car, and put the cash where it matters – or give your time to help those closer to home who urgently need your support? Why seek public approval for giving to worthy causes?

The sight of showbusiness multi-millionaires cajoling the public to part with their hard-earned cash makes me uncomfortable. It is always the poorest in society who give the biggest proportion of their wealth to good causes, but they support the charities that have a personal connection with their lives, not the ones that make celebs appear altruistic and therefore more popular with the public. Sure, there's a huge reach to be had by pairing celebrities to causes – but not when their personal reach is desired more than that of the cause. It's a cynical approach, especially when the point is missed completely. What matters most is the amount of benefit achieved per pound donated, rather than the percentage of each pound sent.

I say this because I now know how it works. Michael's resolve from Kashmir was so dramatic that it has indeed helped thousands of ripped-apart souls destroyed by forces beyond their control. He quietly but firmly declared, 'I'm a designer – that's all I've ever done and I love it one hundred per cent – and now it's time to put some of that love to good effect. Let's cross the great divide from hedonism to humanitarianism. Onward!'

Selling everything we both possessed, we founded the first company to design and manufacture an innovative range of shelter, sanitation and hygiene products for the world of international emergency aid. Michael's industrial design experience gave him unique access to materials that flat-pack and freight effectively.

This equipment is now in the front line of humanitarian aid in Haiti, across Africa and around the world from Nepal to New Guinea, from the Philippines to South America. Our work never stops, we do it promptly and efficiently, for the simple devastating fact of life is there will always be disasters and displaced people who need help and deserve dignity.

I've now learned to put a complete stop to misplaced empathy. I try to help those who can't help themselves – the victims of true circumstance in war-torn, battle-scarred countries – rather than rescuing those who refuse to help themselves. Sure, it's difficult to navigate through life without feeling overwhelmed, alone and isolated at times. But it's important to define the borders between mental illness and 'rubbish life' syndrome.

Over-defining life, rather than just living it and learning from life's events, has spawned a current trend to almost celebrate mental health problems, to join the club; that it's cool to be fucked up. But let's all be aware that pharmaceutical companies know exactly how to identify an aspect of everyday life that can be turned into a medical condition with a marketable treatment attached to their multi-billion-pound business.

My vainglorious modelling years have been a rollercoaster ride of glamour, discovery and financial independence. I travelled the world alone, met extraordinary people and knew the pleasure of mayfly fame – my day in the sun. I was lucky, no question, that my looks defined me for that decade, and I'm ever grateful for a face that fitted those times. And for that 'high' called travel which clouded my pain and forced me to live life in the present, not mourning my past or projecting the future. Trusting things would work out the way they're supposed to without me always trying to control the outcome.

But I've also seen the frailty of life at every turn and cannot remember a time when I was unaware that those I love could die at any moment, and that God will shout my number, bingo style, when my time is up.

I have seen how meaningless glamour is for its own sake, that it's time we demystified the myth of impossible perfection. That we don't need the carousel of consumerism whizzing around at full pelt – this insane addiction to consumption – to have a satisfying life. We can be happy with less.

My partner didn't need rescuing when we met – and neither did I. *Always* drawn to exciting 'bad boys', my degree of analysis has changed. I used to believe that connecting with me inevitably led to an early demise, but that's because my unfocused life attracted me to those who live too dangerously for ongoing happiness. By finally facing what damaged me and slowly mending, I now know that creativity, electricity, mystique, fun and fulfilment *can* exist perfectly within a partnership – without having to be crazily extreme.

At last I've rescued myself from that frozen past. The trunk is unpacked. I'm no longer what happened to me but what I chose to become because of it, and writing this book hasn't defeated me. Facing and owning those memories has strengthend me, made me less frightened of love, helped me to learn and understand why conditions of the mind are so complex, why people suffer the ultimate mental pain I never had to deal with in my time among them.

And as I sit here with this man I love, who writes beautiful poems and always makes me laugh, there is nowhere on earth I would rather be. Because I have travelled the cosmos trying to find this special place called home.

Thank you for sharing my voyage of hope, survival and joy. May it help to open a vital window into an oft-closed world.

Because life is all that counts in the end.

Let's embrace it.

Nothing matters more.

THE SONG

She said she had a way of telling
what was right from what was wrong.
I said that's most impressive,
could she put it in a song?
She replied her strong point wasn't singing
but she could recognise a rhyme,
and if I'd care to ask the question
She'd try and find the time.
Yes, singing's never been my strong point,
she liltingly replied.
I said, I suspect you've hidden talents,
I'd be happy if you tried.
And she wrote a song of substance
about right and wrong and state of mind.
I said that's really most impressive,
but it somehow doesn't rhyme.
Are you saying that I'm wrong? she said.
No, I'm saying you're not right:
do not confuse your rights and wrongs,
or mistake your days for nights.
She said, I'm sick of moral questions:
let's stick with smells and sounds and sights,
as truth is true, and lies are lies,
so there's no need to fight.
I said, that's really most impressive:
now I've heard you sing your song,
your talents truly do you justice –
I'd be pleased to sing along.

Michael Messenger, 1995

ACKNOWLEDGEMENTS

Head Shot would not have happened without the incredible support of my friends and backers who believed in it so profoundly. I'd like to thank you all for inspiring me to 'get on with it' and for making that possible.

The Unbound team gave me the freedom to write the book I wanted to write. They saw past the traditional single genre restriction and 'got the big picture'. My brilliant editor Ella Chappell encouraged, supported and motivated me – and produced a great final edit. Many thanks also to Sarah Barlow for her excellent proofreading, and the design team for understanding the essence.

To the photographers, archives and magazines who gave me permission to publish their photographs; it was a total pleasure to bring your work (and the good times we had) back to life after fifty years. Mega thanks – the drinks are on me.

Most of all, my eternal thanks to Michael Messenger for giving me all the love and kindness that I treasure so much. He inspired every day of the writing process with his fatalistic strength, great humour and constant support for this book and its writer.

349

Unbound is the world's first crowdfunding publisher, established in 2011.

We believe that wonderful things can happen when you clear a path for people who share a passion. That's why we've built a platform that brings together readers and authors to crowdfund books they believe in – and give fresh ideas that don't fit the traditional mould the chance they deserve.

This book is in your hands because readers made it possible. Everyone who pledged their support is listed below. Join them by visiting unbound.com and supporting a book today.

Jane Eriksson
Richard Evans
Peter Fearn
Pascal Ferrier
Martin Fischer
Abby Fletcher
Barbara Fletcher
Tom Fletcher
Marianne Foster
Laura Franklin
Andrew Gibson
Susan Godfrey
Martin Goode
Jo Grace
Caroline Graham
Jane Griffin
Ben Harris
Cat Harvey
Susan Head
Alice Hiller
Neil Huddleston
Arshad Hussein
Sarah Iqbal
Per Jensen
Dan Kieran
Anna King
Harry King
Richard Knyvett Hoff
Angelina Kumeri

Norman Kwang
Pierre L'Allier
Paul Stephen Lafferty
Ginny Lawson
Robert Leach
Gill Liddell
Hanna Linsey
Nikki Livingstone-Rothwell
Mac Macintire
Alice Marshall
Lucia Martinez
Mary
Max McCann
Mary McCarthy
Beverley McClure
Frank McMillan
Boyarde Messenger
Jo Miller
Richard Miller
John Mitchinson
Erika Montijo
Bel Mooney
Alison Moore
Linda Morand
Rita Mori
Andrew Morris
Susan Morrison
Carlo Navato
Ellie Nixon

Louis Nixon
Linda Ogilvy
Christine Pack
Samantha Parnell
Ankit Patel
Justin Pollard
Ariane Poole
John Powell
Samantha Powell
Martin Quinn
Lesley Rich
Janet Richards
Mike Robbins
Paula Roberts
B S
David Samuelson
from SevenDayDoctor
Linda Severino
Faith Simpson
Anne Smith
Lucy Spencer
Julia Stephenson
Sam Stephenson
Mary Stewart
Kate Sullivan
Natalie Summerlin

Richard Sutherland
Heather Taylor
James Taylor
Darnella Thomas
Fiona Thomas
Emily Thornton
Julia Todd
Alex Varley-Winter
Sam Vaughan
Rebecca Verlander
Yvonne Vitos
Rebecca Walker
Roger Walton
Catherine Ward
William Ward
Karen Weber
Diane Whitehead
Daniel Williams
Phoebe Wilson-Sims
Nicko Wong
Max Woodhead
Jess Yelling
Emma Young
Harry Young
Jane Young